the
Scriptures
have the
Answers

inspirational writings by:

Ben Blank

ISBN: 0-9714539-3-4

For additional copies visit your local bookstore or contact:

The Blank Family
 3230 Strasburg Road
 Parkesburg, Pennsylvania 19365

Carlisle Printing
OF WALNUT CREEK LTD

2673 Township Road 421
Sugarcreek, Ohio 44681

phone | 800.927.4196

Contents

Contents cont.

Preface

"…for I know that my Redeemer liveth…" Job 19:25

This book that you are holding in your hands is one no one had envisioned just a very short time ago.

But then, no one dreamed Dad would be leaving us so soon.

We knew he retired from farming and carpentering some years ago due to his health. And, more recently, we knew how he grieved for Mother and longed to be with her in Eternity after she passed away February 20, 2008.

But despite all this, Dad had a very busy life with his writing and research, correspondences, his many appreciated visitors, meetings, book auctions, and occasionally an out-of-state trip.

We barely realized Dad's health was declining so rapidly until he had a 2-day hospital stay. And what a shock to all of us when he died peacefully in his sleep a little over a week later—May 27, 2009.

It is difficult to adequately describe with written words the impact of a loved one being ushered into the timeless hereafter.

A deep sense of loss and grief is mingled with gladness for our loved ones whose wish to leave this earth with its pain, sickness, and sorrow, has at last been granted.

We do not want to grieve as those who have no hope, but follow the One they followed. And thank God for the legacy and many good memories left for us.

And just as we stand back and appreciate a lovely quilt that has been completed, and at last taken out of the frame, so may we view the life of our loved ones gone on before us…. Even though there are flaws, there are often patterns and examples we may wish to consider for our own. And sometimes they are different and unusual.

Dad had an interest in the written word that not all busy farmers do. He was able to pursue this even more when he retired. But as in farming he did not use corn pickers, sprayers, riding plows, etc., he also did not use typewriters or word processors. Instead, he did his writing with pen and pencil and used large amounts of yellow sticky notes to arrange and rearrange his thoughts, before writing the final draft on notebook paper.

He wrote a number of articles that were printed by *Pathway Publishers*, but then branched out to book writing. *"The Amazing Story of the Ausbund"* was published in 2001 after extensive research, writing, and re-writing. That was followed by *"Creation to Ressurrection"* in 2005. Work was started on another book about New Testament times and the early church fathers. Meantime Dad helped oversee

Preface cont.

the translation of "*Das Wahre Christenthum*" by David Beiler as he felt it was a needed book that would reach a wider audience in the English language.

After Dad's writing came to an abrupt halt when he passed away, many hours were spent mining through his writings. Articles he had written for *Pathway Publishers* from 1973-1986 were unearthed. He had sent them a copy of a letter written to a dying friend and neighbor. Soon he was asked to write a monthly column for *Family Life*. Dad was reluctant, but at last agreed to do so with God's help, and Mother's support.

It was entitled "*The Scriptures Have the Answers*," and as we read over them, we had to think of a prayer Dad had quoted in the introduction of his second book. It read, "If we promise to use it only to Your glory, dear God, will You give me the gift of clear and unconfused thinking?" Was his prayer answered? We hope so.

But now Dad has gone to meet the Author and Finisher of his faith. Some day it will be me. Some day it will be you. If even a very small portion of this book helps just one soul prepare for that great day, his work will not have been in vain. And, in the words he often quoted: "May God be given all the honor and glory."

—The Blank Family

The Scriptures Have the Answers

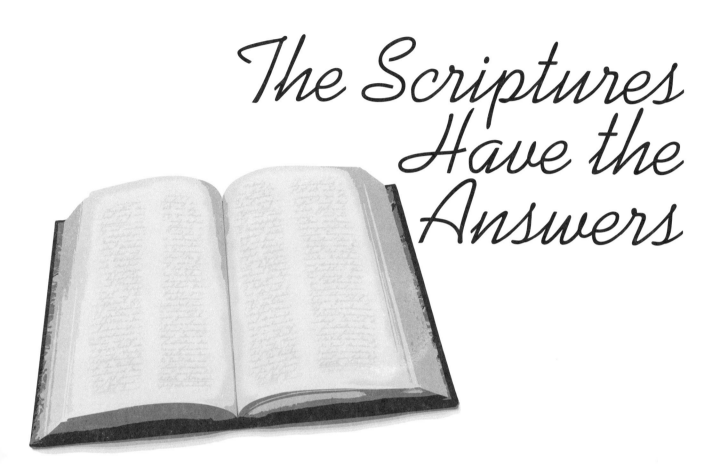

The following articles were written by Benuel Blank for Pathway Publishers between 1973 and 1986.

Dying to Live

This is the first article Ben Blank sent to Pathway Publishers in 1973. It was based on a letter someone had written to his neighbor Levi Stoltzfus, who was battling with cancer. Levi received the letter in his last days.

Dear Friend,

We are writing to let you know that our thoughts are often with you the last few days. When we first heard that you weren't well, we didn't believe that it would take long till you would be back to your usual work and strength again. When time passed by, it pained us to know that you were still weaker, but we still couldn't believe that your sickness would last long. The time has now come that we would like to think that you will regain your health again, but we now know that only a miracle from the Hand of God will enable your frail, sick body to ever get well again.

We hear that you now accept the fact that the Lord may be using this sickness of your body as His means of calling you home. All of us will some day have to leave everything that we own, yes, even the body that we are living in, the body that we could say is really only loaned to us to use while we are making this pilgrim journey through this world. We live here on earth for our allotted time and then pass on to that land of which there is no return, to be only a memory here to those who knew us.

God has given man dominion over the earth. Men have changed the appearance of this earth with their planting and building and machinery. Some men have risen to great heights of power and wealth but no man, from kings and presidents to serfs and slaves, from millionaires to beggars will ever escape that end of the life here on earth, called death. Even those who will live until the second coming of Christ will be no different from those who die before that, in the sense that they will have to leave their mortal bodies and will never again return to this life.

There are no exceptions, there are no loopholes in the fact that we will all have to die. The people who lived here on earth, let's say, two hundred years ago have all passed on; and the time will come that every single person living today will also be gone; such is the way of the stream of human beings passing through this world. If there were only one chance in a million that a person would not have to die, many men would spend all their time and money to find that exception, just to be able to live here on earth forever. This stream of humanity has always been changing faces. Those people who lived here one hundred years ago are unknown to us. In the same way, in another hundred years who will live in the homes we now live in? Those who would till the same soil that we now till could well be of our own descendants.

There is really nothing on this earth that we can see that is eternal. There is nothing here that always stays good and new; wood eventually decays, metals tarnish and rust away, even concrete and stone will also eventually crumble and break away. Our bodies are no exception. We all know what our survivors will do with this body of ours, when due to accident or disease it will no longer be fit for us to use.

The end of our life here on earth can come in many different ways. Our walk through the world could be likened to walking through a winding trail through a woods where we would have no way of knowing what lies beyond the next bend in the trail. For some, it seems the last stretch of the road is straight so that they can see what is coming; others will walk along, totally unaware of what is before them, till the road will make a sudden bend, and there will be the door of death that we all have to pass through to enter into eternity.

It is good that we do not know what the Lord has planned for us. We may be making plans for tomorrow, for next week or for next year, but the Lord may have other plans for us. When we are starting in on the last full year of our life; when we lay down our tools on the evening of our last full day's work; or when we are starting in on the last mile of our way, we will probably be unaware that it is so. It is good that the Lord has made it thus. For us it is only necessary to take one day at a time, and try to live each one well, and then trust that the Lord has planned the future for what is best for us.

Because we cannot see into the future, the future may look dark. We are able to look back on the road that we have traveled, but we cannot go back. We cannot stop. We keep on going forward with time, but future happenings are veiled from our sight. All that we know about the future is what we can read in the Bible, and since the future is in God's hands we can rest assured that all will be well for everyone who tries to do what is right.

We can read in the Bible where death came from. Our first parents, Adam and Eve were warned that death would be the result of disobeying the will of God. We can think that the punishment of being driven out of the Garden of Eden, away from the presence of the Lord, came as a shock to them, but when the day came that they saw one of their own sons laying dead before them, beaten to death by his spiritually dead brother, they probably realized as never before what they really had brought upon themselves. They had feelings just like we do and if anybody ever cried and wept until they finally fell asleep, they probably did the night after Abel was killed.

We can see death in the world of Nature around us. The cold winter wind comes and slays the green foliage and bright flowers that colored the summer landscape. The seeds that we sow in the earth will soften, decay and crumble apart. The caterpillar will shrivel up into an ugly lifeless looking crust shell.

But we can also see the evidence of a resurrection. After the cold blasts of winter are over, the sleeping seeds and buds of last year's greenery will again awaken and grow to be fresher than ever. The seeds that we sow in the earth will die into a new life, just as fruitful as in former years. The caterpillar, crawling slowly from one place to another, living on leaves, will some day make a unbelievable change. It will burst out of its shrunken, crusty chrysalis and will fly away on its beautiful butterfly wings, sipping that most delicious of all foods, the nectar of the flowers.

If we would be creatures whose life span would be very short, say of only a few months, and if we had no way of knowing better, we would probably become frightened in the fall of the year when the leaves would fall from the trees, when life in the forests and fields would seemingly be all killed when the first frosty winds of winter replaced the warm days that we had been used to. If we would have a life span of only a few hours, and had no way of knowing otherwise, we would also become frightened when daylight would cease and the shadows of night would fall upon us.

Our life here on earth is short compared to eternity and if we compare a thousand years of our time as being like a day to God, our time here on earth would not be longer than a few hours long at the most. The minds of human beings cannot comprehend something that it has not had a similar experience with, so it is no wonder that we cannot begin to realize what eternity is really like. We have no more an idea what the eternity before us is like than does a new born baby have an idea of what its life before it is like.

Were it not for that Christian hope in a resurrection, the thought of death would surely strike terror in our hearts. Our loving Father above will not use death as the means of bringing his children to extinction to annihilate them; but will cause it as the means to release us from this world of pain and sorrow and bring us Home to Him. God decreed to our first parents and to all their descendants that they would suffer pain, sweat, tears and sorrow, and then drove them from His holy presence, and put them under the death sentence for their sins. But in His great mercy, He also used this death of our mortal bodies to bring us into His presence, and to end the pain, toils and suffering of all those who accept His plan of salvation. He has made this possible by coming down among men and letting them sentence Him to death. He arose from the grave three days later and thus could Paul the Apostle write: "O death, where is thy sting, O grave, where is thy victory? (I Corinthians 15:55).

One song writer has expressed his gratitude to the Savior in these words: (*Family Songs and Hymns* Number 54)

O, I long to see Him, Look upon his face;
There to sing forever, of His saving grace;
On the streets of glory, let me lift my voice;
Cares all past, Home at last, Ever to rejoice.

As you are laying on you sickbed, hundreds and hundreds of unanswered questions probably come into your thoughts. Will the prayers for my recovery still be answered, or is it God's will that my life soon should be drawing to a close? If so, what will my last moments be like before my body makes its final struggle? What will I see when I open my eyes on the other side of the grave? Then there is the question, the thought of which has dampened many sick-bed pillows: How can I leave my children and my loved ones? How will things go when my place is vacant in the family circle? You have the assurance in the Bible that the same God who "in the beginning created the heaven and the earth" (Genesis 1:1) and "in whose Hand thy breath is" (Daniel 5:23) also is "the Helper of the fatherless" (Psalm 10:14) and "relieveth the fatherless and widow." (Psalm 146:9). It is hard to find a better prayer for committing yourself and your loved ones in God's care than that closing paragraph in the first evening prayer in the "*Christenpflicht*" prayer book.

Doubts will also probably find their way into your thoughts. It has been said that anyone who has ever believed has also had doubts. Suppose the atheist, the non-believers are right when they say that death is like the extinguishing of a flame that will then be cold forever. The atheist will say that it is impossible that the dead will again have life, but do they consider that they now have a life that was awakened out of the dust? That we should be alive at all is a greater miracle than the miracle that will take place when the Lord will awaken and raise from the earth and from the sea the souls of all the people who have ever lived and will give them indestructible bodies that will never again die.

The thoughts from the twenty-third Psalm can be a comfort to anyone who has ever feared the time when he will have to leave this world. Note that the writer of this Psalm does not say "the valley of death" but he says "the valley of the shadow of death." We know that a shadow can look fearful but really a shadow is often much larger than the object in front of it, especially in the evening; and can not do any harm. We cannot reach those great and glorious heights on the other side without first descending downward through that valley. But we do not have to go alone; if we can have that wonderful hope, "thou art with me", what have we to fear? The result of living a God-fearing life is to "dwell in the house of the Lord forever."

The Lord may not only be using your sickness to bring your thoughts more to things eternal, but your relatives, neighbors and friends are also doing more thinking about such things since you are not well. You think that your end might be near, but many of us who are hearty and healthy could full well be in eternity before you are. You have time to read and to think and to ask God for forgiveness when many of us who need it much more go on with our daily work and so often do not even think to thank God for our health and to ask Him for forgiveness and help. You have asked us to pray for you, but my dear friend, we feel that it is much more necessary for you to pray for us.

For all of us that day of our departing from this earth is one day closer today then it was yesterday. Let us all live as if each day could be the last. If we would know this morning that we would not be here to see the sun rise tomorrow morning, what would we do? We hope that we would go on for just one more day, in a quiet way, with our work; with now and then a prayer in our hearts; with love for those around us, and then when we would lay ourselves down like a tired child, for a last sleep, we hope we could then say, "Lord let thy will by done, put my hand into Thine."

God be with you,

from a friend and neighbor.

P.S. To "*Family Life*" readers a few weeks later: One of our good friends in the neighborhood has now been laid to rest. The following poem "Sundown" by Burt L. Taylor often comes to mind: (from the book "*1000 Inspirational Things*").

Sundown

When my sun of life is low,
When the dewy shadows creep,
Say for me before I go,
"Now I lay me down to sleep."

I am at the journey's end,
I have sown and I must reap;
There are no more ways to mend -
Now I lay me down to sleep.

Nothing more to doubt or do,
Nothing more to give or keep:
Say for me the children's prayer,
"Now I lay me down to sleep."

Who has learned along the way -
Primrose path or stony steep -
More of wisdom than, to say,
"Now I lay me down to sleep?"

What have you more wise to tell
When the shadows round me creep?...
All is over, all is well ...
Now I lay me down to sleep.

Faith

"Now faith is the substance of things hoped for, the evidence of things not seen.
Hebrews 11:1

Thus the Apostle Paul puts into words for us what his idea of faith is like. Many, many sermons have been preached and many books have been written on the subject of faith, but there is probably no where else such a great sublime truth is put into such a few words. The German translation may give us a thought partly hidden in the English when it says in effect; "what a man hopes for and doesn't doubt that which he doesn't see." One word that we often use comes very close to this meaning of the word "faith": that word is *trust.*

Suppose we would have no trust at all in other people. The opposite of trust is suspicion, worry and anxiety. We would be like the boy who was going along on a voyage on a ship on which his father was the captain. Instead of enjoying the ride and doing the duties assigned to him, the fearful boy was often down in the engine room making sure for himself that the crew had the steam pressure up; next he was looking over the navigator's shoulder to make sure that the charts he was using to map out the trip were correctly marked. Instead of being all over the ship with his worries, he could have made the voyage much more pleasant for himself and for the other passengers if he would have faithfully done only his own duties and then left his father, the captain, see to it that each crew member did what he was supposed to do and let the things that he did

not understand to his father.

We could also liken faith to the compass in the pilot's room in a ship. We can be sure that our forefathers who came across the wide, deep ocean in the little sailing ship of that time could have seen first hand what trust is really like. When the days and nights were clear the captain had the sun and the stars to give him the sense of direction to pilot the ship. But the weather is not always clear and balmy now, nor was it then. Storm clouds sometimes came up, and at such times the nights got very dark. We can just see the pilot at the wheel on a dark, rainy, stormy night putting his faith on the compass at his side. The compass and the small light next to it was all that he needed even though the outside world was as dark as pitch. That pilot's trust in his compass which was responding to an unseen magnetic force is an example of faith in the evidence of things not seen.

(To the editor: I wish that I would have the illustration that I happened to see once a long time ago. It showed a pilot standing at a ship's steering wheel with a compass and a small lamp at his side. All that could be seen outside the window was the dark night and the driving rain. The lines on the captain's face showed courage and not a trace of fear. The memory of that illustration made an indelible mark on my thoughts in my younger days.)

Another example is when you go across the fields to a neighbor's home. When the day is clear you can see the path the whole way across. Now our life is not like that. We cannot see what is before us. Our life is like going over on a dark, moonless night. We don't have to see the path the whole way to keep from getting lost. All we need is the light at the neighbor's window to guide us, and a small light around us so that we can see where to take the next few steps. Then we don't need to have anxiety that we will stumble or get lost. We can think this is the faith that the Psalmist David had in mind when he wrote about God's word being "a lamp unto my feet and a light unto my path" (Psalm 119:105).

We could also say that faith is like the wings of a bird. You may have often seen a bird on the very top of a tall tree on a light twig on a stormy day. You might think that the bird could be shaken off, which it could, or the twig could snap off. The bird is fearless because it knows that if something does happen, it has wings to fly.

Faith is also the remedy for depression and despair. We all have enough of failures, fear, shortcomings, and maybe just plain stubbornness in our nature that if we would just let it come to us we would despair. The world and the outlook around us can also look so hopeless and dark to us at times. One writer has given us a formula for what to do about such thoughts: Look within and be depressed, Look around and be distressed, Or look to God, and be at rest.

The Bible is full of examples of people acting by faith. It also tells us of the results of not having faith. That classic eleventh chapter of Hebrews has many examples of lives who were guided by that gift from God: faith. The story of the widow's meal in 1 Kings 17:10-16, the story of the widow's oil in 2 Kings 4:1-7 and that of Peter crying out for help to his Lord when he was sinking in the water (Matt. 14:30) (He was sinking because of his lack of faith.) are just several stories of hundreds of examples. Their stories make it easier for us to understand what trust and faith are like. Reading them more often could also make it easier for us to live up to them.

We should remember that reading these accounts in the Bible does not do us any good until we put their principle into practice in our own life. When you are reading in the Bible, don't let your thoughts wander on how this or that would apply to someone you know. What you are reading should be taken as being written just for you. If we would be able to memorize the Bible all the way through, forward and backwards, we would not be helped by it until we started practicing its principles and making them part and parallel of our own life. There is an old saying to that effect; "He who reads and reads and never does, is like he who plows and plows and never sows." It's also the planting and cultivating that helps to make the harvest.

God has put us on this earth with a will of our own. We are free to make our own choices, but then we are also responsible for the results that follow. Just like Adam and Eve were forbidden to eat of the fruit of that one tree in the garden of Eden, so God set up boundaries which are not good for us to cross. This is not to keep happiness out of our lives, it is really for our own good. The peace and joy of living a humble Christian life is something so deep and so satisfying and so enduring that we don't want to miss it. For everything good that God has established in this world, Satan will set up a hollow substitute beside it. The "happiness" which we may be led to believe will come after trying out that fleeting pleasure of this world and having riches and honor is as nothing compared with what Jesus has for us when He said that "I am come that they might have life and that more abundantly" (John 10:10). The thought suggested in the German translation of this verse is "life and a full satisfaction."

Could we give one more example of how faith works? You may have already read about the experiment that the people who study animal behavior have often tried out. They will place a bowl of food on one side of a fence and a hungry animal on the other side. It is possible for the animal to go along the fence for some distance to an opening and then get to the other side. Some kinds of animals will do nothing but walk back and forth opposite the fence from the food. When their hunger becomes severe they will push and beat against the fence in their determination to get what they see and want. They would actually die of hunger rather then go out of sight of the food to go along the fence to the opening to the other side. Other animals will soon discover that it is useless to try to push through the fence and will try going along the fence till they find an opening, even if it means having the food out of sight for a little while.

Can you see this illustration applied to your own life? We all want, in fact, we all need something satisfying in this life. We all have an inner longing for lasting peace and contentment that is lasting. Most of our actions are an attempt trying to find this goal. If we rebel against the authority set over us we are like the animal beating against the fence. Faith will know that there is a better way.

If we try to get this satisfaction by going out and trying what the world has to offer, be it riches, fame or pleasure, we will surely be disappointed. When we are setting a trap we always try to bait it with something that the animal we want to catch will like. Satan is out to trap us in the very same way. We are not going to make a list here of the bait that Satan uses in our time; each of us knows what his own temptations are. There are two kinds of temptations: some to give in, some to give up.

There is an inexhaustible supply of help available to withstand temptation and live a better life. The Lord does not expect us to live a better life without His help; in fact, we will fail if we try to do so in our own strength. God did not put us in a world so full of temptations and trials that it is impossible to live a holy life. With His help we can do it, but there is one condition. We must ask for His help and let go of our worldly pleasures and ambitions so that He can take hold of our hand and lead us.

God has broken the chains of sin in many, many lives already, and He can do the same for you. When we pray the Lord's prayer we say, "thine is the Power," now let us let Him use that power in our lives. Hold nothing in your life from God. Start with prayer. That is faith. Tell Him that you know what you are doing is not what it should be. Tell Him how much you still love your sinful living; then ask Him for a fragment of His divine power to see things differently and to live a better life. We read in Luke 18:8 that God's help will not be long in coming if we really want it, so we know that if we don't get help it is really because we are still too proud to ask for it and we still want our will before God's will.

How do we know what God's will is? God is more eager to show you His will than you are to know it. Don't we too often come to God to find out His will merely to decide if we want to do it or not. This is not faith. Because we can be sure that what God wants us to do is really what is best for us and is really what we are put on this earth for, let us all make a new commitment to our Creator and say in faith, "Show me Thy way, I want to follow." He will then supply all you need to do the work that He has for you. Let us remember the closer we are to the Guide the better is the guidance and the peace that comes from following that guidance. "Thou wilt keep him in perfect peace whose mind is stayed on Thee, because he tusteth in Thee" (Isaiah 26:3).

Right now the rest of your life is before you. We can never tell what tomorrow or the future may bring, but God knows. Life often takes unexpected turns. There are circumstances over which we have no control. Our lives are really like the dark and stormy nights when the stars to steer by are hidden from sight. Here is where you and I need faith. We may have difficult days, but let us remember, our difficulties will never have God baffled. All that we have to do is to step aside with our self-will and in faith let God take over. Faith will not dissolve mountains of difficulties, but faith will move them out of the way.

We know that our life here is not our final destiny. Eternity is so real, so long, and so full of either torment or happiness that we had better do some serious thinking and doing about it.

Really, why do we wish for the things that the world has to offer? They do not last; they will be destroyed with the world. We are living in a world that started out as a peaceful garden, but through the sins of men, their greed, selfishness, wants and lust, will end up being an incinerator. But here let us thank God that He has given us all an opportunity for living in that home in the "new heavens and the new earth, wherein dwelleth righteousness" (2 Peter 3:13).

Even if we will live to be very old, we can still say that our life here on earth is going toward the end. As we stand at the helm of our ship going through the storms of life we need the guidance of One who knows the way. That song writer had faith when he looked forward in hope and penned:

I've anchored my soul in the haven of rest,

I'll sail the wide seas no more;

The tempest may sweep o'er the wild stormy deep,

In Jesus I'm safe ever more.

Let our prayer be like that in the (din Lieder buch) *The Unparteitische Gesang Buch.*

Page no. 292.

Mein lebensfaden lauft zum ende,

Mein pilgerpfad ist bald gethan,

Ach Gott, mir einn geleitsmann sende,

Der mich erhelt auf rechter bahn,

Der bei mir an dem ruder steh,

Wann ich den letzten sturm aussteh.

A Balance in Child Training

3

"He that spareth his rod hateth his son."
Proverbs 13:24

"And ye fathers, provoke not your children to wrath; but bring them up in the nurture and admonition of the Lord."
Ephesians 6:4

John Scott's wife was furious. The hyacinths which she had so tenderly taken care of were all picked off and the flower show was only two days away. Little Allan was just coming around the house so innocently with the flowers in his hand.

"You little brat! You are big enough to know that you weren't to pick my flowers," she shouted, and taking him over her knees, she grabbed a stick nearby and gave him a lashing that the small boy would not soon forget.

"If you ever do it again, I will beat the living daylights out of you," she fumed as she went into the house, leaving her poor son outside crying as though his heart were broken.

The next scene is in an Amish home. Little Melvin, the same age as Allan, was just at that stage when he "got into everything." His mother talked about it to her husband at the breakfast table. "Tie your cupboard doors and drawers shut, then he won't be able to always make such a disarray on the floor," the young husband advised. "He is too young to understand when you tell him to leave your things alone."

That evening Melvin's father saw that little Melvin had found an untied drawer and had the contents all over the floor again. "I will buy him a few new toys on my trip to town tomorrow," he said. "Maybe that will help to keep him a little more content."

This was the way little Melvin was brought up. When he wanted anything, he got it. His parents didn't want to "provoke him to wrath", which was what seemed to happen if he didn't get what he wanted.

So often God gives us a work to do in which we are so inexperienced. Parenthood is one of those. Which is the best method of raising children? Is it to use the rod, or is it to try to reason with our children when they are old enough to fully understand? From scriptures we quoted at the beginning of this article, we see that God is telling us to use both ways, blended in a reasonable balance of punishment and understanding. The two scenes we showed, that of Allan and that of little Melvin, represent the danger of taking only one verse into account. We need to take the two together.

It is so unnecessary to be picking up things after your children all day long, day after day. We, as parents, surely have more constructive and useful things to do than just that. A very small child will soon know what a firm "no" means. The first disobeyed "no" may well have to be reinforced by a slap on the hand. Later, a disobeyed "no" may need a few whacks on that spot so handy for that. We have

11

to give our children a pat on the back now and then for encouragement when they do well, but it is sure Scriptural to give it to them a little further down and much harder when they understand what is expected of them, but still disobey.

A child growing up without a spanking when it is necessary is surely to be pitied. He is a deprived child. A child that is whipped for every little misdeed and never gets talked to in a loving way is also a deprived child.

Suppose your little Sadie has just done something that she has been told not to do. Do not "spare the rod;" she needs a spanking. She needs it severe enough so that she is not just provoked to anger, but not so hard as to be cruel, or just as a vent for the anger of one of her parents.

If she continues to do the same thing again, she has not been spanked enough, or maybe she needs a kind talking-to to make sure she understands. The habit of disobeying starts small, and the bad habits of a small child can get magnified a hundred times until he gets into his teens. So my dear parents, start early. One doctor who has been around children a good bit says that some of the cause of a child growing up and demanding his own way can come from parents running after him all the time with everything he wants before he is two years old.

But my dear parent, just like God loves us even though we are so often ungrateful, don't forget to show your love to your child. When you do spank your child, please don't just go away from him without showing that you are hurt that he disobeyed. A small child spanked hard will cry, not only from the hurt on his bottom, but also from the rejection showed to him when he disobeyed.

When you have spanked him, let him know that he now has had his punishment for what he did, and take him on your lap. Sometimes he just won't be able to stop crying. Take him to the window and show him the neighbor's cows. Talk to him about the cows. If it is dark, take him outside and show him God's moon or tell him to look up and see the stars that God has made. He will usually stop crying immediately, and although he will stifle a sob now and then, he will cuddle up to you and love you. Oh, such moments are such a precious time for both the parent and the child.

If we happen to own a piece of machinery that is valuable, we will take the time to care for it the best that we know how. Anybody who has a garden or a field, and thinks anything of it, will try to plant good seeds in it, and will take the time to keep the weeds down. We will never have anything more valuable than the dear children around us. There is nothing else that we have that we can take to heaven with us. Let us, with God's help, take the time to "bring them up in the nurture and admonition of the Lord."

Make a Joyful Noise

4

"Let the word of Christ dwell in you richly in all wisdom, teaching and admonishing one another in psalms and hymns and spiritual songs, singing with grace in your hearts to the Lord."
Colossians 3:16

We may sometimes wonder if our way of having our church services is like the way they had church services in the times of the apostles, those men who had actually seen Jesus and later started the churches that are still going today.

We can rest assured that it is. The verse quoted above gives us an idea of a church service in those times. The word of God was taught and then, as in our services today, the people sang together to the Lord. Singing was part of the worship.

Two of the evangelists, Matthew and Mark, make mention that Jesus and his disciples sang a hymn when they had finished the Last Supper, the forerunner of our communion service. We have old writings handed down to us from the first century of the Christian Church that tell us about the singing of Christians when they assembled. One such is a letter that Pliny, a governor in one of the Roman provinces, wrote to the Roman emperor, Trajan, asking what to do with those who were brought before him and accused as Christians. One of the faults and errors that they were blamed for was that "they were wont to meet together on a stated day and sing among themselves a hymn to Christ as God." This letter was written less than one hundred years after Christ was crucified.

In those days the Roman emperor was revered as

a god, so it is not hard to understand why the early Christians were persecuted as they were.

The persecution of the church in the 16th and 17th centuries did not quench the singing of its members. We read in the *Martyrs Mirror* (page 590, English) that when Gotthard of Nonenberg and Peter Kramer, a minister and a deacon of the Anabaptist church were being led out to their death, they sang joyfully while nearly all of the bystanders were weeping. On a farewell letter from prison, Jelis Matthyss (page 675) writes to his wife that he has a "joy and a comfort in me that I cannot well describe to you." He writes that "the consolation of His Holy Spirit made my heart joyful, so that I could not refrain from singing a hymn" (page 678).

We read of one instance (page 131) where the soldiers surrounded the place where Christians were meeting and began to pile wood around the building in order to burn the building and all the Christians within. Before the wood was ignited, they gave the people worshipping inside the chance to come out, sacrifice to their gods and thus spare their lives. We read that not one of them responded. They all remained together with one accord, singing and praising Christ, as long as the smoke and vapor permitted them to use their voices.

When we read of such instances of the joy of

singing, doesn't it shame us to think of the times when we have sat in church while others sang praises and prayers to God, and we were just half-heartedly helping, with our thoughts somewhere else, or maybe even sleeping, or maybe visiting with the one next to us. This could be evidence that our joy is not in glorifying our Maker, but that our joy, if we have any, is only the shallow joy in things of this world.

We have instances in which people have left our plain churches and have gone to worship in churches where there is more of a display of joy among the members. In Psalms 81:1 we are told to "sing aloud unto God, our strength, and make a joyful noise unto God of Jacob." (In other words, the God of our forefathers.) We can do that in our own churches. We can do it without turning our backs on our forefathers' teachings and examples of living a plain life. We could, however, be to blame for driving such people from our churches by failing to express the joy that there is in living a Christian life.

Christ tells us in John 15:11 that He came so "that my joy might remain in you, and that your joy might be full." We surely don't have to go to other churches to have a "spiritual experience." Rich spiritual experiences and joy can be ours by wholeheartedly helping with the singing in our own churches and gatherings. Or, if we just don't have the talent for helping along, we can at least try to keep our thoughts on the rich, deep meaning of the words being sung.

Those grand old songs handed down to us in our hymn books have in them what it takes to stir our hearts with a new hope and courage in times of trial and sadness. In times of joy, if we will but let them, God can use the words to help us better remember His peace, joy, grace and love. They have an inspiring message for us that the hollow, shallow songs of the world will never have.

Whenever we have the chance after this, let us help with the singing until the chorus reaches up into the rafters and let us help with our thoughts until they reach up to God. "In the midst of the church will I sing praise unto thee" (Hebrews 2:12).

The Danger of Horse Power

5

"But he (the king) shall not multiply horses to himself."

Deuteronomy. 17:16

Thus the children of Israel were warned by God that when the time came that they would have a king ruling over them, that king was not to have lots and lots of horses and in the verse following, he was also told not to "multiply wives to himself that his heart turn away; neither shall he greatly multiply to himself silver and gold."

The third king that the children of Israel had over them, four or five hundred years after these words were written, did not heed this command. 1 Kings 4:26 tells us that Solomon (the king who built the first temple of God) had forty thousand stalls of horses for his chariots. This disobedience was then followed by also disobeying the words in the next verse. It is hard to believe that King Solomon, who was endowed with enough wisdom and understanding to write several of the books of the Bible that are still so helpful to us, could fall away in his old age from what he himself taught. He later turned his heart away from God, the One who had given him his wisdom and wealth, and with his wives worshipped other gods. He then even tried to kill the man God had chosen to be king after him.

Everything in the Bible was written for some purpose. Here we read about the dangers of having many horses, then when we think about it, who has more horses than the plain people, who use them on the roads as a means of transportation instead

of a car? The fields of an Amish farmer will have a team of horses working in it, while his neighbor has none.

Are we disobeying a command in the Bible?

Traveling by horseback, or by chariots pulled by horses was the fastest mode of transportation in Bible times. Kings rode on horseback; it was considered lowly for a man to ride on the back of a donkey (Zechariah 9:9). Thus God put into the laws of Moses restrictions on the use of a horse, the fastest and most kingly way of travel in those days. It was not the horse in itself that was evil, but the use that was made of it, and the status that was attached to it.

Donkeys were then often used by the common people in those days instead of horses to go from one place to another when it was too far to walk. Oxen were used to work the fields. There was often only one team of oxen in a whole village; the people took turns to use it. In one of Jesus' parables, he tells us about the farmer who bought five yoke of oxen at one time (Luke 14:19). He had so much going that he did not even have the desire to come when he was invited to the King's wedding supper.

Could going after the world's goods in a big way also have the same effect on us in our times? Read any modern farm magazine and you will get advice on how to do things in a big way. They always have stories on how such and such a man became wealthy by producing more than the average man does by using modern methods in a size unheard-of just a few years ago. What would Jesus have to say to us if He would be here with us in our times of affluence and plenty? He would say to us just what He said to the generation that He lived in.

He told them to, "Take heed and beware of covetousness; (greed) for a man's life consisteth not in the abundance of the things which he possesseth." (Luke 12:15). He then gave for us that example of the man who was planning on building a bigger storehouse for all his material goods just the day before he died. He was still planning on having years of ease and merriment with the increase that God had given him when the death angel suddenly struck him down.

There was once a man in our time who by hard work plus good fortune had become quite wealthy. Suddenly a series of misfortunes caused him to lose it all. When his non-Christian friends came to visit him, they expected him to be bitter over his great loss. He was now a very poor man.

They were surprised at his attitude. He said, "It will now be easier for me to die when my time comes; I will not have so much to leave here. The Lord gave and the Lord took away. Blessed be the name of the Lord."

Let us have more of that attitude toward our material possessions, our mammon. We certainly want to work and earn what we can, but let us not forget that when we say, "Thy kingdom come," we are to let the Lord set up his "Reich" and we are to forget about setting up one for ourselves here on earth.

Let us then stay with making a living in a humble way. We don't have to have all the luxuries that the world has. Let us stay with ways that can be done

with "horse and buggy" methods, as they have often been called by modern writers.

But we also want to remember that the animals that share the earth with us are flesh and blood like we are. They have feelings of thirst and hunger, tiredness and pain just like we have, and we are to do what we can to take care of them. It is also not right to have more to do than what our horses can do. We are not to drive them like Jehu, of whom the Scriptures say that when he drove in his chariot; "he driveth furiously" (2 Kings 9:20). The words in German say that "er triebt vie venn er unsinnig vare," or "he drives as one who lacks understanding."

Our domestic animals are willing servants when they are treated kindly and with sense. One old saying goes like this, just as if a horse were talking: "Uphill wear me, Downhill spare me, On the level let me trot, In the stable forget me not." When a man becomes a Christian and has than a new Master, his animals should also feel the difference.

We are not to be conformed to the world. That includes our dress, but it surely also includes our way of making a living. We can believe that it also includes our way of traveling on the road, and our way of working in our fields. What means of travel today is highly esteemed among men? Which means of travel today corresponds with what horses stood for in Bible times, and which means corresponds with the lowly donkey?

Our neighbors may pass us on the road with all that "horsepower" under the hood; and while he works his fields with machinery that has so much more "horsepower" than we are using, let us be content to stay with our work in a small, honest, and humble way, and not "multiply horses to ourselves." If we understand the spirit of that command, we will realize that it is surely just as dangerous today as it was long ago in the time of King Solomon.

6 Judged by Our Clothing

"And it shall come to pass in the day of the Lord's sacrifice, that I will punish the princes and the king's children, all such as are clothed with strange apparel."
Zephaniah 1:8

Is the way we clothe ourselves so important that we could get punished by God for wearing "strange apparel"? Or does this verse just refer to the "king's children?" Does that not also include us, for we want to be Christians, and as such we are the "King's children," for there is no greater King than our heavenly Father.

The way we dress is important. Dress, or the way of dress, is mentioned over 1400 times in the Bible, so it must be something of very great importance to God that He caused so much to be written about it in His holy word.

Read the story of Achan in the book of Joshua. Here he saw in Jericho, among some other things, a garment from the city of Babylon. He confessed later that he coveted it, took it, and hid it. He probably had visions in his mind of sometime walking around and wearing this pretty and costly coat that he had been forbidden to have. He probably had intentions of later getting his garment out and showing it off. Such is human nature that he could just see in his mind the people admiring him when they saw him wearing such beautiful and costly clothes.

He never got the chance to wear it. The law at that time decreed that he should be stoned for his misdeed; not for wearing it, but as the Word says, "because he put it among his own stuff." In other

words, he owned clothing such as the people of Babylon wore at that time.

Babylon is referred to in the book of Revelation as the world. The story of Achan is only one instance in the Bible of how serious a misdeed it is to dress like the people of the world dress. Isn't it our pride that causes us to want to dress to be looked up to? At such times, we have the same spirit in our hearts that Satan had when he was still an angel in heaven.

Satan was cast out of heaven when he wanted to "exalt his throne above the stars of God" (Isaiah 14:13), and when his "heart was lifted up because of his beauty" (Ezekiel 28:17). Satan was proud of the way he looked. That pride made a devil out of an angel and will forever keep him out of heaven. Pride will also keep us out of heaven unless we have a change in our hearts that shows a change in the way we clothe ourselves and our children.

The trend of the styles of the world are always away from modesty and Christian reserve. That is why we have a dress regulation or Ordnung in our plain churches. It is a call for a decent and discreet way of dress. It is Scriptural to have such regulations on the way of dress. The epistles of Paul contain many of the regulations that were necessary to be mentioned in his time. It is also necessary to use church discipline for any member who weakens or attempts to wreck such guidelines by not being willing to support them.

One of the trends in today's styles is for a woman to wear the model of dress that a man has. Deuteronomy 22:5, severely condemns this practice. For a man to put on a woman's garment, or for a woman to wear that which belongs to a man was an abomination or a hateful thing unto the Lord. This surely should not leave a doubt in our mind as to how our Lord and Creator feels about what we wear.

One of the aims of the modern, worldly ways of dressing is to attract the attention of the opposite sex. That alone gives us all a very worthwhile reason to stay within scriptural standards and church regulations. Jesus condemned those who have thoughts of adultery as much as those who are actually in the act. We know that in the act of adultery, two people are involved in the sin. When the adultery of the heart (Matthew 5:28) takes place, there are also often two people involved. The one is the man who has the evil thoughts. Who is the other?

The other person in this adultery of the heart is the woman or girl who is dressed in such a way as to call attention to her body. One writer has said that the clothing that neither conceals nor reveals is the kind that leads the thoughts to that of lust.

The prophet Isaiah mentions some of the things that the haughty or proud daughters of Zion were wearing in his time. Among other things he condemned "glasses" (Isaiah 3:23) which the Revised Standard Version gives as "garments of gauze" or a partly transparent material that was in use at that time. (He does not refer to eyeglasses; they were not in use until several thousand years after his time.) He could well have been speaking to us in our days when he also writes about the "well-set hair" that he saw on the people at that time.

We know that "Demut" or plainness is a command of the Lord. The commands of the Lord are never impossible. God never commands us to do something which cannot be done. With His commands come offers of help to obey them. We can start to trust and obey God whenever we make up our mind to do so. Those who say," I am afraid I won't be able to live a Christian life at this time," (which also includes a different way of dress) are really saying, " I don't want to live it." Anyone who truly wants to live for Christ, can, with God's help, do so.

Oh dear mother, on you depends so much on how the future members of the church will look—like Christians or like the world. When you are shopping at your favorite dry-goods store and when you are sewing for your family in your favorite sewing nook, you are in a ministry that no other person can do. Think of the seriousness of your influence on the little children on your lap. They are now at that age when they look up into your face to see if what they do pleases you or not. You surely don't want your small innocent son, who now holds up his hand to yours for guidance and protection, to grow up and go out into the world and get lost there. You don't want your pure little daughter to grow up to be a bold, or immoral woman, so please don't dress her like one.

If you are concerned about the drift of the church toward the world, do something about it. We are apt to think that the way the people of the world around us dress is what is weakening the church Ordnung, but it isn't that. Really, the most dangerous decay comes from within the church itself from members who will not support a Christian standard of dress.

Why do we so often fear that people will reject or accept us by what we have or by what we wear? Do not let your children down by helping Satan with the temptations that he has for them. That is what you are doing when you put clothing on them that will start them off on the way of pride, vanity and self. Do not betray the trust that the Lord had in you when he chose you to be the parent of one of His precious little ones.

We may sometimes feel there is little we can do for the betterment of the world for our descendants. But there is one important thing that we can all do, and that is to witness to the world around us that we will not go along with their ungodly way of dress. Let us all make the resolve "as for me and my house, we will serve the Lord" (Joshua 24:15).

Human Nature

7

"If the prophet had bid thee do some great thing, wouldst thou not have done it?"

II Kings 5:13

Human nature is more or less the same the world around. It is still today very much like it was about three thousand years ago when the story recorded in the fifth chapter of II Kings took place.

Naaman, who was what would be called a "big wheel" in the court of the Syrian king, had contacted leprosy. They were at the point where they were ready to try anything, so away to the land of Israel he went. When he got to the prophet's home, the prophet didn't even come out of the house, but sent his servant to tell Naaman to dip himself in the Jordan River seven times and be healed.

This was more than the proud human nature of Naaman could take. He had expected Elisha, the prophet, to come out of the house and put his hand over the diseased place and call on the name of the Lord and heal him that way. Another thing that irked his feelings was the bathing in the Jordan River. He thought of the clean waters they had back home, and here he was to wash in that muddy river that flowed through the land of Israel.

The Bible tells us that Naaman turned away in a great rage. One of his servants, however, asked Naaman to think the matter over, humble himself, and do as the prophet had told him to.

Naaman obeyed, and was healed.

A similar happening took place in 1870. The engineers who were planning to dig the St. Gothard tunnel beneath the Alps Mountains to shorten the railway line between Lucerne, Switzerland and Milan, Italy needed a little help with their blueprints. They came to a surveying instrument company in Philadelphia and asked the experts there to take a look at their plans and check their calculations.

"They seem accurate," one of them said. "However, to be certain you should take them to Joseph Shirk, who lives near Churchtown, a village in eastern Lancaster County, about fifty miles west of here."

When they arrived at Shirk's farm, he was out doing his spring plowing. "I can't stop my plowing, but if you leave your plans here and come back the day after tomorrow, I will look them over for you.

The engineers were almost sure they were victims of a hoax. They were not sure if they wanted to trust their plans for this important work with this humble-looking Mennonite farmer. But against their better judgement, they left their blueprints there.

Shirk stayed up the next two nights until after midnight, carefully checking their plans and figures. When the men came back several days later, they were amazed to find their calculations, lines, and coordinates corrected, and even more surprised at his charge for the work—one dollar.

They returned to Europe and, using the corrected plans, began the work of digging the tunnel from both ends. When they broke through at the middle, they found that Shirk had been off in his calculations by only half an inch in the nine and one-third mile tunnel.

This is often the way it goes with situations in our own lives. We come to many problems that at the time seem to have no simple, easy way out. Then we come across some passage in the Bible that we know could be the answer, but we are afraid to try it because it seems too simple. We are looking for something that we feel should be more complex and complicated. We will mention a few examples. You could probably add a hundred others.

A boy turns sixteen and starts going with the young people. He soon sees how some of the boys seem to be leaders in the gang, and gets an ambition to be one of these. So he decides that if he takes a drink (just a little, he thinks) he, too, could be funny and the "life of the party." That is how he starts being a slave to the demon alcohol.

Or he thinks that if he gets a car and takes the other fellows and girls for a ride, he will be popular. He then has a shallow idea of popularity and is playing with a temptation that has taken young people, and later their descendants after them, down the road forever from a church that stands for non-conformity to the world.

Or he gets the idea (from no one but the devil himself) that if he wears his hair patterned after the ways of the world, he will be looked up to and be somebody. Or he will be deceived into believing that if he dares to dress himself with clothing that is not patterned after the modesty and reserve of a Christian "Ordnung", he will be accepted into the inner circle of the leaders of the gang.

In other words, he is seeking the answer to that problem that all people (not only young people) have—he wants to be accepted and have friends. But the answer to that problem is so simple that few people will believe that it really works. It is in those few words from the Bible, "A man that hath friends must shew himself friendly" (Proverbs 18:24). In other words, to have friends, you must be one. You must let it be shown that you are friendly.

That is the answer to our quest of friends—to think more of others than of ourself. It is shallow and cheap reasoning to think that lasting, deep, and durable friendships can be built by trying to have or do things to impress others. The sooner that a person will learn that, the sooner he will have friends. Maybe he will not be attracted to those who think a person has to be "wild and daring" but that isn't the kind of friends we want anyway.

We are not looking for friends who are always in a shell thinking about themselves, or for those who always put on a false front, so we will have to take off ours. If we are sincere, we will find that those who are sincere will be our best friends. If we can stop trying to impress people and forget about "keeping up with the Jones," if we will listen more to what other people say and think less about what we want to say, we will find friendships in sincere people that are deep, satisfying, and lasting. We need friends for their trust and companionship, so we must practice the Golden Rule and be that kind of friend. Then we can be a help to one another and find a contentment and joy in being around other people. We will come to the point where we will thank God from the heart for having sent us this type of friends.

So let us look for the answers to the problems in our life in that Book of Books, the Bible. Many of the answers found there are so humble and lowly that we may get the idea they couldn't work, but they do. Naaman, the leper, first thought that he could only be healed by doing some great thing, but later found out that the laying aside of his pride to follow the humble advice of the prophet did work after all. Those tunnel engineers of 1870 didn't believe that a farmer-surveyor with little formal schooling could be a help to the problems they faced. They thought that only some impressive expert could understand the difficult mathematics of mountain surveying, but later found out differently. In the same way, it is amazing what the humble, but great precepts from the Bible can do for us.

Human nature may rebel against trying some of those timeless principles found in the Bible, but the fact remains, they are simple and honest, and they do work, because they come from our Creator, God himself.

The Duty of Parents
8

"And these words, which I command thee this day, shall be in thine heart: And thou shalt teach them diligently unto thy children, and shalt talk of them when thou sittest in thine house, and when thou walkest by the way, and when thou liest down, and when thou risest up."

Deuteronomy 6:6, 7

These verses of scripture give anybody whom God has chosen to be a parent something to do. It has been said already that silence is golden. This is surely true at a time when more words would only ignite a quarrel between two people. But just as the Bible says there is a time to keep silence, it also says there is a time to speak (Ecclesiastes 3:7).

If there is a time to speak it is surely when we are around our children. Those children came to us as a gift from God. We dare not make excuses and say we don't have the talent to speak like some do. The Word of God places on all parents the grave responsibility of talking to their children about matters that pertain to their salvation. With our children, the ministry and duty of being their first teachers came to us parents. We must tell and show them what is right and what is wrong. A child who is properly disciplined by his parents finds it easier to discipline his own life when he is older.

This verse teaches us about the necessity of first having God's Word in our own hearts. One version (modern language Bible) gives us the same thought in a slightly different way. "These words…shall be written on your heart, and you shall impress them deeply upon your children." The German version tells us, "…Und sollst sie deinen Kindern einsharfen und davon reden," which strengthens for us the thought that we should do this teaching in an earnest way.

In fact, the word "diligence" means "constant, careful, painstaking effort."

This training should start early in the child's life. The mother and the father of a small child who is not even old enough to talk should speak to him in a loving way again and again. It should not be just one endless, meaningless prattle, but enough to let the child know that you are aware of him and care for him. Point out to him interesting things to see or hear. It is also your duty at this age to tell him what to do and not to do, and then gently but firmly enforce it. If children are to grow up to be obedient, they must first be instructed. A very young child is very lovable and cute, but is also selfish and has a nature that can grow evil if left to itself. The sinful nature of us humans can rapidly grow out of hand, even in very small children. Making a fuss over a child's cute sayings and actions will not be a help to him for the good when he is older.

When the child begins to talk, then the questions to you will also begin. You don't need to explain everything to him down to the smallest detail, but you will have to give him satisfactory answers for his questions. He may begin to enjoy the attention he is getting, and start asking questions that are too simple for his age level. If this happens, instead of giving him the answer, you may have to quietly ask him if he doesn't know the answer himself. If the questions get too frequent, maybe he is just thinking up questions and not listening to your answers. If so, ask him the same question a short time later to see if your answer registered in his mind.

Be sure and spend lots of time with your child at this age. If you have no time for your child now, he may someday have no time for you. That is a dear price to pay for being too busy to spend some time with your children. Young children ask many questions. If we don't give them answers to their questions now, they probably won't give us answers to our own questions when things are turned the other way, in their teenage years.

When our children are with us at home, do we perhaps spend too much time providing for them in material ways and neglect the children themselves? Have we been so anxious to give our children what we didn't have when we were growing up, that we have neglected to give them the more important things that we did have? What we do for our children when they are young will make a big difference whether they will be satisfied with what they have or whether they will grow up always wanting to have the best and most of everything. A writer once put it very aptly when he wrote, "On this Christmas don't just give your child what he wants most, but give him what he needs most—some of your time."

Children at any age need discipline and punishment for willful wrongdoing. But here we have to keep things in balance. If we punish our children in the heat of anger, we may be making them turn away from us, rather than away from the wrong they were doing. We are not to let them grow up without reproof and punishment, but we are also not to be like a harsh taskmaster to them. A good pattern to copy is the way the Lord deals with us. In His great love He brings trials into our lives to discipline us, but then He daily gives us more good than we could ever earn in a lifetime.

The bringing up of children does not always turn out right. A few years ago there was a city church which, due to the death of their minister, got a new pastor. He and his family moved into a home close to the church. The oldest boy was a teenager who somehow got into wrong company and eventually stopped going to any church whatsoever. The church people liked their new pastor very much, and were concerned about his family. One of them met the errant son on the street one day. She stopped to talk with him. She told him that he was missing so much by not coming to church.

"Your dad always has such interesting and helpful sermons. You should be there to hear them," she told him.

"I get to hear more than enough of his preaching at home," the young boy curtly replied. Evidently he didn't appreciate his parents' efforts to help him. What has gone wrong in places such as this is not for us to judge. His father may have wanted his son to be a "good" boy so that other parents would think he knew how to raise children. This would be a wrong attitude. He may not always have acted out of love for his son's soul, and may have been so harsh that he provoked his son to anger, which is something we parents are to avoid (Ephesians 6:4 and Colossians 3:21).

Then again, God has given us each the freedom of choice. When children come to the age of accountability they may choose to turn their back on all the good teaching they received from their parents. The Bible says, "The son shall not bear the iniquity of the father, neither shall the father bear the iniquity of the son" (Ezekiel 18:20). God holds us each responsible for our actions, so let us as parents heed the advice of the writer of Lied No. 44 in the *Ausband*:

"Wollt ihnen sharf vorhalden,

Gott's Word und sein Gesetz,

Darnach Gott lassen valten."

(Admonish your children with the word and law of God, then let the power of God take over.) If we can do this until the end of our days, we will have done our duty.

No Money in Heaven

9

"Save now, I beseech thee, O Lord; O Lord, I beseech thee, send now prosperity."
Psalms 118:25

These words sound as if the writer of the Psalm is in deep trouble. It sounds as if he is burdened with unpaid bills and doesn't have anything with which to pay them. It sounds as though he is heading for financial disaster and wants God to bail him out.

It sounds a little like the old story that was making its rounds some time ago. There was once a man who overspent himself. When the bill collectors came and threatened to sell him out if he didn't pay by a certain time, he became frantic.

He remembered the story in the Bible of the widow who had no money to pay her bills and was told that her two sons would have to be sold as slaves to satisfy the debt (2 Kings 4:1-7). A miracle from God by the hand of the prophet Elisha caused the oil to increase until she had enough money to pay the debt and enough for herself and her two sons to survive.

"If God could help her, maybe He can also help me," the desperate man thought. So he prayed.

Now, as the story goes, when an angel brought the man's request for money to God, the angel asked, "What shall I take down to the man to answer his prayer? The gold that we have here in heaven cannot be taken to earth, and we don't have any money here, for we have no need for it."

"There is something you can take to this man to answer his prayers," the angel was told. "Bring him health and strength to do the work that he has to do. Put some ideas into his mind as to how he can take better care of some of the gifts that have been given to him. That will have to be the answer to his prayers."

So the man didn't get money from heaven to pay his unpaid bills, but he received something else that was worth more than any amount of money. He got health enough to do the work that God wanted him to do, and he got the miracle of common sense and clear thinking.

The wish for great wealth is really a desire and appetite of the flesh. Prosperity has always been hard on Christianity. That well-known evangelist of the 18th century, John Wesley, had no hope that prosperous Christians could long keep their faith as it should be lived. He once wrote, "I fear, whenever riches have increased, the essence of religion has decreased in the same proportion. Therefore I do not see how it is possible, in the nature of things, for any renewal of true religion to continue long. For religion must necessarily produce both industry and frugality (thriftiness and careful spending), and these cannot help but produce riches. But as riches increase, so will pride, anger, and the love of the world in all its branches."

When we compare our times with those of fifty or so years age, we live in prosperous times. The times that we are living in could well be a sign of the last times, because Christ told his disciples in Matthew 24:7 of the "teure zeit" in the last days. This could mean famines, but it could also mean the ever higher prices that we are experiencing in our times. The runaway inflation of money throughout the whole world in which money is worth less and less all the time, and its rapid decrease in value sets the stage for some people amassing fabulous profits and for others going down financially almost before they know what really happened. "The Lord maketh poor, and maketh rich" (I Samuel 2:7).

We have churches that are being started in our day that believe that God wants everyone to be prosperous. They say if you aren't prospering financially, there is something wrong with your relationship with God. They believe that if you will only change your way of thinking, you will become prosperous. God's blessings and financial success mean one and the same thing to them. And the rich members of their congregations give. When they decide to build a beautiful cathedral costing millions of dollars, they give, and the result is they soon have a pretty ritzy place in which to worship.

We believe that money spent in such a way is being spent foolishly. Jesus said that we will always have the poor among us (Mark 14:7). If they believe that God will cause everyone who is good to be rich, they would have been uncomfortable having Joseph and Mary among them. They were too poor to buy a lamb to sacrifice soon after the birth of Jesus, but they had a sterling character that was worth more than any amount of money.

The Bible makes it plain that the love of money and wealth is not good. It tells us that "The love of money is the root of all evil" (1 Timothy 6:10). It goes on to say, "which while some coveted after, they have erred from the faith and pierced themselves through with many sorrows."

At another place Jesus said that "The care of this world and the deceitfulness of riches choke the word and cause a man to become as a seed never bearing any fruit" (Matthew 13:22). Riches bring with them many temptations that we otherwise would not have. "Labor not to be rich... for riches certainly make themselves wings: they fly away as an eagle toward heaven" (Proverbs 23:4, 5).

But still we are deceived into believing that if we would have plenty of money we would be happy. We forget that happiness and contentment are something that no amount of money can buy. We are deceived into believing that a big bank account would enable us to buy all our wants. Oh, if we would only have more, we could buy bright, new equipment and gadgets and playthings for grown-ups. We could be the owner of lands and real estate and we could buy the best foods and have clothing in the latest styles. We could fix everything up just like we would want it, and we could travel and have long vacations and we would be secure in our old age. In other words, we are deceived into believing that wealth brings with it everything that we desire.

If we have such thoughts, it is about time that we re-examine our goals and ambitions in life. We are not showing the contentment of the writer of the twenty-third Psalm by such thinking. "The Lord is my shepherd, I shall not want." In other words, if we are under the care of the Good Shepherd, Jesus, we shall have everything that we need; we shall not wish or want for more. Hebrews 13:5 is for all of us, "Be content with such things as ye have."

If the Lord has blessed your efforts and you have prospered, give the credit to where it belongs; not to your own management abilities, but to the Lord, who gave to you those abilities. Don't be proud of what you own. Financial weather can change almost overnight.

We can be rich in material goods, but bankrupt in spiritual values. It is what we are in the Lord's eyes that really matters. He has an answer to us in Revelation 3:17 if we get proud of what we have, "Because thou sayeth, I am rich and increased with goods, and have need of nothing; and knoweth not that thou art wretched and miserable, and poor, and blind and naked."

It has been said that seven out of ten people in the world are too poor to earn enough to feed themselves and their families properly. There are people in other lands dying of starvation, so it is necessary that we become better stewards and caretakers of the gifts that God has given to us. Owning land, getting the tools and equipment that we need for our work and fixing up what is needed is not wrong at all if we use common sense and heed that advice in Phil. 4:5, "Let your moderation (Maszigkeit) be know unto all men."

If you are one of those that is having trouble making ends meet; if the money is always all gone before the end of the month is here, don't despair. Count the blessings that you do have. Maybe God knows that being a "success" would make you proud, so He is removing that temptation from you. Maybe He is teaching you to be dependent more on Him for you daily bread and needs. Maybe He is letting you go through all this to teach you not to again spend your money too foolishly, or maybe He wants you to appreciate those friends who are a help and those who understand.

So let us keep busy. Busy hands make happy hearts. The Bible does not approve of laziness. "If any would not work, neither should he eat" (2 Thessalonians 3:10). We want to make proper use of the time and material goods that God gives us. That tired feeling after having done an honest day's work is a good feeling and seeing that loan slowly but surely being paid off is a feeling of accomplishment. There are no happier families than those that work together and are busy, but still let us keep in mind that it is destructive to a happy and contented life to live and work with more and more material goods being our goal.

If we desire riches so that we can get whatever we want, the next generation will be much more so. Our young people can not altogether be blamed for getting things that they want but should not have; if we parents have as a goal in life to get and have everything we want.

So let us take heed what kind of prosperity we wish and work for. The prosperity that the Psalmist prayed for was the same prosperity and good success that was promised Joshua in Joshua 1:7-8 for meditating and observing (thinking over and doing) the laws of God. It was the prosperity of the spirit. That prosperity is what really counts.

Let us then all work and pray for that kind of prosperity. We need material things in this life; we really couldn't live without some of it, but let us not work so hard for the abundance of such that we neglect our families and our salvation. That work comes first. God will not always supply us with everything that we wish for. He loves us too well for that. In His great love He gives us everything that we need. Let us use it wisely.

"Seek ye first the kingdom of God and His righteousness and all these things shall be added unto you" (Matthew 6:33).

10 The Strength of Words

"Then they that feared the Lord spake often one to another."
Malachi 3:16

"But exhort one another daily, while it be called today."
Hebrews 3:13

Nearly all of us live in this world in homes with other people. Even those few human beings called hermits, who prefer to live far away from other people all by themselves, have some contact with other people at some time or other. The rest of us who share homes and living quarters with one or more people as a family can hardly imagine how it would be to live alone and not see or hear another human being for weeks or months at a time.

There may be people in our immediate families whom we see and talk with hundreds of times in a day; then there are many other people whom we know, but do not see very often–those whose paths do not often cross with ours, but the fact remains we are here on earth with each other and we need each other. "It is not good that man should be alone" (Genesis 2:18). All of us are dependent on others for hundreds of our needs and necessities. How true the verse in Romans 14:7, "For none of us liveth to himself."

Our relationships with people that we meet and know are all different, but God wants all of those relationships between human beings to be such so that we can be a help to each other on our journey through this life. He gives us instructions in His Holy Word on how to do this. The two verses quoted above are only two of the many found in the Bible. Our conversation, or talking with other people, is one way that we can be a help to one another.

In talking we make use of words. Without words or some kind of communication, we would know very little about what other people are thinking and feeling. Like all other good things, words can easily be overdone, but what would the world be like without words?

We need words to have and keep an understanding between people. Because they could no longer understand each other's words, the people of Babel could not continue building. Our work here is to help each other in the building of good in this world, and if we don't have an understanding with each other through words, our work will suffer.

We all need encouragement at times and at other times we need reminding and even sometimes criticism from other people. How could this be done without words? Sharing our joys and pleasures with other people doubles them. Sharing our burdens and troubles halves them. How could that all be done without words? Genuine appreciation and encouragement is not fully expressed without words.

Words and talking are a little like eating. Eating is a necessity, but it surely would not be good to sit at the table eating all the time. There is "a time to keep silence, and a time to speak" (Ecclesiastes 3:7). Too many words can get boring. One writer has taken the pessimistic view of human relations and has said that there are only two kinds of people, those who are boring and those who are bored. It doesn't have to be this way if we will but remember the Scriptural advice to "let thy words be few" (Ecclesiastes 5:2). It is very true that we can learn a lot from one who doesn't say much. It is also true that there can be a deep feeling of Christian love between people even though the words that are being exchanged are few.

There are always a lot of interesting things in anybody's surroundings to talk about and to start a conversation. Two people with the same interests won't long have silence between them. They will soon be talking about what interests both of them. For some it will be cows or horses; for some it will be about hay fields or about marking out rafters or one of thousands of other interesting subjects. We can learn from each other by using words. If we would all listen more with an interest to what others have to say, and not just think about what we want to say we would be surprised at what we would learn.

But our talking should not be just about the weather and about material things. We can also be a help to each other in increasing our spiritual understanding if we will do some talking about such things. What we think about is what we talk about. "Was des Herz voll ist, des geht der Mund über" (Matthew 12:34). We don't have to wave our beliefs and religion in other people's faces, but then we should not act as if they were only very private matters.

Why do most of us usually wait for the other person to open a conversation? There was once a woman who seemed to have a gift of understanding human nature and seemed to always have a way of getting people to respond in interesting conversation. One of her friends asked her if she had a secret that she used for reaching people that others did not know about.

"No," she replied. "It's no secret. I just try to remember one thing. Deep inside every human being is lonely and wants friends." There is really nobody who does not respond in some way or other to genuine from-the-heart friendship. Friendship can be shown by deeds, but what would a friendship be without words?

The best place to practice this friendship is in our immediate family; among those with whom we daily work and live. How sad to live under the same roof and eat off the same table and hardly ever share our thoughts and feelings with each other. We would be better off living alone as hermits than to live like this. Aren't we too often unkind and rude, or just plain thoughtless to those nearest and dearest to us—those loved ones we live with? Why is our worst behavior so often let loose at home, the most sacred place on earth? It is really false of us to be grouchy and unsociable to those at home and then as soon as we go out the door, to meet other people with smiles.

There will always be many, many opportunities every day when we are with the other members of the family to get an interesting conversation going if we give it a try. But the prime time is around the family table. Families who have little or no talk around the family table except for hurry, gloom or belittling talk about others are headed for trouble. They do not know what they are missing by not making efforts to have a pleasant time together. Do not wait for the future to have this enjoyment with your family and to talk things over openly as they come up. Do it now while you are still together at home.

Time will soon bring big changes. Some may go out into other homes and some may leave home to start their own homes. Some may be called away from this life by the Lord and will never again come back, but the memories of happy home gatherings will always remain. Make use of the fleeting opportunity that you (have right now) to cement the good and lasting relationship of close-knit, satisfying and enjoyable home life. Whoever you are, don't wait on the others to make the start—you yourself can start right now. You will have regrets in later years if you don't. Your good humor, if it is really genuine, will be catching to the others. Then you yourself will be later helped by them at times when you are in a low mood.

It should not be true that a husband and wife or parents and their children, or brothers and sisters live under the same roof day after day, but at heart live in two different worlds. It is so unnecessary to have what is called a break-down in communication and sit at the same table with each other and find no words to reach them. Words can help to make a climate in which love can grow and result in an exchange of deepest understanding.

Talk things over. Talk things over openly and honestly. It takes words to bring resentment to the surface and to resolve quarrels. We don't need to "boil over" but there will be times when we need to use words to bring those bottled-up feelings to the surface. A build-up of resentment can cause rebellion between members of a family, but with the grace of God it doesn't have to stay that way. A quiet, frank and open discussion may be all that is needed, and that takes words. Loving and understanding words will melt away the walls of indifference. Showing and expressing appreciation for what others do for you will result in a change of attitude that is next to a miracle.

The words that we speak will have a far-reaching influence. Words that we send out have power, some for evil and some for good. What we are in our hearts cannot remain hidden, because our words that get past our lips reveal what is really in us. "For by thy words thou shalt be justified and by thy words thou shalt be condemned" (Matthew 12:37).

It is really a sobering thought when we think of the responsibility that rests in the words that we use. We know that "every idle word that men shall speak, they shall give account thereof in the day of judgement" (Matthew 12:36). But on the other hand, words that help to build up goodwill and understanding among the members of a family, a neighborhood, or a church are not idle words. As the Scriptures remind us, they are to be used "often" and "daily". Let us resolve to use God's gift of words to help our fellow pilgrims and to glorify God.

A Cheerful Countenance

11

"A merry heart maketh a cheerful countenance."
Proverbs 15:13

Many of the artists who have drawn pictures of Jesus in *Bible Story* books show Him as having a sad or having a faraway look on His face. We look at those pictures that they have painted and then we may also get the idea that Jesus never smiled or laughed. When we think of all the evil that He could see in the hearts and actions of men, we can believe that He had plenty of reason to wear an unsmiling and sad look on His face.

But there was also another side to His character. Small children flocked to Him when He was here on this earth. A person who is a chronic worrier and who always has a gloomy look on his face will not attract small children like Jesus did. Children will shy away from grown-ups who never smile or laugh, so it is not irreverent to believe that there were many times when Jesus had a smile on His face and a little light humor in His talk.

The Scriptures record for us that "Jesus increased in wisdom and stature, and in favor with God and man" (Luke 2:52). That passage gives us reason to believe that because He was in favor in His young days with men, He very likely was a typical, lively, busy, fun-loving boy, and because He was in favor with God, He did not let His wholesome fun turn into mischief, mockery, or sins of any kind.

We can also imagine that He was an interesting

visitor to have as a dinner guest after He had grown into manhood, because the Gospels often record Him as being invited into different homes. A gloomy person who always looked on the dark side of life would not have been so often invited.

One of the prophecies in the Old Testament that describes the Christ who was to come, pictures Him as "a man of sorrows, and acquainted with grief" (Isaiah 53:3), but in the next verse we read that they were not His griefs and sorrows, but that they were ours that He bore. On the very evening before His death on the cross, He told His disciples that after their sorrow they would have a joy that "no man taketh from you" (John 16:22).

There was once a Christian who was trying to tell a man who was living in sin to go along with him to church and to start living a different life. He would then experience for himself the peace and joy of being a Christian.

"I would be more interested in your religion if more of its joy would show in the faces of those who go to your church," the man remarked. Evidently he was not interested in accepting a faith which did not prove to be a joy to those who practiced it.

Yes, it is necessary that we do not spend our days in gloom and pessimism. Oh, we do not want to go to the other extreme of, "Let's eat, drink, and be merry, for tomorrow we die". With an All-powerful God available to help us with the cares and burdens of life, it is wrong for us to be fearful and gloomy all the time and to always walk around with a long face. Some seem to think that if you are very good, you must always be very serious, but it is not that way. Christians can also have fun, but in a far different way than the world does.

Of course, it is possible for people to act happy and to force their laughter and smiles just to try to hide the heavy, burdened heart inside. You might have read the story of the doctor who nearly always had a good degree of success in talking with depressed people and helping them back to normal life.

One day a very sad and depressed man came to him. He poured out his troubles and laid bare his unhappiness to the doctor. He unfolded his fears and talked of the burdens that were making his life nothing but a series of joyless days.

After listening to the man's troubles for a while, the doctor said to him, "I have a suggestion that may help you. You are thinking too much of your own troubles. You need something different. There is a circus at the other end of town this evening. Take the evening off, go there and watch Simbo, the famous clown, do his acts. After watching his funny stunts and hearing his jokes for a while, I am sure that you will forget some of your own imaginary troubles!"

The doctor was pretty sure that he had just given the advice needed to start a change in the thinking that would help the poor man sitting at the other side of the desk from him. But the man lowered his head, and with a tear in his eye, said, "It won't work, Doctor, for I am Simbo, the clown."

Yes, our life here is serious business, but it is not so serious that we shouldn't be able to see the humorous and amusing side to many of our daily situations. There is nothing like a little intelligent laughter to relieve some of our tensions and pressures in our relationship with others. The Bible tells us that there is a "time to weep and a time to laugh" (Ecclesiastes 3:4) so it is not wrong or sinful to cultivate the habit of sensible laughter.

Most of the people who are chronic worriers and have mental problems are people who cannot or will not laugh. They have not learned to laugh at themselves: they take themselves too seriously. Looking at the humorous side of life has helped many to shake off the worst forms of gloom and has helped them get over days when the moods were pretty low.

A bubbling sense of humor is as contagious as the mumps or the measles. We need people everywhere with a good humor that is catching to those around them. A family where goodwill and humor are shared is a happy family. A group which laughs, not nervously and not at other people, is a relaxed group. Just like the moving parts of machinery need oil to keep down the friction, so do we need humor and goodwill to ease us over some of the tight spots in our relationship with others.

God gave us several senses, one of which is a sense of humor. Small children usually have it, and if grown-ups don't have it, it has been lost somewhere along the way, or has not been worked on to improve it. A little humor, light and often, is part of contented and happy family living, and will leave memories that time will never erase. Children who grow up in homes where goodwill and humor are never shared are deprived of some of the real necessities of life.

We have more than enough people in the world who are ever so busy and have so many worries that it is showing in the haggard and hurried look on their faces. We now have too many faces who show nothing but serious business and who hardly ever light up and break out in a smile. We need more people with a twinkle in their eyes, and a bright up-look in their hearts that shows up in faces that can easily smile. Such a face is like a bright spot in the clouds on a dreary day.

Such a countenance comes from a heart that does not find its joy in the clowning and silliness of the shallow entertainment of the world, or in amassing a fortune. Such comes only from the heart of those who are contented with the deep little joys of this life that come from Him who said "that my joy might remain in you, and that your joy might be full" (John 15:11).

Husbands in a Happy Home

12

"Live joyfully with the wife whom thou lovest."
Ecclesiastes 9:9

All of us know that the average housewife does a lot of work. Recently someone has figured out that in the course of her housekeeping days, the average housewife washes and hangs up enough wash to fill a wash-line about fifty miles long.

Think of it! Try to think of a place about fifty miles from your home and then try to imagine the work that the average woman will do to fill such a length of clothesline in her lifetime. Some of it will, of course, be hung out on fair and balmy days, but much of it will have to be washed and hung out when the weather is cold and freezing and at other times when the weather is hot and sticky.

Now the rest of this article is going to be written to the men.

Do we really realize the work that our wives do for us? Doing all the sorting, the washing, the ironing and the mending for the clothes on that fifty-mile length of wash-line is just a small part of their work. The average housewife works a hundred hours or more a week at her job of making a home. But then, if the work that they do is done in a Christian state of mind, they do it all willingly if they have the health to do it. The work that they do is a labor of love. Shouldn't we do more to show our appreciation for what they do for us?

Many of us know that happy sound of a woman singing at her chores. Is there a sound that gladdens the heart more than the sound of a faithful wife at work singing some of the songs that she learned in her school days, or some of the songs that were sung at the young people's singings in her younger days? There will never be a better way for our young children to learn the sacred songs that we sing in our churches than by hearing their mother sing them above the din of the washing machine. The fortunate husband who hears his happy wife sing while at her duties has a blessing and a jewel that no sum of money can buy.

If there is a husband who has seldom or never heard that sweet sound, maybe he is the one who is at fault. By making life a little more cheerful and joyful for his wife, he might be able to sometimes hear that heartwarming sound and be cheered himself at times when he needs it.

There was once a trucker whom we will call Jerry. He told a friend how he had come out of a broken home. He told of how he remembers his father and his mother having their heated arguments and loud disagreements. Later they parted and were divorced. He talked with tears in his eyes about the hurt that he went through.

Jerry later grew up, met a nice girl and got married. He confided to a friend on the happy home life that they were having after having lived together for a number of years.

He said that he did not want his children to go through the trauma that he had gone through. Early in his marriage he decided to show and also tell his appreciation to his wife for what she did–something he had never heard his own father do.

When his wife cooked a good dinner that he liked, he made it a point to tell his wife that he appreciated her meal. He told her that he appreciated it when he came home to a well-swept kitchen. He told her that he appreciated the work that she put in keeping his clothes clean and neatly mended.

It surely did not take much effort to show his wife that he appreciated the little things that she did for him. It was not hard work for him to help her out a little when she needed it, but he got rewarded many times over for doing so. In his own words he told a friend that although they had their little disagreements from time to time, their home was a little heaven on earth compared with what he had as a boy. He had learned a secret that his own father either could not, or did not want to learn. He learned to fulfill his wife's deep longing for appreciation.

What was the result? The result was that she did all that she could for him, which meant a happy home life for both of them and for their children.

A marriage counselor once made the remark that he believes there is only one truly happy home for every ten marriages. The average for our plain people would certainly be higher than that, but we have to wonder if there are families where the husband and wife just live together with very little in common–really being divorced in spirit. It does not have to be that way if we will only appreciate each other and the little things that are done, and learn to talk things over freely.

There is a lot of truth in the statement, "The best thing a man can do for his children is to love their mother." One court judge who has had a lot of experience with youthful lawbreakers, has said that in the hundreds of cases that he has had, every single one of them came out of either a broken home, or out of a home where the father and mother lived together but showed evidence of not getting along together. He strengthened his statement by also saying that he did not know of a happy home that produced a juvenile delinquent. How necessary it is to work together to build and keep a happy contented, and satisfying home life.

One more verse from the Bible that may be a help, "Husbands, love your wives as Christ also loved the church, and gave Himself for it" (Ephesians 5:25). Christ gave His life for the church. Your job is now to give the rest of your life to your dear wife and family. If your home life is not what it should be, talking things over with each other and with God in prayer will not fail to make an improvement.

Dear husband, work with your wife, laugh with her, talk things over with her, admit your mistakes and failures, listen to what she has to say, and pray with her, and above all, be her friend. An unknown poet has put into words one of the reasons why we should work to build a happy home life; one that will leave pleasant memories behind us:

"Bear this in mind, when God decrees,
   that loved ones now must part,

Fond memories will make us smile,
   light up the grieving heart,

So we must cultivate true love
   during our years together,

So when the storm of parting comes,
   we can withstand the weather."

God's Beauty

"And God saw everything that He had made, and behold it was very good."
Genesis 1:31

"He hath made everything beautiful in His time."
Ecclesiastes 3:11

In this earth we are surrounded by the beautiful and marvelous things that God has created. There are many lessons that God wants to teach us with the awe-inspiring and wonderful things that He has made.

All of us have at times stopped and marveled how beautiful the landscape looks in the fall when the leaves are changing their colors. How dull it would be if they were all to shrivel and wilt like they do when a tree with leaves gets cut down. God has created the leaves in such a way that they show off a splash of colors before they let loose and fall from the trees. Here and there is a tree with bright yellow mixed with flaming red. Over there is one with the foliage a dull purple all over. Some have not changed color yet and are still a bright green while others are past their prime and have all their bright colors gone and are a dull brown.

The effect of all these shades and hues of color from a little ways off is a thing of breath-taking beauty. A bed planted with different kinds of flowers is another example. Each one has a beauty all its own. There are the pansies that always smile at you, even at times when your moods are so low that you have a feeling that no one else has a smile. Then there is the lily-of-the-valley, which does not have a large or colorful flower, but which has a fragrance which is unforgettable. God has made them all different. All are beautiful in their own way.

That is the way it is with us human beings, too. Each human being that has ever lived is somehow different from all others. Let no one think, "Why am I like the tree that is a dark purple all over? I wish I could be like the tree next to me which has been given such bright shades of yellow and gold." Just as the autumn landscape needs all the colors to complete the beauty, in the same way God needs all of us, every single one of us to make His plan complete. He needed someone just like you in His creation. That is why He made you looking like you do, and having the talents that you have.

The bright colors of the sunset are another form of God's created beauty. The snow that falls silently during the night and covers the earth with a pure white mantle is another. There is no limit to the beauty that God has made for us to enjoy.

There is the little wren that sings with all her heart, just as if she knew that God is caring for her, and her family. There are the stars in the sky, that God keeps in their precise orbits. All that we can do when we look up into the heavens on a clear night is to humbly say with the Psalmist, "The heavens declare the glory of God and the firmament sheweth His handiwork" (Psalms 19:1).

Jesus saw and noticed beauty when He was here

on earth. He remarked on the beauty of the lily (Luke 12:27). It is easy to see that they have far more glory than all the beauty that man tries to put on himself, on his feeble frame that will soon turn to dust. Jesus must have noticed the beauty of the green grass, which has a simple beauty all of its own (Luke 12:28).

He must have noticed what the beauty of smiles do.

Yes, God's beauty is all around us. Oh, how true is the verse that says, "His work is perfect" (Deuteronomy 32:4). If it would not be for sin and the curse and corruption that came with it, and for the greed of men, the world would be a beautiful place to live in.

But God has other plans. He has a new heaven and a new earth planned (Revelation 21:1). We know very little of the details as to how everything will take place. It is not necessary that we know much. What we do know is that the beauty of the place will be beyond description in the language that we use here on earth. The Bible says that "Eye hath not seen, nor ear heard, neither have entered into the heart of man, the things which God hath prepared for them that love Him" (1 Corinthians 2:9). We know that the beauty of heaven will be far beyond anything that we have ever seen or heard of here on earth, and it will have far more splendor and glory than anything that we can even imagine.

The glimpses that the Bible gives us provide us only a faint idea and only a dim shadow of what heaven will be like. That place will be a happy place. There will be boys and girls playing in the streets (Zechariah 8:5). Here on earth gold has been fought over and has been slaved for. There it will be as common as the materials used here to make roads, for the Word says that the streets will be paved with it (Revelation 21:21).

God himself will be there and live with His people. He "shall wipe away all tears from their eyes; and there shall be no more death, neither sorrow, nor crying, neither shall there be any more pain, for the former things are passed away" (Revelation 21:4).

The earth and all its beauty was made by God in only six days. Hundreds of years have now passed since Jesus said that "I go to prepare a place for you" (John 14:2) so heaven must be beautiful beyond description.

If we do not get to live in heaven after our life here on earth is finished, it will be because we have let our sinful and selfish nature keep us out. God cannot have people like that living there. We will have no one to blame but ourselves if we want the pleasures of earth more than what God wants us to have.

The home that God is preparing is a place where only righteousness will dwell (2 Peter 3:13). That place will be worth living a God-fearing life. That place will be worth all the trials and struggles against temptations that we have here on earth. "After this life with all its strife, Heaven will surely be worth it all."

The Commandment 14 for Wives

"Teach the young women to be sober, to love their husbands, to love their children.
Titus 2:4

The Scriptural advice in the verse above to young women to be sober, which in this case means to live quietly, modestly, and orderly, can easily be seen to be a teaching that is necessary. But at first thought, the advice to young women to love their husbands and children may seem to be so unnecessary. Why, of course, every young bride loves her new husband! How could she but help to love the young man who treated her with all the courtesy and respect fit for a queen throughout all their courtship days? It would seem unnecessary to tell the wife of a young married couple to love the one who she spent a lot of time talking with and planning for a happy future.

But God knows the weaknesses of human beings. He also knows that we must always be on guard against the enemy of our souls who will make every attempt to destroy the love in a peaceful and happy marriage. There is not one marriage that will be exempt from the enemy trying to drive a wedge between the love of the man and the wife. God knows that it is necessary to keep reminding us; that is why He caused the above verse, and many others like it, to be written in His holy Word.

Someone has said that all marriages are happy; it is only the living together afterward that causes all the trouble. If the marriage relationship does later get to be only that of indifference, or even if it gets to the point where it has deteriorated into bitter tears and heartaches, there is still hope if both of the partners want to make it better and are willing to work for what will make it better. The marriage relationship was designed by God to be holy, so with God's help, it is never beyond repair if both want to have it repaired.

It is love that brings the two together in the first place, and it is love that will keep the two hearts together afterwards. When that first love gets forgotten through lust or even from just the grind and monotony of everyday living, it is going to take a miracle from God to get it back again. But, thanks be to God, the God whom we worship is a God who can do miracles.

When the cold, freezing and icy landscape of wintertime changes into spring and the God-given breath of warm air and gentle rains causes the grass to grow and the flowers to bloom; that is a miracle. God can change a marriage in the same way. Chilling indifference can be changed into warm love. Human nature cannot love that which is not lovely. It will take the grace of God for a wife to keep on loving and understanding, even if her nature rebels at doing so. You can't just wish for a change; you have to work and pray for it.

How about the part of the verse that reminds young women to love their children? At first thought it would appear to be unnecessary to tell a mother to love her children. Is there a mother anywhere who does not love those dear, innocent children who have just arrived from the hand of God? Is there a mother anywhere who would not sacrifice anything to make them comfortable and happy?

One of the verses in the Bible asks if there is a woman who can ever forget her child (Isaiah 49:15). There is probably not a mother anywhere who has given up one of her children in death who does not think of that child again and again, and who will not have a vacant spot in her heart as long as she lives.

But there is much more to loving a child than just seeing that it gets fed and is comfortable. Letting a child grow up always having his own way and getting everything that he wants is not really loving a child. A child soon learns if he can get Mother to wait upon his every want and desire. A child who has everything but a mother who sometimes says no, and enforces it, is not a child who is getting the right kind of love.

A mother who loves her child will, of course, think that he or she is the most wonderful child who ever lived. Children's first actions and their first words are so cute. But the child had better not know that the mother is thinking such thoughts. There are hundreds of ways to plant a little of Satan's pride into that tiny heart. If the mother helps that pride to develop and grow, it will be well–nigh impossible to root it out in later years. It is love to encourage and to show appreciation to a child. We all need a certain degree of appreciation and encouragement to keep us from sinking into depression and despair. What children do not need is applause and flattery. That will only feed their pride, with the result that they will grow up always making efforts to be noticed.

There is one form of pride in our days that some seem to think does not matter any more, but it does. That is pride in dress. Dear mother, putting other than plain and decent clothing on the dear children in your care will show what is in your heart. You are trying to tell all who see that you want your children to "be more" than other children. If that attitude of yours develops in your child, the time may come in later years when you will often think back on how easily you could have avoided some of your heartbreak back in those days when he was on your lap and in your care. The young mothers in our churches are really the class of people who have the most influence on the future of the church.

A mother who loves her child will also teach him to pray while he is still small enough to sit on her lap. What is learned at the mother's knee will never be forgotten. That little prayer that the mother teaches her young child at her knee when he is tired before he goes to bed will be remembered many times when he is grown, wherever he may be. That prayer may well be the last prayer he will have in his thoughts years later when he is taking his last breath in this life.

Dear young mother, you will never have anything more important to do than to make a home for those children entrusted by God into your hands. When your children are grown, they will forget that some of the corners in your house did not get swept regularly; but they will never forget that you had time to talk with them, and to do things with them, and to answer their questions. They will remember if you shared your thoughts with them. They will remember it by also sharing their thoughts with you in their school years, in their teen years, and later when they have homes of their own.

There is a short verse that sums up the whole of our duties here in this life: "Only one life, 'twill soon be past, Only what's done for Christ will last."

15 The Responsibility of Children

"Honor thy father and thy mother."
Exodus 20:12
"Children, obey your parents in the Lord, for this is right."
Ephesians 6:1

There is a story which has come down to us from the olden days when the grain crops were still cut by hand.

The grain was ripe and this teen-age boy and his father, and two of his father's servants had started to harvest several days earlier. Now this morning the boy and the servants had started early in the morning. They could probably finish today.

The ripe grain fell at their feet as they made their rounds across the field. The boy also expected his father to be out in the field helping after he had the rest of the barn chores done. But all forenoon he did not show up.

As the sun climbed higher and higher in the sky that forenoon, the day became very hot. Every time the three of them came around the field again, the boy was pretty sure that his father would be out to help, and he also hoped he would bring them a fresh drink of water from the spring. But every time they came around, he was still not there.

When noontime came, the boy and the servants hung their scythes on the low-hanging branches of a tree beside the field lane. They were just ready to wash up before going into the house for dinner when the boy's father came out of the house. "Son," he said, "could you go down the road to the village store for me?" Giving him a paper with a short list on

it, he said, "Your mother needs these things before we can eat dinner. Would you go and get them?"

That was nearly more than the young boy could take. He was hot and tired, and he was hungry. Here he had been looking for his father out in the grain field all forenoon and he had not showed up. Surely his father could have found some time that forenoon to go the half mile to the village store for what they had needed. But just when he was almost ready to put his angry feelings into words, he noticed that his father looked very tired.

He suppressed his anger, and said, "Yes, Dad, I will go."

On his way back from the village, one of the servants came running to meet him. "Your dad, just passed away," he said.

At first he could not believe it, but it was true. His earthly father had left his tired mortal frame and gone to his eternal reward. Oh, how glad he then was that he had obeyed his father's wishes and had not talked back. He would have regretted it till his dying day if he would have had to bear the memories of having sassed his father in his final earthly moments.

There is another old story of a boy whose mother had died. He lived with his father and brothers at home until he was seventeen years of age. By what could have been called a chain of unfortunate circumstances, and against his wishes, he was placed in another home far away from the one he had known as a boy.

Although he was treated well at the new home, we can be sure that his thoughts often went back to his father and brothers. He now lived in a very rich, godless, and worldly home. He missed the religious training that he was accustomed to.

Now, there are no young people who are never tempted to do wrong. This boy was no exception. There in that home where he lived he was tempted to do a thing very much against his conscience. In his loneliness he could have given in and thought that no one in his family would ever find it out anyway. Because he stuck to his convictions, he was falsely accused and put into prison. Later he did a good deed for one of his fellow prisoners, who then, right away, forgot all about it for a long time.

That boy could have said that life is just not fair. He could have given up his convictions and lived a life of sin, or he could have given up in despair. He had plenty of reason to do so. If he would have done either he probably would never have been heard from again. As it was, he was later richly rewarded for honoring his parents and his God, even though his mother was long since dead, and his father was hundreds of miles away.

By now you will probably have recognized this as the familiar story of Joseph in the first books of the Bible. That story goes to show us that it is possible for a young person to live a godly life and to honor father and mother under the most trying circumstances. Although he had to stand alone, without family or friends to be a support for him, with the strength Joseph got from God he could say no to temptation and he could stay cheerful and helpful even when he was unjustly treated. He learned what we all have to learn, that respecting and honoring our parents is not always the easy and the popular thing to do, but with the help, strength, and power from God, it can be done.

Everybody living on the earth has had parents, a father and a mother. The Bible has instructions for the living of a holy life for everyone. It has instructions for parents and it also has instructions for children. The instructions for children are to honor their parents. That includes each and everyone of us, no matter how young or old; no matter if our parents are living or not; no matter if our parents see our actions or are a thousand miles away. Even if you happen to have had godless parents, you can still honor them by living a God–fearing life.

Satan knows that he will have a lot easier time influencing the generation after us if he can first get us to be disobedient to the good example of our parents. He does tempt us hardest to disobey our parents when we are young. He knows that it is easier to get us to disobey in our young days than is is to get us to disobey when we get to be old enough to be parents and are mature enough to see what disobedience leads to. (Although it is also possible to be dishonoring to our parents when we are old enough to be parents ourselves. Very much so. The temptation then is even more sly and subtle than in our young days.)

So no matter what our age, we don't want to do things that are dishonoring or disobedient to our parents. If we do, it is just as if we are giving our younger brothers and sisters, our nieces and nephews, or the neighbors children who are younger than we are, and including the unborn children of the next generation, a license to also be disobedient.

It is not only the blight we are putting on our own lives if we are disobedient, but it is also the bad influence that we have on others that makes not honoring our parents such a great sin. Jesus explains in Matthew 18:6 how great the evil is to offend and to cause one of His pure, innocent little ones to sin. God has put us on this earth to further His cause of righteousness. That is lost if we do not honor our parents.

You would not have lived very long if the women whom God had ordained to be your mother had not spent many a sleepless night caring for you when you were helpless and fretful. What would you be if you would have grown up without the discipline and love that you got from the man whom God had chosen to be your father? Who else would have had the practical love to earn what you needed for your food, clothing and shelter when you were too young to do it yourself? Even though your parents' love was often far from perfect, that still does not excuse you. Now you are to return that love by honoring them.

So, to all you dear young readers, if the Lord sends you health and strength and will tarry in His second coming till you are grown, you and those of your generation will have your turn to till the soil and take care of the livestock, to do the building and to work in the shops, or to do what you are to do to make a living. But most important of all, you and your generation will then be responsible for strengthening the homes, schools and churches, and to raise and be a good example to the unborn generation coming after you. If you obey, honor and respect your parents, the Lord's blessing will rest on your work so that the next generation may well respect and honor you.

Listen, Young Man

16

"Remember now thy Creator in the days of thy youth, while the evil days come not, nor the years draw nigh, when thou shalt say, I have no pleasure in them."

Ecclesiastes 12:1

Young man, when are you going to make up your mind?

Not everybody is like you. We have many other young people who are making up their minds to lead decent Christian lives. As they grow out of the age of childhood innocence, they feel a need for a Savior to rescue them from their own sinful natures. They know there is a more satisfying way to live than to chase after the shallow things Satan and the world have to offer. They willingly submit themselves to baptism and to the fellowship of the plain non-conformed church of their forefathers.

But you, my dear young friend, have time and time again been putting that step off, even though you know deep in your heart you have already put it off too long.

Evidently you do not see enough of the dangers which come when young people sow "wild oats" in their young years. It is one of the lies of the devil when people say that "just a little of such living doesn't hurt anybody. It helps to get it out of the system."

How wrong they are!

Why don't we call that harmless sounding "sowing of wild oats", what it really is? It is a life of rebellion and sin to God–the Creator of your life and of mine.

Just like that strong drink that you again and again are pouring down into your system. When you took that first drink, you remember well enough that it tasted awful and you knew you were starting in something that you should have left alone. You knew that drinking would sometimes cause you to empty the contents of your stomach on the floor in front of you. You knew it would make you do crazy, disrespectful and sinful things you wouldn't do when you were in your right mind. That alcohol in your blood stream will slowly but surely destroy some of your brain cells, which will never again be replaced. Think, young man! As you go through life you will need all of the sound mind that God has given to you.

Young friend, can you tell us what is so glamorous about filling your body with the poison found in beer and whiskey bottles? There is surely no fun involved when you think how it often caused its victims to lie in a drunken stupor and have a headache and a depressing hangover the next day. Then so often the addiction to alcohol is a start in the downward spiral to the using of drugs, which has already wrecked many lives beyond repair.

But instead of being brave enough and manly enough to say no and walk away when you were offered the first drink, you followed what you thought was the leader of the crowd. You showed

40

everybody what a number-one coward you really were. Are you still too much of a weakling to stand up for what you know to be right? When are you going to stop acting like some dumb cattle being driven to slaughter and start standing on your own two feet?

Young man, you need to start associating with a different kind of company. We know you now think the decent, plain-dressing bunch is too common for you to be seen with. But the prayers of those people is what you need, and the Almighty God who is helping them to find a true fulfillment in their lives is the only place you will get the power to put a stop to your reckless living before it is too late.

The devil is out in full fury trying to keep you from remembering your Creator in your youth. And he is succeeding when he is getting you to keep the leisure part of your time, even on Sundays, filled to the brim with sports and amusements of the world. There are surely more constructive ways to use the time that God gives to you than to waste it away in such empty and shallow ways.

The amusements which the world is offering to you can be very destructive indeed. For one example, do you realize what you are doing when you go to see and hear those sensual moving picture shows which, in later life, you are going to wish you could forget?

Listen, young man, those shows are not going to leave your moral thinking undamaged. Even if you later "settle down" and get married, those evil passions which you developed and cultivated in your young years are not going to be so easily forgotten. They will be permanently recorded in the back of your mind and are not going to be as harmless as they seem to you now. They will leave you with a warped ideal of love which is poles apart from what a true, solid, and stable love can be. Those illicit desires and lusts can make you do things later that will leave you with lifelong memories of heartbreak, shame and remorse.

Keeping your mind filled in your young years with the devil's garbage that comes out of movies, television shows and cheap romance story books can have a way of keeping your future home life from being contented and your future married life from being satisfying. Those evil lusts awakened in

you can keep you from ever having the genuine love which is centered in one person only. A true home with a Christian foundation, such as is required for the proper upbringing of children, cannot be built with anything less than this godly kind of love.

This "settling down" just to get married, which is getting to be so common in our days, is so often not the sincere repentance and the new life the Bible teaches that we must begin while here on earth. How can such be a true conversion if the change does not come from the heart, and from God, and is done jut because it is getting to be considered the normal thing to do before getting married?

And do you realize you are playing with a fire that can soon be fanned out of control, if you keep running with the group that has cars, radios, musical instruments, cameras, and all the rest that goes along with these?

There is a very good reason why the plain-dressing non-conformed church of our forefathers kept standards and limits on how much modernism would be tolerated among its members. It doesn't matter if you are with the tough, rebellious crowd or with the group who goes around trying to appear more spiritual while losing out on plainness - you are in dangerous company. Before you realize it you will start having doubts about Christians being non-conformed to the world. You are on the way to becoming another person discontented with the simple and plain way of life - the true spiritual way of living that Jesus taught to His followers.

What can happen is you may soak up such a desire for more and more of the world's little gods that you will someday have no room left in your inner being for contentment and for what is meaningful in life. You are filling your system with ever-increasing desires that will leave you with an empty unhappiness. You will miss out on the abundant life that Jesus wants you to have. God gave you the gift of life, and put you on this earth for a much higher purpose than the selfish squandering of your means and your time for luxurious and worldly living.

The longer you are with misguided people, the longer and harder is going to be the uphill struggle to completely come back to the way of contentment. Not only can your own spiritual life be wrecked by the craving for more and more of the world's gadgets and modernism, but it is a well-known fact that going to a more liberal church is just about like a one-way street. Changing churches so that you will be allowed the desires that have crept into your heart is like giving the next generation a license and permission to go even further with the drift into the world. If you trample into the dirt the convictions your parents had, don't be too surprised if your children will someday do the same to yours.

And then another thing, young man. Who are you trying to impress with those loud clothes and those cowboy boots and the worldly hairstyle? Are you hoping some frivolous young girl with a short, immodest dress and pinned-back prayer veiling will consider you as good husband material? If you are trying to get her hand in marriage by attracting her in such a way, how will you still be able to say on your wedding day that you believe God has drawn and guided you together with the help of your faith and prayer?

Do you think that such a girl will make a true Christian helpmeet for you? Do you think she will make a good, praying mother for the children God may someday entrust to you for their training? Will the two of you someday provide a home with the Christian atmosphere required for the proper upbringing of children? The chances are getting to be very slim that the two of you will ever raise a family who will have firm Christian convictions.

Listen, young man, there is much more to life than young people living out their youthful days in sin, then getting married and later raising a generation of children who will be just as bad or even worse. Your bad examples are being noticed and will be copied by others, and thus kept going by others as long as there will be people on earth. The behavior of the next generation of young people will be influenced by how this generation lived - good or bad.

If the Lord tarries and if He will spare your life for a while, you will find it hard to believe how soon the time will be here that you will be at the same age your parents now are. The heartbreaks that you are now causing to your praying parents is evidently not too much of a concern to you now.

But the time could come, and could come too soon, when those stabs of heartbreak could be yours. Then you will know how deep and how sharp those pains can be. You will then know what the Bible verse means when you will say of those joyless days in your future, "I have no pleasure in them." What you are sowing now has a harvest of bitter tears and heartaches to reap later.

Dear friend, God could someday use you in the miraculous way He has to create new life, and you may someday have a son of your own. If the Lord tarries, and if that son stays healthy, he would someday be exactly the same age you are now. What would you say, and what would you do if he spent away the best years of his life as you are now wasting away yours? Would you want him to be rebellious and disrespectful to you and your wife as you are now to your parents? How much hope would you have for him if he were to be killed in an accident and would suddenly have to leave this world?

But God has not promised to you that you will live to be old. He has not promised you another year; no, He has not promised you that you will even become a day older than you are now. You might be closer to God's deadline for repenting than you realize. There are many young people now in eternity with their broken bodies in their graves who never got the chance to become as old as you now are.

Young man, your parents and the church have prayed, have coaxed, and have pleaded. Perhaps it's about time to tell you that if you don't soon make up your mind to become a worthwhile member of the church, maybe you would better go and keep away from our other young people. Your influence is having an adverse affect on too many of our otherwise innocent youth.

Even the Bible tells you to go and do as you please. But then it tells you how responsible you are for doing so. "Walk in the ways of thine heart, and in the sight of thine eyes, but know thou that for all these things God will bring thee into judgement" (Ecclesiastes 11:9). In a somewhat similar way, when Jesus saw that Judas had already made up his mind to carry out his evil intentions, He didn't try to coax him out of it. He saw Judas was beyond coaxing and challenged him with "That thou doest , do quickly" (John 13:27).

Yes, we know there are many who say we are to love you back into our circle. They say the love of the father of the Prodigal Son never wavered, no matter what his son did, or where he went. That is true; he loved his son until he came back in spite of all his son's enormous and ungrateful waste of time and goods. But the greatest deed of love that the father did was to build a home life that his son remembered when he was down and out. The remembrance of that home brought his son back. It was not that the father went to the far country to force his son to come back.

So, my dear young friend, we are not going to force you to come back and live a better life. We can't make you believe and be baptized so that you will not be dammed with the world (Mark 16:16).

It is up to you. It is an opportunity that God is still leaving open to you.

Make use of it as soon as you can.

The Titanic and the Church

17

"Repent, and be baptized, every one of you in the name of Jesus Christ for the remission of sins, and ye shall receive the gift of the Holy Ghost."

Acts 2:38

There could hardly be any of the readers of *Family Life* who have not once, or perhaps many times, heard of the tragic disaster that took place on the high seas 70 years ago this year. The ship, the Titanic, which had just been built, sank to the depths of the Atlantic Ocean on her maiden voyage.

This ship was built to be the most luxurious and largest ship in the world. She was designed to be unsinkable with watertight compartments separated by partitions called bulkheads, which were watertight well above the waterline of the ship. This was so that if one, or even two of the compartments got flooded, the ship would still stay afloat. This was a new idea in shipbuilding at that time.

On this clear, cold night the ship was plowing through the water, the crew hoping to make record time on her first ocean crossing. Some of the most influential and wealthiest people in the world were aboard, many of them wanting the distinction of being along on the Titanic's first trip.

A little after midnight an iceberg was sighted almost directly in front of the ship. The captain managed to avoid hitting the iceberg head-on by swerving the ship to one side. The ship scraped the iceberg, making a long gash far below the water line of the ship. The cold sea water started pouring into the holds of the ship, much faster than the pumps could pump it out.

After the captain found out the extent of the damage, he had a hasty conference with the builder of the ship, who was also aboard. Not only one or two, but the three front watertight compartments were being flooded through the rip along the sides.

The truth dawned on both of them. If the ship had hit the iceberg head-on, she would have been badly damaged, but would probably have been able to stay afloat. They knew that in a short time the front compartments would become waterlogged and the front end of the shop would sink. The water would then pour over the top of the next bulkhead into the next compartment, and soon that would be flooded. There was no other way; the ship that was built to be unsinkable was doomed to sink, probably in a few hours.

The more than 2,200 people that were on the ship were the captain's next concern. He gave orders to the crew to awaken the ones who were sleeping and to get the lifeboats ready.

The crew got the first boats ready to fill up and leave the ship. But strange to say, most of the passengers still couldn't believe that the ship that they were standing on, so solid under their feet, would sink. Hadn't they been told that the Titanic, the big floating city, could not sink? It did seem like a far-out idea, getting out of their warm beds to step off of the big ship into a shaky little boat and paddle away in the middle of the night. It is no wonder that the first lifeboats that were sent off hardly got filled with people.

A disaster like this was not even remotely expected so there were not enough life boats provided on the ship for all the passengers. Only a third or so of the people on board had room on the lifeboats. The rest of them were left to go down with the ship when the last lifeboats left the ship. They were rowed away from the suction which the sinking ship would make and also away from the crowds of desperate swimmers who could soon swamp a little boat.

The sight that the people in the lifeboats watched with horror in the next hour or so was unforgettable. As the front end of the ship slowly sank below the water the hundreds of people still on board grabbed for anything that they could hang on to when the decks got too steep to stand on.

The waterlogged front end kept sinking until the back end of the ship was standing almost straight out of the water. It didn't stay in this position very long till she slipped our of sight into the cold depths of the ocean. "There she goes!" Somebody shouted. Some of the lifeboat passengers wept openly at what they were seeing. Others were too stunned to say or do anything.

The survivors in the lifeboats were just far enough away by now that they could hear the cries for help coming from the people who jumped off just before she went down. The chorus of the hundreds of people who were perishing was a sound that they would never forget as long as they lived. It didn't take very long till all was still and quiet because even a good swimmer did not last long in that icy, frigid water and soon followed the ship done to a watery grave.

Don't we have the same problem is a spiritual way very much like when the first lifeboats were being launched when the Titanic was sinking? That is the problem that is in nearly all of our churches in our days in that so many of our young people want to "sow wild oats" awhile before they are baptized and live a godly life.

Talk to about anybody in any of our churches and you will get the same story. "We have a number of young people who are old enough to be baptized but not even half of them came for instruction." There have been instances where nine out of ten who would have been old enough to be baptized preferred to live a life of sin for awhile. Of course, some of them come to be baptized later, but sadly, too many of them never get it made.

Putting off to be baptized after we have grown out of our childhood innocence is living in the danger of being called away from this life and then having to answer to God as to why we did not deny the sins and lusts of the flesh. Sin is doing something which we know to be wrong. It is just as wrong to be living in sins before being baptized as it is afterwards. There is also the danger of forgetting the warnings which God sends to us to forsake our sinful life. Our sleeping conscience will then never prod us into coming back from our life of sin. Then there is also the danger of coming back but still being so unconcerned that our attitude will spread to the next generation that is coming on. There is surely more to this life than spending the young part of our life "sowing wild oats" and then later raising another generation that is just as bad, or even worse.

What are we parents doing about it? We may excuse the actions of our own children and say that they are young yet and don't seem to know any better and don't seem to realize the seriousness of it all. Of course, we are not responsible for what our children do if we have told them and warned them, and they still go on in a rebellious way, but doesn't it give us away that we did not lay the seriousness of it all before them, if we excuse their actions in this way and say that they do not know any better? Jesus made the seriousness of baptism pretty clear on one of the last times that He talked to His disciples when He was here on earth. "He that believeth and is baptized shall be saved; but he that believeth not shall be damned" (Mark 16:16).

It took faith for the Titanic's passengers to step off the big ship and away from it's comforts when they were told that it was sinking. Some of the passengers did hurry back to their cabins to get some of their belongings, but when they got back the lifeboats had left. Those people were then left to go down with their cherished possessions when the ship sank. If we keep putting it off, it will also be too late for us someday to forsake the world and it's sins and lusts of the flesh. The time to be baptized into a church which stands for contentment with less of the world's luxuries and pleasures is when the Lord lays it on our hearts to do so. Every time that we put it off it will become easier to put it off still longer.

Of course, baptism can be cheap and shallow. Some of you may have read the story of the commander of an army in the Middle Ages who was ready to go to battle. He found out that a number of his men had not yet been baptized. He gave orders for the whole army to march through a river while a priest was blessing the waters, thinking that in that way everyone would be baptized. We know that baptism is not that cheap.

Most of the state churches in the Middle Ages made laws requiring all babies to be baptized when they were just a few days old. Those small children who died before getting baptized were in some places not even allowed to be buried in their regular cemeteries because they thought that they were lost. How sad. What chance would you and I have if those innocent children would not make it to heaven?

Even in our days there are often advertisements in the newspapers that let the public know that they will hold a baptismal service, inviting anybody who wants to come and be baptized.

But even in our churches the holy rite of baptism can be made to have much less meaning and power than God intended it to have. One is when someone will put off getting baptized because his friends are putting it off, or because someone who is older is not ready yet. We can be a help to each other, but to decide to submit to baptism would still be an individual decision to make. If we do so only because we know that our parents wish for us to be baptized it is also not as it should be. We should be willing to be baptized and join the fellowship of believers because we want to do so ourselves. Just getting baptized into a church because it is feared that the government will draft the non-members of a non-resistant church is also a cheap and shallow reason to be baptized.

Yet another abuse of baptism that is creeping into our churches is when young people get baptized in some other church where some of the desires of the carnal nature are allowed. They say that they plan on later coming to the church of their parents and then live a plainer life. Some will make it back, but some will not, and thus lose for the next generations the examples and teachings of humility of dress and living that our forefathers worked to keep up.

What would our churches be like if everyone got baptized in another church? Isn't the danger of losing sight of the teachings that we were taught too great? Won't we start to thinking that some of the modern things of the world are not as evil as we were taught that they were? What will happen if we associate too freely with those who take the crucifying of the flesh and blood too lightly?

Then also, God knows that the church needs the doctrine of avoidance, so that the examples and teachings of backsliding and discontented church members do not spread into the fellowship of believers. Will the teachings in Numbers 15:30 and 31, Romans 16:17, I Corinthians 5:11, 2 Thessalonians 3:14 and Titus 3:10 be passed on to the next generation or will they be corrupted beyond repair? Let us keep to a fellowship where the examples and teachings of Jesus on the humility of plain living are both taught and practiced.

So my dear young friend, God needs you. The church needs you. Getting baptized is not to keep happiness out of your life. There are still many, many people, young and old, to whom the plain churches are a shelter of peace, joy and contentment in a troubled and evil world. Come in and join them. Their churches are far from being perfect, and never will be perfect, but where can you find a church that is grounded on more of the Biblical principles of humility and contentment that Jesus lived and preached than in the church which our forefathers, the Anabaptists, worked to establish and uphold.

Hundreds of those Anabaptist were tortured and killed because they would not give up that which they believed. Where have our churches lost the vision that the persecuted churches of the Martyr's Mirror had? We read of young people desiring to be baptized even when they knew that being found out would mean torture and death for them. We read of young people in some Communist countries in our days who would rather endure persecution than give up their search for a noble purpose for their lives. In our land of government freedom it is so unnecessary that this blight of young people unwilling to give up their lives of sin should continue.

Let us then repeat, "He that believeth and is baptized as shall be saved" (Mark 16:16). Just like the people in the Titanic's lifeboats were picked up the next morning by another ship and taken to shore and saved, so will God's people be saved from going down with the world on the morning of the great resurrection. But then also in this life will they be saved from their sins and be a witness to the Saviour who died for all of mankind who will accept His salvation. Being a witness for Jesus does not necessarily mean for us to ask everyone who we meet if they are saved or if they are newborn Christians. Being a witness for Jesus means much more than that. It means living a quiet way of life that proves that it is possible to be contented without so many of the luxuries which the world thinks it must have. The world, with its television, radios, automobiles and the ever changing styles of dress and the hundreds of other things that it has will never know of the deep and satisfying joy that can be had in the plain and simple way of living. The plain way of living is like the life which we believe Jesus would live if He were still on this earth, which He still is, in the followers of His examples and teachings. That way of living and baptism should go together.

Baptism is a symbol of the pouring out of God's Spirit of love, peace and power, and of the living of a new and better life. Baptism is a symbol of the washing away of the sins of the past and the guilt and condemnation that goes with them. Is there any verse more fitting to all who are grown out of the innocence of childhood, but are not yet baptized, than the words which were said to Paul before he was baptized, "And now, why tarriest thou? Arise, and be baptized, and wash away thy sins, calling on the name of the Lord" (Acts 22:16).

The Clock of Life

18

"And it is appointed unto man once to die, but after this the judgement.
Hebrews 9:27

Early in the year of 1848, a happening occurred that was to change the lives of many people living at that time. The Territory of California was just beginning to be settled by white people. As there was a good demand for lumber for building, one of the settlers started to set up a sawmill. An employee who was working in the tail race that led the water away from the mill wheel happened to see a gleam of something among the sand that caught his eye. He picked up the piece, which was about the size of a dime, and found out that it was really a nugget of gold.

As the news of his find spread, and as more bits of gold were found here and there, many people became intensely excited. They deserted their shops and abandoned their work and swarmed to the hills and mountains to find gold for themselves. They clawed at the sand in the creeks and dug along the rivers in the hopes of making an easy fortune. The sawmill stood there unfinished - the great California gold rush was on!

When the news of men making easy riches reached the eastern part of the United States, many of the people there, especially some of the young men and unmarried boys made hasty preparations to go west to California as soon as possible and try their luck in the mining camps.

At this time there were no railroads crossing the continent, so the overland route to the West was not an easy one. One company in particular, a group of about eighty men and boys who had pooled their money to buy mules, wagons, and supplies to go to the gold fields, were soon to find out that the road was a long and hard journey, such as they had never before experienced.

Not all of the eighty people in this company who started out were destined to live until they arrived at their journeys' end out west. On one occasion the wagon train came to a river that was too deep to go through with the wagons. They followed the river upstream for a while until they could find a shallow place where they could ford across.

One seventeen-year-old boy decided to save himself the long round-about way by swimming across the deep part of the river. When he was only partly over, his companions saw that he was having trouble, and then saw him sink out of sight. Although they tried to save him, he did not make it, and was drowned. His body was recovered afterwards by his friends, and buried beside the trail with only two boards from one of the wagons marking the head and foot of his grave.

Part of the trail to the west led through the great western prairies, where even though they traveled for days, the distant horizon did not seem to get any closer. It was while they were crossing those plains that seemed to be so endless, that this same company suffered the death of another one of its members.

A carelessly-handled shotgun went off unexpectedly, with the full blast hitting one of the young men in the hips. There was nothing that those who were with him could do to save his life. As his life was bleeding away he told his comrades that he did not mind the thought of dying as much as the thought of lying all alone out in that great empty land. When he died about four hours after the accident, he was gently wrapped in a blanket, and buried in a deep grave.

These two youths came to experience what everybody who lives on this earth will some time experience - that is dying. Even those who will be living when Christ comes again will experience the leaving behind of their mortal bodies, just like a dying person does. The life of our flesh and blood will some day cease.

There was once a stranger who came to town and asked what the death rate was there. He was told that the death rate there was the same as it is everywhere else - it was one to each person. Even though there have been many rich people already who would have given all of their fortunes to have their life extended, death is one experience that all of us, rich or poor, small or great, both the ordinary and the famous, will not miss. There may be other things that the smart and the clever and the rich will find loopholes to avoid, but not so with dying.

We know that death will not always wait until a person has all his life's plans completed. Our plans and God's plans are so often not the same thing. Those two young people with the high hopes of making easy riches in the California gold fields never even got there. Their allotted days were up before that. When our time is up, there will be nothing that anybody will be able to do to keep this life going. On the other hand, if God wants us to be here yet for one of His purposes, He will somehow protect us and we will live as long as He wants us to live.

No, death does not come to all people at one certain age. The ages of the departed that are carved on the gravestones in a cemetery will show all ages from just several days old or less, to a hundred years old or more. No matter how young your age now, there are many, many people who were laid in their graves younger than you now are. You have now already seen more of this life than they ever had or ever will.

Some people will get to be old, feeble, and sickly, and weary of life, but they are still here for a purpose. Others depart from this life when they are yet young and are still making plans for the future. These are often people whom we may feel are sorely needed by their families.

Some are only here for a very short time, indeed. There have many been born who have opened their eyes to this world, and then only a short time later they have closed them again in death, just as though this world was not fit for their pure little eyes to see. Such are a little like the first snowflakes that lightly fall when it starts to snow. They come to earth, but do not last long. They no more than touch the earth, and are soon gone. God sometimes takes those who are just like an unopened flower bud home again to Him, because their purpose for living in this life has then been fulfilled.

We can daily read in the obituary part of the papers the names of those who have passed to the great beyond; that place from which there is no return. We glance over the names, but it does not mean very much to us if we did not know the people any way.

But now and then a name is there of someone we have perhaps known well. Then it comes close. It comes closer yet if word comes to us of someone in the neighborhood or community who has gone the way of all flesh. It comes another step closer if that one has also been a close friend or relative to us. Even closer than that is when death comes to the immediate family, and claims a father or mother, or a brother or a sister - or a married partner.

But death will someday come even closer to all of us. It will come to the home where you are living, and on that day, it will not be somebody else. It will be you.

So far it has always been somebody else who has gone through that door, which separates this life from the next. Although nearly all of the details of what lies beyond that door will never be known to us, while we are in this life, God saw to it that not all of what is on the other side is unknown. God's Word, the Bible, gives us enough that we know an eternity will follow our time here on earth. We also know that there will be only two places for us to be spending those unending ages - the endlessness of which our finite limited thoughts cannot even begin to grasp. All who are living on the earth now; all who have lived in the past, and all who will live here in the future will spend eternity in one of two places. Not a single person will be left out. We will spend that time either in heaven, the home of God, or in hell, separated from God. The life of our inner being, called the soul, was started here on earth, but will not end here.

There will be a resurrection of the dead. No matter where they have died, or when, God will use His power to bring all the dead to life again. Some of the early Christians were thrown to the lions, some were burned to ashes, but they will still all be there at the Judgement Day. Some have died at sea, and were slipped overboard for burial. The forms of many now lie as dust in many unmarked graves all over the world, but God has not forgotten a single one of them. Jesus promised His disciples that after He would arise, they would see Him again, and them "because I live, ye shall live also" (John 14:19). Oh, what comfort and hope in those words of promise.

Our time here is too short to be doing anything but the work that God has put us on this earth to do. We are here as stewards or caretakers of the material things that we use as we go through life.

But at the same time, we can also be doing much more than that. We are also here to further God's cause of peace, righteousness, and love, just as Jesus did while He was here.

Our allotted time here is too short to be leaning toward the world. "Where the tree falleth, there shall it be" (Ecclesiastes 11:3). Let us not for one moment think that we can lean toward the world, but still fall the other way when our life here is cut off.

We all make mistakes. We may have the opportunity to correct some of our mistakes and make them right again. But one mistake that can never be corrected is to waste the time which God has granted for us to use here on earth on anything else but for His honor. A wasted life here is a wasted eternity.

An unknown poet has put a lot in a few words:

The clock of life is wound but once,
And no man has the power,
To tell just when the hands will stop
At late or early hour.

Now is the only time you own.
Live, love, toil with a will.
Place no faith in tomorrow for
The hands may then be still.

Who Can Know the Future?

19

"...tell us, when shall these things be? and what shall be the sign of thy coming, and the end of the world?"
Matthew 24:3

While Jesus still walked on earth with his disciples, they were wondering when the end of the world would come, and asked Him to tell them of the signs that would appear just before the end.

There was nothing wrong with asking those questions. Jesus did not just shrug off their questions as unimportant, but answered with illustrations that are still very helpful to us today.

Questions very much like those which the disciples asked have been asked and wondered about ever since. The second coming and the end of the world are mentioned many times in the Bible. Ever since the times of the apostles many of the people of the Christian church have studied and have tried to figure out what the Bible is teaching on that subject. They are seeking answers to questions that have never yet been fully explained.

Oh, of course, there have been hundreds of books written on the subject, both in our day and also long ago. In our day we have some who claim to be able to understand the Bible prophecies. These people say we should all be able to predict all the events of the future. They have written many books and articles on the subject. They especially like to take the last book of the Bible, the book of Revelation, and just like taking you by the hand, will show you exactly how the events of the future will unfold.

Are they always right?

Just a generation or so ago, when Adolf Hitler was ruthlessly and unmercifully making his bid to be the ruler of all the world, there were people who were sure that there was the man who had the mark of the beast. They were sure that the man mentioned in Revelation 13:18 who had the number 666 was Hitler himself. They were sure that they had the wisdom and understanding to confidently point to him as being the man of the "thousand-year kingdom." (This kingdom is mentioned about a half-dozen times in the twentieth chapter of Revelation.) Hitler himself knew enough of Scripture to boast that the government which he had established and was leading would last a thousand years - much longer than any government in history had yet lasted.

Hitler's government lasted twelve years and three months! His dictatorship, that for a short time extended over the greater part of the continent of Europe, fell to pieces and the life of Hitler fell with it. Those who explained Bible prophecy to say that Hitler was the man were wrong. They went back to their Bible for a different explanation.

Then we have the verse in 2 John 2:18 which tells us that when the anti-christ shall come - "...Whereby we know that it is the last time." Who is this anti-christ? Some of the early Christians were almost sure that the anti-christ was Nero, that cruel Roman emperor who took pleasure in torturing Christians to death. Nearly two thousand years have passed since then, and time still goes on.

Some of those who explain of prophecy today are saying that the anti-christ is an evil ruler who will soon be coming up and will rule all the world with cruelty and wickedness. His wickedness will be such as mankind has never before seen. Some grab the verses in Revelation 9:15-16 (in English) where mention is made of 200 thousand, thousand (200,000,000) soldiers. These soldiers are said to slay the third part of the people in the world in less than a year's time. So people today deduct that this nation is China. That is the only nation with a population large enough to come up with that number of soldiers. So they say that China, and not Russia, is to be feared.

So it goes on and on. If we were to listen to and believe all the prophets of doom in our time, we would all be shaking with fear. This is surely not what Jesus wants us to do. He knew that the people of every generation would have many reasons for becoming frightened and fearful. So in a few words he spoke these words of comfort, not only to his disciples, but to us all: "And ye shall hear of wars and rumors of wars; see that ye be not troubled, for all these things must come to pass, but the end is not yet" (Matthew 24:6).

"See that ye be not troubled." Isn't that a reassuring answer for all Christians in these days of uncertainty and troubles? All of the world events are a part of God's master plan. Just take the prophecy about the beast in Revelation 13. Those verses could well have a literal fulfillment and could mean that a world ruler will come, perhaps yet in our time, or in the time of our descendants. It is also possible that he will require everyone to worship him, and will require everyone to wear his mark which will then make them unfit to reign with Christ (Revelation 20:4). But then those passages could also have a symbolic or spiritual fulfillment which could mean that the pride of Satan is in the human heart is the beast which causes people to mark themselves with the ever-changing styles and fashions of dress and hair-dos of the world. That animal nature in the the hearts of humans from which the sins of the flesh and lust are produced could also be the beast which the Bible is describing to us.

There are other passages which could be going into fulfillment in ways which we do not expect. That which is in our hearts which is not of the humility and love of Christ could be the anti-christ which is marking us by our sinful actions. Then there is the prophecy in Revelation 16:14 and 16 which tells of the terrible and final battle between the forces of good and evil at Mount Megiddo or Armageddon.

Armageddon is an actual place in the Holy Land at which many fierce wars were fought from Old Testament times on down to World War I. This plain between the mountains was of such strategic importance that there is a record of an ancient king having said that the capture of that place was like the capture of a thousand towns. It is quite possible that Jesus sometimes took the route that led through this pass to go from his hometown in Galilee to the temple in Jerusalem.

There could be a great clash there someday, such as the world has never seen before, but it also makes sense to think that the battle that is described is the spiritual life and death struggle that goes on in the battleground of our hearts. Our heart is the place where all sin has its beginning. The prophecies of the Bible could be fulfilled in many ways God knows how and when, but we don't. Get out your Bible and read that verse in Acts 1:7.

It is a little like those who tried to interpret and explain the hidden meanings of some of the Old Testament prophecies before the time of Christ. Many of the details of Christ's coming were plainly foretold by God's prophets hundreds of years before they occurred. But then he came he came in such an unexpected way. Plus his coming occurred only after prophecy had been silent for 400 years.

If Jesus would have been born in Bethlehem, as they had expected, in the palace of an important and powerful king, no doubt many would have heralded him as the Messiah. But who expected him to be born to a very poor couple who just "happened to be" in Bethlehem at that time? And then of all places for the birth to take place - in an animal stable.

Nor did Jesus act like most people expected him to. He was not impressed with the outward show of piety that the Pharisees had. He condemned them severely because he knew they didn't have that change in their inner hearts. Also, he never even tried to challenge the might of the Romans who ruled over the Jews at that time. Actually, he all but ignored them.

"What a way for the Messiah of the Jews to act!" they might well have cried.

The Jews were expecting the promised deliverer to call an army together and drive those hated Roman soldiers along with their despised tax collectors right out of the land of Judea. Even up to the time that Jesus ascended to Heaven, his own disciples still thought he would establish a new kingdom in the land of Israel (Acts 1:6). If he would have promised deliverance from the Romans and established a free kingdom in Israel, everyone would have flocked to his banner.

But as it was, although his suffering and death were plainly foretold, even down to many of the little details, it was not one bit understood until he was no longer here in person. Only after his death and resurrection could it be understood that he had to suffer a death on the cross to save his people.

That could still be very much the way much of prophecy might be for us in our time. The events of history are happening before our eyes, but only after the happenings are over will we be able to see that things came to pass just as God had foretold and planned them.

This is not to say that conditions in the world will straighten out and that things will get better. The words of Jesus in Matthew 24 rule that out. What we do not want to concern us too much about is to try to figure out all the details. Let God take care of that.

It is something that we don't like to think about that men are now able to build a big computer that could keep track of all our past records and transactions. But it is a thousand times more important to be concerned and to repent from our sins because of the record that God is keeping of our lives.

The details of what the future holds for us is not known to us. It is unthinkable that God would ever put people on this earth with the conditions being so bad that it would be impossible to live a true Christian life. He never has, and He never will. Many, many Christians in other days, (and still in our day in some countries) have been persecuted and have given up their lives rather than give up their faith. They knew of the peace and power that could be felt but not seen. They have proven that men can take away one's life, but man can never take away one's faith. It is even possible that we may never again have persecution because Satan can see that he can win more people with a slow drifting toward the world than by using forceful methods. In times of persecution, you are either a Christian, or you are not a Christian.

We may wish for a way to see into the future– clear over to the other side. But that is not for us humans to do. Far better than to see a known way is to put our hands into God's hands and let Him lead the way for us. The future is unknown to us, but it is in good hands – it is in God's hands.

So again, "Let not your hearts be troubled." Even though the events around us may seem to us like a galloping team out of control going downhill with a loaded wagon with broken brakes, God is still in full control of His creation. The true Christian life will never be easy, but with God it will never be impossible. Only in that way of life is there contentment, peace and joy even in tribulation. Only in Jesus can be found rest for our souls (Matthew 11:28). Let us permit the words of Jesus to tell it just like it is: "These things have I spoken unto you that in me ye might have peace. In the world ye shall have tribulation, but be of good cheer, I have overcome the world" (John 16:33).

The Story of Demas

20

"For Demas hath forsaken me, having loved this present world."
2 Timothy 4:10

Very little is known of this man, Demas, that Paul is writing to Timothy about. In only two other places in the New Testament is there reference to a Demas. In all three places where he is mentioned, it is very likely telling us of the same man. He was one who Paul had at one time called a "fellow laborer" (Philemon 24). But later he became so spiritually blinded by the allure of this world that he turned away from Paul to follow his love of the world.

It is known that Demas, along with Luke, was with Paul in Rome (Colossians 4:14). As is well known, Paul spent a good many of his last days in a prison bound with chains (Colossians 4:18, Acts 28:20, 2 Timothy 1:16, 17). What would a man chained in prison do without friends? Evidently Luke and Demas, as friends, often visited Paul in his imprisonment.

We do not know what happened that later caused Demas to love "the good things of this life," as one version puts it. But we can be pretty sure of the result. When Paul writes that Demas had forsaken him due to his love of the world, we can presume he also left the church. The Christian church, just started a few years earlier, and based on the teachings of Jesus, did not have use for a member who loved the world. Nor did such a man have use for the church, which in those days was as different from the world as day is from night.

If Demas was around Paul for any length of time, we can be sure that he knew how necessary is the living and practicing of the true Christian life. He must also have heard tell of the rewards that follow, that are beyond measure, both in this life and hereafter.

But, sadly, he left it all for the love of the present world. Didn't Demas know that the love of the present world would cause him to forget to prepare for the next world that lies just beyond this short and fleeting life?

We know nothing more of this Demas, but we do know of Luke; the one who stayed. Luke was the one who wrote one of the four gospels and also recorded in writing the story of the first church. his writings, like the rest of the New Testament, are priceless to all the generations who have lived since him. The life that Luke led caused him to be later martyred for his faith.

Sad to say, there have been many like Demas since then, right on down to our time. Those people who are left in the church when they are forsaken by people like Demas will never finish grieving and wondering why. We so often have to wonder what we could have done differently so that those who leave would have found contentment and wished to stay.

To those of our dear friends who have chosen to forsake us, we will have to tell you that we shuddered when those frightening words were spoken over you; when "with the power of the Lord Jesus Christ" you were delivered "unto Satan for the destruction of the flesh" (I Corinthians 5:4-5). That day was sadder and more sorrowful for us than the day of a funeral.

But still we hung on to the hope that is expressed in the rest of the verse, "that the spirit may be saved in the day of the Lord Jesus Christ." We have not ceased to hope and pray that you will still cry to God for help to crucify your love of the world and the desire of your flesh so that you will still be saved on the day of the Lord Jesus Christ. When that day comes you will be forever finished with this life and the things that you loved in the world.

Oh, "Demas," why did you turn away? How could you so easily forsake those who wished to live a life different from the world? Didn't you realize what you walked away from when you left the church that stands for non-conformity, as commanded in Romans 12:2?

The Demas of 1900 years ago lived at the time when many of Jesus' disciples were still living. It is possible that he knew some who had personally known Jesus when He was here on earth. He knew that those disciples taught and sought to live according to the ways and teachings of their Master and Lord. One of them writes that we are to "love not the world, neither the things that are in the world. If any man love the world, the love of the Father is not in him" (1 John 2:15).

And to the Demas of today, God saw to it that you were taught, first by your parents, of the humble, contented and plain way of life. Those who taught that way of living to you, along with the Biblical way of salvation, were convinced that God's will for their lives was a walk of life separated and distinct from the world. They were not ashamed to live a life that showed what they believed in. They were convinced that the best Christian witness to a decaying world is to quietly uphold a plain way of life. They gladly lived such a way of life, not because they thought that they had to, but because they felt it was more like that which Christ Himself would live if He were still here in person.

They did not believe that the plain way of life was just weak, obsolete, and out-dated. The powerful influence that they had to others by not blindly going along with all the rapidly-changing lifestyles will never be fully known in this life. They did not think of plainness and simplicity of living as being an impossible burden. Even though they had neighbors and friends and lived among people who did not practice non-conformity, they "lived and let live," but did not permit anyone to explain away the necessity of such living.

Although far from perfect, they sought to live up to what they believed in and were taught by their parents. They did not think that such living would earn their way to heaven. But they wished to follow the footsteps of their Saviour, who redeemed them from their sins. Among those sins they were redeemed from they included the love to the world. We also know that they hoped that the generation following them would find fulfillment in such a way of life.

That which you were taught in your young days was your legacy or birthright. It is very much like the birthright which Esau was born with. We know that later Esau considered this birthright almost worthless, and sold it for a bowl of food, which was soon used up and gone (Genesis 25:33). He considered it of little value. But the day came when he found that the blessing which went with the birthright was also gone. All the tears which he shed in remorse (Hebrews 12:17) over the lost blessing could never bring it back.

An upbringing in a plain Christian home is a priceless blessing. But it is all too often ignored and walked away from in our day. How can so many be ungrateful to their parents and to God for their plain "Old Order" heritage? Oh, don't you sell the blessing that goes with your heritage just for the things in the world that will soon pass away? "But continue thou in the things which thou hast learned and hast been assured of, knowing of whom thou hast learned them" (2 Timothy 3:14).

It hurts to hear someone talk of how "grateful" or how "proud" they are of their plain background, when at the same time they have left it. They have left it because they thought it was too much of a burden to live up to, or because they were deceived and misled into believing that plainness is not necessary for a true Christian life. There are hundreds of people who see later what their choice has brought to them, and would have stayed if they could have seen how things would turn out in the future.

To the "Demas" of our day, we wonder if you didn't see the results that so often followed when others started to love what they thought were "the good things of life." Did you fail to notice that so often the next generation will go even further into the world? It doesn't take long until there is forever no turning back to a life for Christ.

We know that you are familiar with many who are now out in the world, but who have had parents or grandparents who staunchly sought to live a life patterned after the humility of Christ. Such parents and grandparents believed that plain living is a Scriptural commandment and not just a tradition of man. There are many with such a background who are now in the world and who work on the Lord's day just as they would on any other day of the week. You probably also know some who have gone so far that they at least say that they don't believe that divorce and remarriage are wrong. How can so much be lost so soon?

There are others who don't believe, or at least say they don't believe, that it matters how you are dressed, just so that the heart is right. Some even say that if we want to be a witness to the world, we must be more like the world so that they will accept our witness. Their styles and fashions of dress (or at times, their improper undress) are sorrowful and shameful to see. Some of the parents and grandparents who are no longer living would weep until they could weep no more if they would have to see where some of their descendants are now and how they look.

But they are not here anymore to see it. Could one of God's mercies be that He closed their eyes in death so that they did not have to live to see it all? If they would come back to this life they would not be able to believe that some of the people that they would see would be their own descendants.

Dear friends, did we too often shirk our Christian duty as parents that some of you have left us? We know that we have failed many times. Some of you are saying that you have left us because you

thought that you could raise your children better somewhere else. Did you fail to see that there are still many, many of our young people among us who would have been decent examples and good company for your children if you would have stayed with us?

But we do hang our heads in shame that there are still too many of our young people who are a worse influence to others than anybody out in the world could ever be. All that we know to do is to make a new start by doing better ourselves.

With God's help and prayer, we want to tell our young people of the new birth and of the new, better and more fulfilling way of living and behavior that follows that new birth. We must also let them know that we are praying for them for the power from God that they need so that they are able to make the change in their lives that is needed. We sorely needed you to help to make things better and to help to clean out some of the sins and evils that are still among us.

We know that you are saying that you wished to find your home in a more spiritual church than what we seem to be. If you would have left us, and then lived a life closer to Christ and further away from the world, we would have had reason to think that you might have something for us to look into. But when you went on an "ego trip" soon after you left us, and brought home many of the luxuries and conveniences of the world that our forefathers thought best to keep out of the church, we couldn't help but to get serious doubts about your way of life being more spiritual.

It is open for all to see as to what is taking over the central part of your heart. The narrow way "which leadeth into life" (Matthew 7:14) does not have room for living sumptuously every day" like the rich man did (Luke 16:19). The word "sumptuously" is defined in the dictionary as "costly, lavish, and splendid."

We also couldn't help but wonder if there was some pride involved that you did not do more to keep your children plain so that they would seek company with the more decent ones when you were still with us. When somebody leaves the church and then says that he feels better inside than he ever did before, it often is highly suspected it is because he now has some of the material things for which he had been longing and wishing.

We know that some of you have also taken as a handle that too many of our people act as if it were a chore to listen to the teaching of God's Word, and to help with the singing of God's praises. We don't want to ever excuse our laziness and our lack of zeal by saying that the reason that we sometimes get drowsy at church services is because we are such a busy and active people during the week. Give us another chance to do better. Please take those for example who heartily help with the singing and are interested in the services. Don't take for examples those who don't.

We still have many who seek to refresh their souls on the Lord's Day and then live up to their beliefs during the rest of the week. Look at those before you judge us too harshly. There are still many among us to whom our churches are a source of comfort and peace that can not be found anywhere else. We also still have many to whom the praying together with others in church is such a priceless source of power that they do not like to miss being there. Again, we needed you for the good influence that you could have been if you would have kept the faith and stayed with us. You could have done more good by staying with us and helping us than by going out and criticizing us.

Now we will have to let you know of the next step which we are going to have to take. You have been admonished time and time again. But you have still chosen to forsake us and leave us for a closer walk with the world. Even Jesus did not try to plead with Judas when He saw that he had made up his mind to do what he later did, but said to him, "That thou doest, do quickly" (John 13:27). The only course left for us was to excommunicate you from the church, and now practice what Scripturally follows that excommunication – the ban and the avoidance which goes with it.

The human nature in us does not want us to do so, but we have so much Scripture to support that doctrine that we cannot do anything else. Your way of life and your beliefs are no longer a help to us, but could even be deceiving to us and to others. We will therefore have to limit our dealings with you.

We know that some of you who have left us are saying that avoidance and separation are surely not the way of love. You say that Jesus loved the sinners of His day, and ate with them, so why are we avoiding them in our time?

Our answer is that if we have a neighbor who is not even a church goer, and who we know lives in gross sins, we will not hold that ban against him. We do so because we are not to judge those who are without, but we are to judge those who are within (1 Corinthians 5:12).

God knew that nobody can be more of a deceiver than someone "that is called a brother" (1 Corinthians 5:11) but who has fallen away and starts to live a life of sin. That is why such a one is to be separated from the church, so that he does not have as much influence to mislead others. We would not be obeying Scripture if we did not hold the ban or separation against him.

Now we also know that some of you are saying that it is right to ban those who are in gross sins named in 1 Corinthians 5:11, but you say that you are not one of them. You say that you are born again, and that we are wrong that we separate ourselves from you. But Scripture does not stop there. If you are one who has "caused divisions and offenses contrary to the doctrine which ye have learned" (Romans 16:17) we must mark and avoid you.

The same Paul who believed in, and accepted the salvation which Christ brought by grace, also believed in not keeping company with discontented ex-church members. He gave us that verse in 2 Thessalonians 3:14 in which he tells us to note that man who does not obey and have no company with him. Sorry, but we are to reject ("meide" in German) according to Titus 3:10, even if we can hardly bring ourselves to do.

We did not first reject you. You have rejected us and the way of living which we value and hold dear. It has hurt us all to see you so deliberately and carelessly trample upon the doctrines that you were taught. For those who wish to look it up, the *Martyrs Mirror* in pages 32, 33, 37, 43, 807, 808 and 974 in the English edition record for us how the persecuted Anabaptists, the predecessors of today's Mennonites and Amish, Scripturally upheld the ban. They avoided backsliders in social eating and drinking, not just at the Communion table. The Scriptures are as much in effect now as they were then.

We will say it again: it goes against our human nature to place you in the ban. If we say that we love you too much to judge you and ban you because you have been such a good neighbor to us, or because you were a close relative of whom we were fond, then we admit that we have the natural love for you, but not the spiritual.

On the other hand, if we are so angry at you for the things that you have done that we are just glad to ban you, or as might be said, to get rid of you, that is also far, far from the way of love. There is not to be a trace of hate in the practice of the ban.

When one member suffers, all the other members should suffer with it (1 Corinthians 12:26). We are never to count you as an enemy, but to admonish you as a brother (2 Thessalonians 3:15). The people of the church did not put you in the ban and do not avoid you because they think that they are better than you, but because they know that so often the drift into the world speeds up when the practice of the ban is not kept. We believe that the ban is to keep the Scriptural practices in a church from being diluted, or watered down, by erring members.

Some of you have told us that only what we believe and only what is spiritual is what matters, and not our works. You have tried to argue with our belief that we have to be doing good works. Your argument has been that we cannot earn a home in heaven with our good works. That is true. Christ has fully paid for our redemption. It would have been unnecessary for Christ to suffer and die on the cruel cross if we could have redeemed ourselves. But still works will go with faith.

Works and faith cannot be separated. Our works will always show what we are believing in. Works and faith are like a set of healthy twins. They are born and grow up together.

"Remember therefore from whence thou art fallen and do the first work" (Revelation 2:5) which is repentance (Matthew 3:2, Matthew 4:17, and 10:7). The Bible also says that "I will give unto every one of you according to your works" (Revelation 2:23). We also have one chapter which twice tells us that the dead "were judged every man according to their works" (Revelation 20:12 and 13). Let no one tell you that deeds are unimportant, for it is clear that at the end of our lives we will be judged by what we have done.

Now we know that it is so often useless to give advice unless it is asked for. You would probably never ask any of us for advice. But all of us want you to know that you are invited and are welcome to come back to us and to our fellowship. The most touching and the most powerful sermon that you could ever be able to lay onto the hearts of those coming after you, even after you are gone, will be to come back to the church. You will never be able to go back and live your life over again. With time always moving forward, that is impossible and God does not require that of you. What is required is that you start all over again. That is what is called the new birth. You will have to do so while you are still in this life; the length of which is known only to the Lord. We all know well enough to better our lives so that it really would be unnecessary for God to ever warn us again.

Now in closing, the words of Revelation 22:17 come to mind, "And the spirit and the bride say, Come." God's spirit is talking to you through your conscience to come. The people of the church, the bride of Christ are inviting you to come. You are invited to come just as you are. That is right, but there are things which cannot be brought along.

You may have to bury some personal grudges to come. You may have to swallow a mountain of pride to come. You may have to give up some of the good things of this life, that are like idols to you to come. You may have to live a life vastly different from what you are now used to. Your life style, which you now seem to love, will have to change. And you may have to face the ridicule of those who are now your companions.

But really, aren't all of us who are seeking the new birth required to be doing these things? With God's grace, you will be able to get to where you will be tired of trying to drag any hindrances of your soul along with you. If you are willing to be saved from your sins, which includes the sin of loving the world, God's grace can help you do just that.

We wish you the power of God's Holy Spirit and will be praying for you.

When Praying Won't Help

21

"He that is unjust, let him be unjust still; and he which is filthy, let him be filthy still; and he that is righteous, let him be righteous still; and he that is holy, let him be holy still."

Revelation 22:11

One of Jesus' parables, that of the rich man and the poor man, gives us a glimpse of what eternity is going to be like. Eternity is that unending span of time after the time of hours, days and years, as we know it, is over.

That well-known parable gives us the story of what happened to two men who had lived on earth, but had died. The rich man was buried. The Bible does not tell us whether or not anybody bothered to bury the poor man after he was dead.

But the Bible tells us that while the one was in heavenly bliss, the other was in hell, that place "prepared for the devil and his angels" (Matthew 25:41).

Let us note. Here was a man who had lived on the same earth you and I are now living on. He was now dead and buried, but there was still a part of him which was very much alive. In the place where he found himself, he could see, because he "lifted up his eyes" (Luke 16:23). He could feel the terrible misery he was in, and he could cry out, because he pleaded, "Have mercy on me,...because I am tormented in this flame." He could pray because he prayed that someone would be sent with his finger dipped in water to cool his tongue. He could think and he could remember because he thought of his brothers who were still in his father's house.

He was denied all the requests that he had made, even the one in which he prayed for his brothers who, if they were still in his father's house, could possibly have been in their innocent days of young childhood.

That place where the rich man found himself was sealed off. We can note that the hell where he was spending his time and the heaven where Lazarus, the former poor man, was spending his time, had nothing like a bridge between the two. The Bible says that the former rich man was told that "there is a great gulf fixed, so that they which would pass from hence to you cannot, neither can they pass to us, that would come from thence" (Luke 16:26).

In eternity, he that is unjust or filthy will forever stay that way. Those who are righteous or holy will forever stay like that.

How different in this life! A change can always be made. The good can become bad, and sometimes do, but thanks be to God, it is also possible for the bad to become good.

Take that young man, Saul. At one time he was "breathing out threatenings and slaughter against the disciples of the Lord" (Acts 9:1). Not long afterward he was one of the disciples himself.

The jailer, who may have had a part in beating Paul and Silas, (at least we know he "thrust them into the inner prison and made their feet fast in the stocks" Acts 16:24), was going to show these wounded, beaten and despised men that he had them under his authority.

The change that came to him came overnight. He would not have believed the evening before that he would be kindly washing off their bare, bleeding backs before the night was over, or that he would be giving them a good meal in his own house. But that is exactly the way things turned out.

When the disciples came together after the crucifixion of Jesus, they were afraid of the Jews and kept their doors locked (John 20:19). Just several weeks later we find them telling others about Jesus. They were doing this boldly and openly, and even right in the temple and to the very people who had arranged for Jesus' death on the cross. And they were no longer afraid.

People can change. People can change in a short time.

Then there are the thieves who died on their crosses, on each side of Jesus. If we could have lived in Bible times and would have know these thieves and the lives that they led, we probably would have had no hope for them. If we would have been close enough to have seen them die for their criminal acts, but would have been too far away to hear the words that the one had with the Saviour, we would still have said that they both died without hope.

The story is not meant to make us think that it is good to put off repentance until we are dying. The other thief had the same opportunity, but did not do so. That story is to teach us to let God, who knows everything, do the judging. We know too little to judge others. And that story is there to teach us that a person can change, even when others who have the same opportunity, don't do so.

There is hope for all of us when we read such accounts of people who changed. We can also change, but first we must want to. If we will only let God work, we can change. There is something like the miracle of a slow, steady growth to becoming better, but there is also something like the miracle of a big change that takes place almost overnight.

When someone lives in sin, it is always going to be God who will sometime stop that person from going on with his sinful living. It has often happened that a person living in sin on one Sunday evening completely stopped doing any sin by the next Sunday evening. He died during that time and God stopped his sinful living.

But thanks be to God. He also stops willful, sinful living in another way. It is possible for God to make a big change in a person's life in one week's time if that person wants it done. It will take the miracle of God's power and grace to do it, but it is possible.

A change for the better is going to take prayer. The prayers of the rich man in hell did not help him any more. He should have prayed for himself and for his brothers while he was still living. After the finality of death, prayer will no longer help. Heaven and hell will be locked – there will be no going back and forth.

Let us pray for ourselves and for our brethren while we are still in this life. That is the only time that prayer will help. What are we waiting for?

60

The Search for Contentment

22

"Be content with such things as ye have, for He hath said, I will never leave thee, nor forsake thee."
Hebrews 13:5

You may have already read or heard the old story of the territory of land that had been opened up for sale. The story has been around in some form or other for quite a long time.

As one version of the story goes, a nobleman had a vast tract of land that he wanted to sell. The land agent who had been put in charge of selling this land had an unusual way to go about it. The prospective buyer was required to give the bag of coins containing the purchase price to the agent before he started. The agreement was that the buyer would start at one spot and all the land that he could go around in a day's time on foot was the land that he could have. It was also in the bargain that he was to be back to his starting time before sunset, or he would forfeit both the purchase money and the land.

Many were the young men who wished to have an acreage of ground to live on and to till, so as to make a living for themselves and their families. Many of them got their farms in this way. Many an older man who wished to own a small plot of ground to work on it his retirement years and to pasture a small herd of cattle also came to buy land. Taking along the stakes supplied by the land agent, they paid for and then marked out nice-sized tracts of land for themselves and their families.

However, not all who came to buy land were contented to get only what they needed and could use in a small way. One day a young, energetic man came who had visions of becoming a big and rich landowner. On that day he started as early as possible, as soon as the day broke, to stake out his purchase. He walked as fast as he could.

Seeing the wide and level land before him, he became very much excited about the prospect of becoming the owner of a large and extensive plantation. Nobody else from far and wide would have a spread of ground larger than his. His brisk walk soon had taken him far from where he had started. He could hardly stop going.

When he saw that the sun had crossed the noon point of the day, he knew that it was high time for him to make a swing to one side before he started back. His land would now have one long border, but it would also have to be wide. What good would a long and narrow piece of ground to be him?

So he jabbed one of his markers in the ground and turned to his left. As he hurried to cover as much ground as he could, he came to a wide expanse of land which looked to be as fertile as any land that he had ever before seen. Why not hurry a little faster and get more land while he was at it anyway?

So hurry he did.

61

He was jogging along at a trot now, and watching the sun out of the corner of one eye at the same time. He went as fast as he could and as long as he dared before he placed another marker and turned toward his starting point.

At this point his troubles began. Not until now did he realize how tired all his efforts had made him, and how exhausted he was. The ground over which he needed to walk was becoming swampy. He was bogging down to his ankles. It was only with much effort that he could keep moving forward at all. He just had to reach the starting point! He just had to reach it before the sun went down.

Feverishly he plodded through the muck. Shortly before the sun set, he was still pretty far from his starting point. Sometimes it looked as if he would never make it. At other times it looked as if he would yet make it if he would just run a little faster. Never before in his whole life had he made such an effort, so desperate was he. He did not want to lose both his money and the land.

But he did not quite make it. He was within sight of, but not quite at the place where he had started that morning when the sun sank down behind the horizon.

The exertion of the long day proved to have been too much for him. He fell over dead.

When his friends later buried him and had mounded the earth over his grave, they could not help but think about what had happened. They were all thinking the same thought, "All the land that this man has now is this small spot just big enough for his grave.

This story has more than one moral, or lesson, to it. We all know that it takes work and industry to make a living for ourselves and our families. The Bible never excuses laziness. "If any would not work, neither shall he eat" (2 Thessalonians 3:10).

But as in anything else, there are extremes. Unbridled and unchecked ambition for more and more in natural possessions and riches does not fit Jesus' description of a Christian life. "Where your treasure is, there will your heart be also," He says (Luke 12:34). If there is one thing that has been the seed of much evil, it is the sin of discontentment.

Many a young man has found this out the hard way. Going recklessly and unwisely into a deep debt to "keep up with the Jones's" or just for the sake of bigness has often been the cause of later struggling through the mire of desperate financial difficulties when the debt had to be paid off.

There is something like going too far into debt when the going is still easy. Then, too, so often only after the children of such a family have left home do the parents remember with regret what they missed by not having taken the time to enjoy their children when they were still small. Another thing is that the spiritual values that are not planted in those years usually never get to be planted.

Besides the financial danger, there is also a spiritual danger in always being discontented. Oh, how many young people do not realize how hard is the way back when they start to be discontented with a plain and simple way of living and begin to follow the allure that the world has to offer. Many, many of these later secretly wish to come back. But they have gone too far out to do so. They never get it made. Too late they find out that the way out into the world is too often a one-way street. All this anguish started by being discontented.

It is very much like Adam and Eve, who could have been happy and contented in the beautiful garden that God had planted for them. Here God planted and caused to grow "every tree that is pleasant to the sight and good for food" (Genesis 2:9). This included the tree of life, which if they only would have reached out and eaten, they would have lived forever (Genesis 3:22). They were not just allowed to, but they were commanded ("Du sollst essen," says the German translation of Genesis 2:16) to freely eat from all these good trees. God wanted them to be happy and contented.

But with all this goodness available, and within easy reach they still chose to eat the fruit of that one forbidden tree. They ate of it even after they were told that to disobey would be the cause of their death. They ate of it after they started cultivating the thoughts of discontent that Satan had planted into their hearts.

When we ponder and think over this story of what happened to our first parents of so long age, we probably think that if God would only give us such a chance in our days, we would be obedient and contented.

But would any of us have done any better?

Are we doing any better with the good that God does give us?

Here we are living in this life with so much God-given good around us to be thankful for. God has blessed us with thousands of times more than we deserve. God daily shares so much with us that it is a sin not to be grateful and contented with it. How little would we have if we only got what we were worth?

Isn't it about time that we shorten our lists of material things that we think we must have, so we can more appreciate and be thankful to God for what we do have? Isn't it about time that we, as Christians, quit seeking for all those things that are only used for selfish or vain purposes anyhow? Isn't it about time to be more satisfied with what we have, and less satisfied with what we are?

Isn't it about time that we ask God to free us from the slavery which the love of possessions and our discontent for more is bringing into our lives? Only then can we experience the freedom of being fully satisfied and contented.

It is a mistake to think that contentment would come from having everything that we could wish for. It would not. Contentment is a freedom and a feeling of fulfillment and happiness that comes from being satisfied and thankful to God for what we do have and letting Him decide what our needs are.

Bitter discontent and unhappiness are often found in places where we would least expect to find them; in people who seem to have everything that they could desire. But on the other hand, contentment is often found in very unlikely places. One such place was in the prison where the Apostle Paul was chained day and night, just like we would chain an animal so that it could not get away. We would hardly expect a man in such circumstances to write the words which contain the secret of happiness: "For I have learned whatsoever state I am therewith to be content..." (Philippians 4:11).

The Pangs of the New Birth

23

"Marvel not that I said unto thee, Ye must be born again."
John 3:7

The poor, almost helpless creature makes another struggle, but it is so weak from the efforts that it has already made that it falls back and pants heavily for another breath. It finally thrashes around some more and makes a few more loud peeps, but the way things look, it can't last too much longer. It looks like it's strength and energy are all spent.

What we are describing sounds like a death, but it is not.

It is a birth. It is a description of a chick hatching out of an egg.

It is interesting to watch a chick or a small bird being released from the egg shell in which it had been confined. From the time that it pecks a small air hole through the shell to the moment that it makes that final supreme effort, it is all a painful struggle.

At that time it is not the cute, fluffy chick as we know it when it is a day or so old. It looks more like it has barely survived a near drowning.

Even after it is freed from its shell, the chick usually lies on its back or on its side kicking and struggling. It takes a little time to painfully unwind from the curled position into which it had been cramped.

But if it is to live, it must go through that struggle. There have been many times when people, who meaning to be kind, have helped a small chick with its efforts by breaking away the shell to make it easier for the chick. But such chicks have rarely survived because that first struggle is necessary if it is to live. It is nature's way to exercise those muscles that they never before used.

This miracle of new birth takes place in nature all around us countless times every year. Every feathered creature that you have ever seen has had to go through those birth spasms and throes at the beginning of its life.

Even all those creatures to which God gives life without being hatched from the hard shell of an egg have to go through a struggle to live. The small calf or the small colt gasps for its first breath and thrashes around until it can stand on its own feet goes through a struggle that is anything but easy.

But even if such creatures could think and would have a memory like man does, those first desperate gasps and painful struggles would soon be forgotten. When the colt soon afterwards makes its first frisky romp around its mother, the first difficult moment of being brought into life is forgotten.

In the same way, none of us will ever recall even faintly our gasp for air and our first cries of discomfort on that day when God awakened us into life on this earth.

64

Even in the plant world, birth is a struggle. The little bud that is cramped inside the heart of a seed is not born without a struggle against the hundreds of odds which would smother or kill it.

When the moisture, light and temperature conditions are right, a force called "life," a power which nobody really understands, triggers the seed to start its growth. At that time it is weak in that it is so tiny, minute and fragile. It is strong in that it has a persistent impulse to survive and grow if given a chance.

Only by growing after its birth is it possible for blossoms, fruit and more seeds to be produced. Only then can the thread of life which started at creation be passed on. Only life can beget life.

We can only marvel at God's creation of new life. We stand in awe at God's miracle of the awakening of life out of materials which were only part of the common soil. How wonderful is life from which comes both the birth and the growth which takes place after birth.

As we know, being born is not enough. There has to be a continuous growth if any good is to come out of a life. Spiritually, it is the same way. Wouldn't it be better if we were just as concerned about our growth since our new birth as we were about being born again? It is the fruit that is produced that counts. God gives us the new birth to get us started with the work that He has given us to do while we are here on earth, and then, as His children, to have a part in that eternal inheritance in heaven.

In the religious circles of our day, there is much talk and much is being printed about the new birth. Of course, this is good. Without the new birth, Christianity would be impossible.

What is not good in the popular gospel of our day is that there is too little or no emphasis on what should follow that new birth. In nature there are countless seeds born every year which never produce any fruit. They get smothered or dried up and killed before they get to produce much growth. The spiritual new birth also easily withers and dies if it is not given any attention, and Satan will do his best to see that it gets neglected.

Again, being born is not enough. Anything born soon dies if a healthy growth does not follow.

So much is often said and written on the joy and the peace which follows the new birth.

This is also good. There are too many of us who do not have God's joy and peace because we carry too many of the three kinds of cares with us. We are so burdened with yesterday's, today's, and tomorrow's cares that we forget that we do not have to carry those burdens and cares alone. If we have nothing but joyless days, it is not because God wants His children to live that way.

What is not good is if little or nothing is said of the struggles and trials that also follow the new birth.

One of these is the pain of turning back and away from any companions which have an evil influence on us. Another is the dropping of ways of living which cause us to drift slowly but surely into the world.

The old nature does not want to make such a drastic step. The old nature, which is to be crucified (Romans 6:6) when the new nature is born, does not die right away, but writhes and struggles like a dying Roman criminal who is being punished for his wrongdoing. The crucifying and sacrifice of our self-will is part of the new birth.

The laying down of our pride and the things that we are proud of is one very hard struggle that comes with the new birth. Writes Paul to Timothy, "Be not thou therefore ashamed of the testimony of the Lord" (2 Timothy 1:8).

How often our pride makes us ashamed to live and dress like a plain and modest Christian. Plain clothes and a simple quiet life are certainly a Christian testimony which can have more far-reaching good influence on others than anything that we can ever say. A testimony does not necessarily mean for us to go up to a stranger and ask if he is saved.

Another part of the new birth which is painful is that of being ashamed when we think of the doings in our past life. That is what makes so hard the confession, which is necessary for repentance and the forgiveness of past sins (I John 1:9). Jeremiah tells us about the people of his day who didn't care about their past misdeeds. "Were they ashamed when they had committed abomination? Nay, they were not at all ashamed, neither could they blush" (Jeremiah 6:15).

Paul writes to the Romans of the part that being ashamed has in the living of a new life. "What fruit had ye then in those things whereof ye are now ashamed? For the end of those things is death." (Romans 6:21). Being ashamed of our past sins and our past bad example for others is a part of the new birth.

This being ashamed of our past sins and failures is not the same as the condemnation of guilt which is a terrible burden to those who go through it. The remorse for having sinned is part of the punishment which we will have to go through here in this life. God works that in us so that we do something about our past sins. Those feelings of guilt and condemnation are meant to get us to confess and forsake our sins.

When we repent and accept God's forgiveness, we should then also believe that we are forgiven. Our past sins are then as if somebody else had done them, which is as it really is. It was our old nature that did them. The condemnation of guilt can then cease, even if being ashamed does not.

Another pang of the new birth is the change of living and behavior which should show up in our lives. Again, the old nature, not being dead yet, and the new nature, still weak and having its birth pangs, will have a real struggle. Here is where only prayer and the searching of God's Word will get us to the faith and the Source of Power that will enable the good nature to take over.

How long will these pangs and struggles last? They will last as long as life lasts. We are not immune to Satan's temptations as soon as the new birth takes place, but we now have a new help to lead us away from our temptations. Jesus did not escape temptation, so how can we expect to escape it?

Making things right with others is a very humbling test that comes with the new birth A man tells the story of how he was once notified to come to a certain hospital as soon as he could.

He did not know why. He was not aware of anyone that he knew being hospitalized at the time. But he immediately left his work and went. He was directed to a certain room. There, near death, lay a man whom he had worked with years before. The dying man asked him if he remembered a certain incident which had happened years earlier in which he had done some very unkind things to him.

The visitor had forgotten all about the incident until the sick man told him how sorry he was. All these years that he had been so unkind, he often thought he wanted to ask forgiveness, but had never been able to face doing so.

"Will you forgive me for what I did to you?" he pleaded. With tears running down both their cheeks, the one asked for forgiveness and the other freely gave it.

After a very brief visit the visitor left. He wasn't even outside of the main hospital entrance when he was called back and told that his friend had passed away.

The pangs of the new birth will demand a humbleness which the old nature (which is proud and cannot do any good) will not be able to do.

There is also an incident of a woman who had left the plain non-conforming church in which her parents had remained faithful to until their death.

She often had an impulse to come back, but her pride kept her from it. Many were those who, over the years had suggested to her to come back to the church she had left, but she would hear nothing of it. It seemed that coming back to the church of her youth was a test of humility and a laying down of old grudges and pride that she knew she should do, but could not, or would not do so.

Some time later she became sick. Those long days on her sick bed gave her time to think things over. She make a request which must have been very humbling. She asked to be taken back to the church she knew she should have stayed with. She said she wanted to do so before she left the world. She felt she would soon be leaving this earthly scene.

One of the ministers was heard to make the remark that he did not think that the woman was as sick as she thought she was, but he gladly did his part to take her up out of the excommunication she had been placed into years earlier.

As it turned out, she died just a short time later. It seemed that she could die in peace only after she put down her pride and went to the deepest depths of abasement to ask for help with the mistake that she now saw that she had made.

Again, the pangs of the new birth, and the peace that follows.

If we are having no struggle it could mean that we are not being born again, or that we have lost the new nature born of God that we once had. The new birth is not as simple as just signing a card that you have accepted Christ as your Saviour.

It is much more than that.

Let's take the new birth for what it is. It is the brand new garment which God gives as a gift to those who ask for it when they see that what they have is too threadbare to patch up again (Matthew 9:16, Mark 2:21, Luke 5:36). The garment will have to be brand new. Merely improving or mending the old is not enough.

It is the vital spark from which life begins. At the same time, it is only the beginning of a new life which is to grow if it is to produce good fruit in this life and eternal life in the next. May God work in all of us "both to will and to do of his good pleasure" (Philippians 2:13).

A Bridge of Many Stones

24

"And if any man shall take away from the words of the book of this prophecy, God shall take away his part out of the book of life, and out of the holy city, and from the things which are written in this book."

Revelation 22:19

The waters of the Octoraro zig-zag their way between southern Lancaster and Chester Counties as they flow on their way downward toward the level of the sea. For a short distance south of the town of Christiana, the Noble Road follows the banks of the Octoraro. At one place the road and the creek winds around an S curve and then, right next to a bend among the trees, stands a stone railroad bridge, spanning both the waters and the road in one single immense arch.

This bridge was built when the railroads were still in their hey-day as a means of transportation. The tracks of the Conrail, now a part of the one-time huge Pennsylvania Railroad system, still support and guide the freight trains that travel overhead on this bridge. All the long and heavy freights, passing many times daily over the years, have thundered across this stone arch with barely a quiver among the giant stones.

Quite a number of the steel bridges that were built in the same period no longer exist, or have been condemned as unfit to use. Not so, this stone bridge and the many more, some probably even more impressive, which are still around. These bridges, well-built of durable and enduring stone, are still as firm and solid today as they were on the day when their builders gathered up their tools, looked over their work, and called their job finished.

One impressive part of these stone bridges was the skill of those bridge builders of a now bygone era. To the eye, this bridge almost seems to float its stone arch above the utility wires and high over both the waters and the road traffic with plenty of room to spare. What the eye does not see is the tremendous internal pressure of the stones supporting and pushing against one another. Every single one of the hundreds of massive stones has a place and is needed there.

This is very similar to the verses contained in the Bible. For the verses of Scripture are very much like the stones, which are fitted and laid up to make a bridge.

What are the important stones in a stone bridge? Is it the row of stones at the upper height of the arch, called the keystones?

Yes, they are important, The tremendous pressure of hundreds and hundreds of tons of weight presses against these stones from both directions. The rest of the stones could not act as a supporting bridge without that row of keystones, which have been carefully cut to fit into their proper places.

Now suppose those bridge builders would have used only the row of keystones, which are so important, and would have discarded all the other supporting stones. A bridge could not be built that way. Every one of the stones are needed, from the keystones to those which are laying out of sight on the bedrock and are the foundation on which the whole structure is built. So every single one of the stones has an important place.

When we think of verses of Scripture, of course, we can also think of some, which are like the keystones, which are important because all the rest of Scripture seems to lean against them.

Those priceless verses in the third chapter of the Gospel of John and in the first epistle of John which tell us of the New Birth could be thought of as such. Without these verses, we would know very little about what Peter is trying to say in 1 Peter 1:23 about the life which lives forever. We would understand even less of what Paul is trying to tell us in 2 Corinthians 5:17 about the new creature in Christ that lives after old things are passed away.

It is clear that without the New Birth, no one would be able to enter God's kingdom, either in this life or in the hereafter (John 3:5). Perhaps the verses that explain the New Birth are a little like the row of keystones in a stone bridge.

But then, just like every one of the hundreds of massive stones is needed in its place in a stone bridge, so also do we need the rest of the supporting verses that are found in the Bible. One example is the Sermon on the Mount, found in Matthew 5, 6, and 7, which does not once directly mention the New Birth. In it Jesus gave His listeners that masterpiece on the "how" of living a Christian life.

That sermon which touches almost any situation that could come up in anybody's life is just as much for us today as it was for His listeners nearly two thousand years age. He closes the sermon with the well-known parable of the house built on the rock and the house built on the sand. Those who hear His voice and do them, are like a house built on an enduring foundation. Jesus believed in doing.

We need the complete Gospel, not just a part. Start removing the stones in a stone bridge and the whole structure will soon crumble into a useless heap. Small wonder then that God caused a warning to be placed near the end of the Bible on the danger of adding or taking away form the Scripture. The Bible, God's word to man, stands even more solid than heaven and earth (Matthew 24:35). Man is

not to tamper with it. He does so at the risk of his own destruction.

Of course, as anybody knows, this does not mean that an explanation of the Scriptures in our churches will have to include every verse in the Bible to meet the standards in the closing paragraphs of the Bible.

What it does mean is that we are not to take out only one or two verses from the Bible, build on just these, and omit and leave out the other verses that balance it. We are not to make the Bible read to suit our way of thinking.

Yet this can easily be done, and is often done in our days.

One such instance is where Ephesians 2:8 and 9 say, "For by grace are ye saved through faith, and that not of yourselves. it is the gift God. Not of works, lest any man should boast." Reading such a verse alone, could give us the impression that the kind of life we live (our works) will not mean anything to God when He decides who will get to heaven.

But it does.

We can find verses on the necessity of doing works, which seem to directly contradict that verse to the Ephesians and which seem to be saying just the opposite of the verse we have just read.

Take that verse in Philippians 2:12, for example, "...work out your own salvation with fear and trembling..." Reading that verse only, and not the one following it, would give us the idea that salvation depends just on our works. Or take James 2:24, where we read that, "Ye see then how that by works a man is justified (Gerecht wird), and not by faith only."

These verses do not contradict each other at all. They are there to balance each other and to bring out a fuller meaning of what God wants us to know. There is no reason to believe that one verse carries more weight than the others.

One verse is necessary so that nobody will think that he can earn an eternal home in heaven by a lifetime of good works. The other verses are there to remind us that, even as we know that salvation, both now and in the hereafter, is only possible as a free gift from God, we are to know that it is not complete unless we do our part. Our part is to be doing good works; a part that our old nature does not want to do.

If we were to take a pair of scissors and cut out those verses which our old carnal nature does not want to live up to, the pages of our Bible would soon be full of holes.

Much of the popular, watered-down gospel in our day is like reading from a Bible with many verses cut out. Many of the verses are omitted which are so reassuring to us that the plain, simple way of life is Scriptural and not just a tradition of men. The verse on nonconformity to the world (Romans 12:2), the verse on not loving the things of the world (1 John 2:15); the verse on walking the old narrow way leading to rest and life (Jeremiah 6:16 and Matthew 7:14) and the verse on keeping unspotted from the world (James 1:27) are just a few examples of verses that are mostly not mentioned by those who do not seem to be alarmed about the drift into the world by today's Christian churches.

There is much said today about accepting Christ as a personal Saviour. Many even say that is absolutely all that you have to do to be sure that you are saved; nothing else. If we would follow such a gospel, we could live just about as we pleased.

But salvation is not that cheap. It is necessary to accept Christ as a Saviour from our sins, but it is just as necessary to accept Him as Lord of our lives.

If Christ is the Lord of our lives, we will obey His commandments. We will bring forth the good fruit of a Christian life. We will place on the altar our self-will and our love for the world. We will do these good works because of the New Birth and its effect on our lives. This is one result of our faith. Even though we are far from perfect, good works will come naturally.

Why are good works important? Their purpose is not so that people will look up to us as good people. If good works and nonconformity to the world are done with that aim in mind, we are nothing but hypocrites, or pretenders of being good. Such a show of holy living, without an inner change of heart, is only Satan's counterfeit and a false imitation of what God wants us to be.

There is a nobler purpose in doing good works and in not loving the things of the world and in walking the narrow way. The Bible gives us that purpose and reason. We do not want to cut that verse from the Bible.

"Let your light so shine before men, that they may see your good works, and glorify your Father which is in heaven" (Matthew 5:16).

That is the sum and substance of it all. To God and not to us, be all the glory.

When Parents Learn to Listen

25

"For I know that he will command his children and his household after him, and they shall keep the way of the Lord."

Genesis 18:19

"Train up a child in the way he shall go, and when he is old, he will not depart from it."

Proverbs 22:6

Everybody ever born on this earth has been put here by God for a purpose. When we leave the world, we will leave it a little better or a we will leave it a little worse than it was before we came. We will either have encouraged and helped others, or we will have discouraged and hindered them.

Parents are no exception Parents cannot live out their children's lives for them, but the influence of parents in the lives of their children either makes it easier for them to live a Christian life, or will make it harder. Whether we are aware of it or not, our example and our way of life are teaching our children. Someone has once well said, "We may not be responsible for what our children do, but we are very much responsible for what we do, or do not do for them." The influence of parents will make a mark on their children that will stay with them for the rest of their lives.

All children need guidance. A very small child can't just have his own way all the time. When they are small, they don't know what is good for them, or what may be harmful. They need someone to tell them of things that are harmful to their bodies. For example, when they are small, they don't know enough of themselves to stay away from a hot stove. It is the parents who must limit the amount

of candy and sweets that they are allowed to eat. Small children do not know enough to discipline themselves.

When they are older, they need guidance in staying away from things that are harmful to their undying souls. Here is where our examples and our way of living will speak louder to them than will our words. Here is where our own knowledge and understanding of what we are to do and say is far from sufficient. As parents, God has trusted us enough to put those children in our homes for us to raise. The first step is to ask God for help with the great responsibility that is now ours.

Suppose someone would make a list of the things parents are to do in the raising of their children. No doubt it would be a long list. Then suppose you were asked to narrow that list down to the three most important points. One thing that I would want to keep on the list at any cost is what I would call, "Keeping communication open."

Of course, this should start between husband and wife. If they can't "talk things over" freely, it is going to be hard indeed to keep a healthy family communication alive with their children. Communication and conversation are not talking at somebody. It is talking with somebody. Communication is even more than conversation in that it can be done without words being exchanged.

This sharing of thoughts and feelings, (so important in a family) should start early. It is hard for all young parents to believe how soon those small children start into their school years. They will then have new interests. They will share those interests with you if you will but take a little time to ask a few questions, and then take the time to listen to their answers.

They will come to you all enthused about their day at school, if they know that you have an active interest in what they have done. Too often when children come home from school, they are absentmindedly asked how school was that day. Children are not to blame if they get the habit of giving an unthinking, "Oh, all right" to that question. That goes on until there will soon be very little shared with the parents about school happenings.

Much of this failure in "keeping the communication lines open" in a family can be traced to this lack of listening on the part of the parents. Even if someone says very little, there is always a message in what they are saying. It is ten times more important to listen and think on what is being heard than it is to think about what we want to say. It is more important and harder for us to learn to listen with interest than it is to talk. Talk usually takes care of itself; thoughtful listening doesn't. It is not possible to have a real close-knit family relationship which is sensitive to the feelings of others without practicing this art of listening.

When your children come home from having been with their friends, be sure to ask a few questions about what they were doing. It is not always necessary to do this right away – in fact it often works best if you wait a while. It will take a little thought on your part to ask a few questions that will stimulate a response on their part. What most of us forget is that it then takes more thought to listen to the answers to those questions than it does to ask the question.

All this will take some thought and some time. If your child ignores you and doesn't share anything with you about what goes on at school, or when they are with friends, you could be to blame for having acted too busy and too disinterested when they were younger. At that time they probably would have talked to you if you would have known the importance of listening.

If they are helped to get the habit in their school years to share their joys and disappointments, they are more likely to also do so when they are going through their teenage years. You are missing out on a lot of joys of parenthood, if you act too busy to care. The dollars that you are making while you fail to be an understanding and concerned parent are costing you hundreds of times more than they will ever be worth.

When children are young is the time when communication between them and their parents is either built up or is wrecked. If it is wrecked, it is almost always because the parents did not believe that it was important enough to take time to really communicate. You need to care enough to take a real interest in their interests, problems, and concerns. The joys, as well as the fears and struggles that they are going through, are real to them. They need to talk to someone about them, someone who is interested enough to listen. It is hard for children to stay rebellious to, or to try to outsmart someone who has a genuine understanding for them, but who is also firm and loving at the same time.

Of course, the Bible tells us the same thing, and much more, in just a few words: "Fathers, provoke not your children to anger, lest they be discouraged (Colossians 3:21), and "Ye fathers, provoke not your children to wrath, but bring them up in the nurture and admonition of the Lord" (Ephesians 6:4).

This last verse does not give a parent room to become permissive, or to allow children everything that they want. For that does not gain a child's respect for his parents. Children need the security of parents who will, if necessary, have a firm "no" to some of the things that they want. All children, even those of teen age, will become confused if they are not sure of the limits allowed by their parents.

There also comes a time in a child's life when it is necessary to have some frank talk about at least some of the facts of life. It is not necessary to explain everything in detail, but it is necessary to have answers that they are satisfied with at their different age levels. Far better is it to first learn some of those facts from an understanding and prudent parent than to learn them from their peers behind the outhouse at school. Let them learn early that such things are not to be made fun of and laughed at. The miracle of God's creation of new life is not to be taken lightly, or to be abused. Let them know that the purity of such things will be lost if they are talked about too openly or at just any time. If only children would be taught that such things are not only to be secret, but they are to be kept sacred.

Yes, to all of you dear young parents – your God-given ministry to your children is going to take a good bit of your time. A story comes to mind of a young man who had a small son. The young father was always very busy.

His small son often tagged along behind him, and as small children are, he was full of questions. The father often didn't take the time to give him satisfactory answers to his many questions. His impatient answer often was, "Don't ask so many questions. Don't you see that I am busy now?"

One Sunday forenoon when the father was still out in the barn, hustling with his many chores, the mother of the small boy took him on her lap. As was her custom, she opened a Bible storybook and showed him the pictures and as best as she could, explained the stories and answered his many questions.

She came to a drawing of Jesus ascending to heaven. The boy listened with interest as she explained how the time will come some time when Jesus will come again and how they will all want to go along to that beautiful place.

After a pause, the small boy looked up into her face and in all innocence remarked, "Dad probably won't go along, will he? He will probably be too busy."

With a tear in her eyes, the young mother thought, "Don't small children say things pretty bluntly sometimes?"

Oh, if only all parents would realize the seriousness of the mission that the Lord has called them to carry out. That mission is to build a Christian home. God places those precious immortal souls in human homes, but wants them back again some day. Let us take heart and not despair, for we know where we can get help for the awesome task that lies before us. We must have Christian homes if we are to leave a Christian influence on those who live there.

The home is the greatest influence that a growing child will ever have. A home should never be a place where unhappy, disturbed and bitter parents and children had only a continuous "tug-of-war." It should not be just a place to live, eat and sleep. A Christian home is a place where parents and children are helping each other on a pilgrim journey to a better land beyond this life.

After the minutes and hours that were given you to use today are almost spent, take a little time this evening to think over your day. Did you do something for each of the other members of the family out of gratitude for what they did for you? Did you have at least a little interesting talk together at mealtime with the others who share your home with you? Did you have a little laughter today, light and easy, with everyone included? Then, most important of all, did everyone at home gather together for prayer to God?

If any of these were missing from the day that is now gone, your day was not complete. Before you go to sleep, ask God to help you and resolve now to have a better tomorrow.

What Can the Girls Do?

26

"And next to him repaired Shallum, the son of Halohesh, the ruler of the half part of Jerusalem, he and his daughters."
Nehemiah 3:12

What part and what influence do young girls have in a church? What can the young girls do for the betterment of the church and for the community where they live? Is there anything they can do to help build up the church?

There surely is! One example of young girls helping to build is found in the story in the Old Testament when the Jews were rebuilding the torn-down, burned-out walls of Jerusalem.

The Jews had just returned to their homeland from their 70-year captivity in the far-off land of Babylon. The glorious and mighty Jerusalem of their forefathers lay in ruins. They found the walls around Jerusalem and the recently-rebuilt temple not much more than heaps of rubble (Nehemiah 2:12-14). To keep out their enemies and the robbers and the Sabbath-breakers (Nehemiah 13:19-21) the wall needed to be built up again.

When we read the third chapter in the book of Nehemiah of the rebuilding of the wall, we gather that each family had a part of the wall assigned to them to be built. It was a nice way to get the work done. If each family did their assigned part, the wall would soon be complete, and would have no unbuilt openings for the enemies to get through.

This chapter is hard to read and is really rather uninteresting reading. Starting at the place called

the sheep gate, which was likely near the market where sheep were sold, the account gives us the names of the people and the families who helped to build all around the wall.

Most of the names are difficult to pronounce. Nobody could ever be expected to remember all those dozens of names. There is, however, one verse, verse twelve, that stands out in a rather touching and remarkable way. It tell us that a man named Shallum, with the help of his daughters, built the portion of the wall assigned to him.

As in many Bible stories, most of the details which would be interesting reading are not given leaving us with a lot we can only wonder about. Since Shallum's wife is not mentioned, didn't she help or was Shallum a widower? We do not know.

We also do not know if Shallum's daughters had brothers or not, because nothing is said of Shallum's sons. Maybe he didn't have any sons or perhaps they were some of the nobles who thought they were too important to help with the "work of their Lord" (Nehemiah 3:5). There is a lot we do not know, but we do know that the daughters of Shalllum, the granddaughters of an important ruler of the city, bent down to the labor of building the wall.

Building and repairing that wall around Jerusalem back in those days, some four hundred and fifty years before Christ, was very much like the building and strengthening of our churches, which needs to be done in our days. There is work for every family, for everybody young and old, for the boys and for the girls.

Those daughters of Shallum who were working with the other wall builders had some of the same problems that anybody today has who is helping to build the church. One was that they got mocked and laughed at (Nehemiah 2:19 and 4;3), but they didn't mind and kept right on building.

Those enemies who lived in the neighboring countryside did not wish to have a wall around the city to keep them out. When they saw that poking fun at the wall building did not stop the workers, they tried other tactics. They tried to get Nehemiah, the founder of the work, to come out to one of their cities (6:2). But he sensed the trap they were trying to spring upon him and kept on working; Shallum's daughters and the other workers right along with him.

The enemies then threatened to come with an army to kill the workers if they kept on building the wall (4:11). They tried to get Nehemiah to flee and shut himself up in the temple so he would be safe (6:10), but he bravely kept on working. Going to the temple to worship was necessary, but staying there all the time, (however safe) would not get the work done of building the wall.

As could be expected, with the threats that the enemies made, the wall builders were afraid (6:9). But they kept working, and prayerfully kept watch at the same time, toiling from early in the morning until late at night (4:21). When the building of the wall was finished (6:15) only fifty-two days after it was begun, those daughters of Shallum must be given their share of the credit, because the Bible record tells us that "the people had a mind to work" (4:6).

What a wonderful lesson for everybody, and especially for the girls who can help to build and strengthen the homes and churches of today. If everybody does their work with a will, our churches and homes can be built and strengthened so that the evil influences our enemy, Satan, wants to bring into our churches can be kept out.

We have another story of three young girls

who made an enduring influence on the cause of righteousness. Those girls didn't go along with the wickedness and sinning that nearly everybody else was doing at the time. They were willing to keep company with three decent young men who could not have been very popular in those days. The three girls later married those three young men, who were brothers.

We do not know the names of those three girls, and know very little of the other circumstances in their lives. But we do know that not going with the popular crowd is what saved their lives when an event occurred which claimed the lives of all the other sinful people that they could have been friends with.

By now you have probably guessed who those three girls were. They were the girls who married the three sons of Noah.

Then we have yet another story that shows us what the changed life of one girl can do. This was the girl, Rahab, who had lived in a very sinful way in her past, but who made a drastic change in her life. She had heard of God's blessings on the Israelites (Joshua 2:10-11), and must have believed there was a better way to live than the way she was living.

She knew without being told that the city where she lived would be destroyed. She made a plea to the spies from the camp of Israel for the lives of her father mother, brothers and sisters, without asking to be spared herself.

The day came when Jericho, the city where she lived, was destroyed, but she and her father's family and all they had was spared. The sudden earthshaking roar of the falling stones when the walls of Jericho fell flat (Joshua 6:20) was a mighty display of the power of God. But it was also through God's power that one house built right on the wall of Jericho was still standing after the dust had settled all around it. The house where Rahab's family had shut themeless in did not go down with the rest.

The girl, Rahab, is thought by many to be the same Rahab (Matthew 1:5) who married into a family through which the Saviour of the world was born hundreds of years later. What an influence the changed life of Rahab had! The New Testament says that she was justified both by what she believed (Hebrews 11:31) and by what she had done (James

2:25). In other words, by both her faith and by her works which followed her faith.

We need more girls like the daughters of Shallum and like the daughters-in-law of Noah among the young people in our days. We need more girls like Rahab who forsake their sins, whatever they may be.

We need girls who are not so overly concerned about their popularity and about the fashions of the clothes they wear, because such things are not as important as some may think. What really counts is the character. That is the part to be concerned about. That is the part that comes from within the heart.

The decay of what should be Christian family living is a greater threat to our churches than almost anything else. It is not altogether true that Christians should not be found in places of pleasure. What should be true is that all Christians should make the home they live in the happiest spot on earth.

Our churches should all be like one big family, but first of all, our families should all be like one small, close church. The character of the girls in our churches could be said to provide the climate so that the families now and in the future will be just like that.

27 The Tempter's Snares

"The Lord knoweth how to deliver the godly out of temptations."
II Peter 2:9

There are not too many things more interesting than watching the world of nature that God has made.

You may have already noticed some cone-shaped depressions about an inch and a half or so across in your garden soil, especially if the ground is dusty from not having had a recent rain.

The next time you see such a pit in the soil, see if you can't find the small insect looking a little like a large tick that lies just out of sight at the very bottom of the hole.

If you have caught him, you have caught an ant lion. If you want to see something interesting put him in a glass fish bowl with several inches of fine dry sand.

Soon you will see him moving backwards in a circle. He will be burrowing just a little below the sand, nearly out of sight. If you watch him you will see him busily throwing up sand by putting his head under the sand and suddenly jerking his head back.

He will keep throwing out sand until he has a clean little cone-shaped hole and will then partly busy himself at the center of the hole. As he quietly lies there in waiting you will see only a little of his two pinchers sticking out of the sand.

Now catch several ants and let them loose in the bowl. As the unsuspecting ants scurry around one of them will be pretty sure to get too close to the edge of the funnel-shaped hole and will start sliding in toward the center. He will frantically dig in the loose sand to try to work himself uphill.

But he is trapped. He is now doomed as the soft sand slides away and he slips toward his enemy—the clever ant lion. As soon as he touches those strong, nearly hidden jaws they will snap shut and that will be the end of the ant. His body juices will be sucked dry and the ant lion will throw out the hard outside shell that is left. He will then quietly stay and wait to seize the next unsuspecting victim.

That is very much the way Satan and his temptations work. They are designed to trap us when we are not aware what is going on. The word "temptation" means to "rouse a desire in or to lure or entice." Satan wants us to have things that are not good for us or to do things we should not be doing.

The lures that Satan sets for us are a little like the lures and bait used by fisherman. They would never catch a fish by dangling a plain hook in the water.

That lethal hook has to be hidden with something that the fish likes to eat or something that attracts his eye. And about the only thing that will keep a fish away from a baited hook dangling close by is if the fish is not hungry. A full and satisfied fish can hardly be coaxed to even nibble at the bait the fisherman wants to catch him with.

If a fish does get hooked and pulled out, the fisherman will not have to use a club to pound its skull to kill it. It is just as effective to pull it out of, and keep it away from the life-sustaining water it had lived in. That alone will cause its death.

Only a hooked and captured fish gets to be fried.

The Bible tells us about Satan's first temptation to man. Because Satan never fails to make use of an opportunity, he got to work soon after man was created. He didn't wait till there were thousands of people on earth to come with his deceiving. He came when there were only two people on earth, and his temptation came to each one separately.

He used the subtle, or wily serpent to help him. There was not a lot of coaxing done. Only three sentences were spoken, but the untruth in those few dozen words started thoughts of doubt in Eve's mind and awakened a desire for something she should have left alone. She got to thinking that God might fail to carry out the punishment for disobedience that He had said He would. She also got to believing that God was unkindly withholding something good from them that would be nice to have. Because she kept looking at the fruit her desire got so great that she reached out and did exactly what God had told them not to do.

She ate of the forbidden fruit.

After she had eaten, Satan did not need the serpent anymore. Having the fruit picked and handed to him by his wife made it pretty easy for Adam to also eat of the forbidden fruit. And that is what he did.

That is still very often the way Satan works. He uses misled people to mislead others. Probably the only time Satan himself came directly as a tempter was when Jesus was on earth. Here was Satan's chance to try to spoil God's plan of redemption for man.

He tempted Jesus with three temptations that really include about all the kinds of temptations that we will ever have, but Jesus stood firm. He did what our first parents did not do. He said no to temptation.

The first temptation was to satisfy His physical hunger. Hunger is something not wrong in itself, but that should not be our only concern. We live in sin if we live only for satisfying our bodily appetites. God has put us on earth for a higher purpose than going after each and every item of luxury and comfort that we may be tempted to possess. If we let our desires and lusts take over, our spiritual life will wither and die.

Satan then tried to get Jesus to let Himself fall down from a very high point of the temple, the place where the people worshiped God, and probably were praying for a Messiah to come. Now that would have really been a great and spectacular way for Jesus to start His mission. Right away, Jesus would have gotten a lot of believers among the throng of people down below Him if He would have appeared to have floated down from Heaven. But that was not His way. He never did anything for the display or show of it.

Then also, although Jesus could have been sure that He would not get hurt, He still took no chances. In the same way none of us should become too sure of ourselves that we think we cannot fall from the faith, because there will never be a time in this life that Satan is through with us.

Then came the last temptation. This temptation includes those temptations which have felled countless people since the world began. Young people see pleasure in the world, and they want some of it. Older people see riches and power and go out after it. If only Jesus would have fallen down and worshiped Satan, He was promised all the glories of the whole wide world. But Jesus had something better.

Now with Satan's temptations around us everywhere, how do we humans have a chance? Is there any hope for us?

We can do what Jesus did. If we only become more acquainted with Scripture we can find something there for every temptation, just like Jesus did. Even though Satan quoted written Scripture in one of his temptations, Jesus always had other Scripture to back Him up in withstanding the temptations.

And we can pray for help. Not until we are ready to pray for God's help are we ready to accept God's help. The power that runs the universe is ready to help us if we are ready to accept it. He will be there to lead us away from temptation if only we ask Him to do so.

What can we do for others who are being tempted? Again we can pray. The church prayed without ceasing unto God (Acts 12:5) when one of their members was being kept in a locked prison, guarded by 16 Roman soldiers for execution the next day. Knowing of Peter's denial of Jesus earlier in his life, they probably prayed for him to remain faithful to the end. God gave them so much more than they asked for that they could not believe it when the answer came. Prayer is our best weapon against temptation.

God will not keep us from being tempted, but will not allow us to ever be tempted above that we are able to withstand. He will "with the temptation also make a way to escape", (I Corinthians 10:13) so that we may be able to withstand it. There is always a way out.

Satan is never able to make us sin if we don't want to and if we stay away from situations which increase the temptation. If we sin we have willingly let ourselves get too close to the quicksand that we knew was there. We are like the ant getting too close to the pit dug by its enemy. "Every man is tempted when he is drawn away of his own lust and enticed" (James 1:14).

God will help you. He will send help to you when you have that overpowering desire that will not listen to reason. But you must turn your back and look the other way. God has placed people in your life to be good company and to help you so that you, in turn can help others. And you will find a fulfillment and a happiness in your life you ever thought possible. Like the satisfied fish with the coated hooks dangling close by, temptation will lose its power over you. Thanks be to God for making the Christian life leading to heaven what it really is. We never have to give up anything that is good for us. It is only those things God knows are not good for us that we have to give up.

The Need of Forgiving

28

"Forgive us our debts as we forgive our debtors"
Matthew 6:12

So many of God's gifts coming to us are not at all dependent on what we do. There are no conditions attached.

We are granted the spring rains and the warm sunshine on which depends the growth of what we plant and hope to harvest. God sends the miracle of the sprouting and growing seeds whether we ask Him or not. It rains on the just and the unjust (Matthew 5:45). It seems we go on getting blessings from above even if we forget to be thankful for them.

His love that made redemption possible also came this way. His love for mankind was not because anybody was worthy of it. "Herein is love, not that we loved God, but that He loved us, and sent His son to be the propitiation (the satisfactory payment) for our sins" (1 John 4:10).

There is, however, one gift from the hand of God that has a condition attached to it. That is forgiveness – something we all have to have. Unless our sins and wrongdoings against God are forgiven, we can never have peace in our hearts in this life. Nor can we hope to have a share in the glories of heaven in the next.

The conditions attached to God's forgiveness are simple and easy to understand. In order for God to forgive us, we must forgive our fellow men. If we don't forgive others, any pardon we received from God becomes null and void. Our debt to God, which is impossible for us to pay, is again heaped upon us.

We are just like the servant in the familiar story in Matthew, chapter 18. This is one of the chapters read every time before we go to the Lord's Supper with each other.

This servant must somehow have squandered a lot of borrowed money or else done some very serious blundering in an investment the king had made, and which the servant was responsible for.

But he was freely forgiven what he had done. He no longer owed the king even one shekel of the ten thousand talents that the king would now have to do without. The king's compassion for his pleading servant was costly. His treasury was now ten thousand talents poorer.

But the servant walked away a free man. He could go home to his dear wife and children who very nearly got sold as slaves because of his misdeeds. He could go home and start all over again. He could walk away completely free from a debt so immense that it is almost impossible to imagine.

Those ten thousand talents that somehow disappeared while he was responsible for them represented a lot of money. Of course, in Bible times the value of a talent varied widely at different times and in different places. Also, Matthew 18 does not state whether the ten thousand talents were in bars of gold or in bars of silver. So there is no way to determine exactly what the ten thousand talents equaled in today's dollars.

Even so, in an attempt to figure out the value, some will start with today's value of the silver in a shekel, which could have weighed anywhere from half to one and a half ounces. Then as it is generally agreed that one talent was worth the same as from two thousand seven hundred to three thousand shekels, they figure out the approximate dollar value of the forgiven debt. Even by figuring the value of the silver in a shekel at sixty cents, which is a very low figure at today's highly inflated silver prices, the sum of the debt comes to millions of dollars.

Then there are others who will take the weight of a talent, a figure which again depends on which Bible reference books they look it up in. They will then take that weight, which probably was somewhere between seventy-five and ninety pounds and multiply it by what gold is worth. It then also makes a big difference if they take gold by its value of thirty-five dollars an ounce a few years back, or eight hundred dollars an ounce to which it had risen not too long ago Again they come to an immense figure.

There is, however, also another way for us to grasp an idea of the great value of that forgiven debt, (Let us remember that this debt represents the forgiving that God has done for us because we have spoiled the investment God has made in us).

We can really get a more accurate value of that debt if we find out what the buying or earning power of a talent represented. As a piece of silver, or shekel, was the payment for a day's wages for an average working man, (Matthew 20:2) and if we figure that a man would have to work from two thousand seven hundred to three thousand days for only one talent, the size of that forgiven debt goes to astronomical figures.

In round figures that man would have had to hand in all the money he could have earned in all the working days of a hundred thousand years! And to think the servant promised that if the king had

patience, and would give him time, he would pay it all back!

Anyway, the point is that although the servant could never have paid the impossible debt, he was now free. His enormous waste and mishandling of property was forgiven.

But the story is not finished – the king's forgiveness was complete, but not final. It was complete in that he did not even demand any money which the servant could later have earned and paid. But it was only final upon the condition that the servant forgive others in debt to him.

The servant's freedom did not last long. He was not worthy of the forgiveness granted to him because he later could not, or would not, forgive the debt of a fellow servant who owed him only a small sum.

What the king did then not only defeats the doctrine of "once saved, always saved" but also tells us what God will do to each of us who will not, from our hearts, "forgive every one his brother his trespasses", (his failures, or fehler in German) (Matthew 18:35).

The king cancelled the forgiveness of the debt and again heaped it upon the man who had proven himself to be unworthy of it. This time nothing is said of selling his wife and children as slaves. The servant was responsible and he was the one to get locked up.

Now for most of the things that we as Christians should be doing we can get help from fellow Christians. What others do is a big help, and makes it easier for us to do what we should be doing. For one example, being around and associating with people who also live a plain and simple life, makes it so much easier for us to live that way. The examples of other people who believe is one way that God uses to make the Christian life easier for us.

But forgiveness is something else. It is true that it is somewhat easier to forgive others if we are around forgiving people, and it may also make it easier to forgive others if they come and sincerely confess and ask to be forgiven. But at the same time, if we still chose to harbor unforgiving thoughts, it will only harden our hearts and whet our anger even to hear others ask for forgiveness. The reaction of an unforgiving heart is just to become more incensed and angry.

So our forgiving of other people is really not too dependent on what others do. The decision to forgive or not is in the final sense up to us. It seems forgiving must come from one of the deepest recesses of the human heart, the part that only we have the key to open and the part that only God can reach. Only God has the power to change an unforgiving heart to one with healing forgiveness, but we must first want to. We should not even be asking for God's help to forgive unless we really want to do our part.

This forgiving business can become one of the hardest parts of living a Christian life, and is often one of the most neglected. An unforgiving feeling in a heart can go on for years. Unless that feeling breaks out openly in a spiteful action, other people may never know of the dark, ugly, and bitter thoughts being hidden there.

But God will know. The stress and wear and tear of bottling up a grudge can be hard on both mind and body. It can drain out a lot of energy and wear down the system and can color every thought going through the mind. It can upset the fine balance God has put into the human body which can then be the cause of all kinds of illness. We are hurting nobody more than we are hurting ourselves if we don't keep our forgiving up to date. God had good reason for telling us not to let the sun go down upon our wrath (Ephesians 4:26). In other words we are to wipe our slates clean of all unforgiving grudges toward others every day.

Perhaps if we do choose to be cold and unforgiving to others we should omit part of the familiar Lord's Prayer when we pray because we are really asking God to grant us the same unforgiveness we are giving to others. We are not worthy of God's forgiveness if we don't forgive others!

If Jesus could forgive those who were pounding nails through His hands and feet, even as they were causing Him indescribable pain, surely we should be able to forgive others who are hurting us far less. And He was innocent; so often we aren't .It's asking very little of us to forgive others who have done nothing more than hurting our pride, that part of us that should be reduced to nothing anyway. God has put those people, who we sometimes think we can't forgive, into our lives for a purpose. How else could we learn forgiving if we had no one to forgive?

The forgiving spirit of Christ which He wants to share with us is like the forgiveness shown by the father of the prodigal son. He was ready with his forgiving love even before his son came back to ask for it (Luke 15:11-32). It is the same kind of forgiving that Joseph had for his brothers who had been so unkind to him. When their father died, Joseph could have taken revenge for what they did to him years earlier, but he did not even think of doing so (Genesis 50:15-21).

The story is told of two neighbors who had a dispute over an incident which angered both of them. The incident, which as is usually the case was at first only a small and trifling disagreement. It could have easily been settled if both would have quietly talked it out and taken their share of the blame.

But the angry accusations of the one was followed by the bitter accusations of the other until things were blown all out of proportion. Both men were determined to keep score of their revenge. Neither one could forgive the other.

One of them became ill, laying on his bed for a long time with a sickness which became progressively worse. But still none of the men were ready to forgive. The vice called pride kept them from it.

One day the sick man died. His body was taken to an undertaker to be kept there until his funeral, a few days later. But before that day came the other man, in his full health, was killed in an accident and was taken to the same room. The two men who in life had not been able to get along with each other, now lay together – still in death.

What a tragic waste of days and years which could have been filled to overflowing with Christian good will! If both men did get the reward of heaven after this life was over, we have to wonder how they could get along together in that eternal place, if they didn't start here.

There may come times in our life when we think we just can't forgive. It is very true, of ourselves, we can't do it. We have to allow Christ's forgiving spirit, which we should give room within us, do the forgiving. Our old nature cannot forgive, but the new nature can.

Corrie Ten Boom in her book, *The Hiding Place*, gives us an incident concerning a difficult lesson in forgiving that she experienced. She had been imprisoned in a German concentration camp during World War II. It is almost unbelievable how inhuman and horrible they were treated by Hitler's S.S. guards. At this one prison camp alone, 96 thousand women died or were brutally killed by the Nazis.

At a church service after the war was over, Corrie met a man whom she immediately recognized as a former guard at the prison camp, where she and her sister had been kept in a cruel way.

As soon as she saw the man, she recognized him for his part in the Nazi regime of terror which had caused the death of her aged father and her sister and the cruel suffering to herself and to millions of other people.

Even though the former guard was now a changed man, ugly and angry thoughts of hate and vengeance boiled inside her at the sight of the man.

Only when she thought of her own sins of thinking such thoughts and when she thought of how Jesus had died, not only for her, but also for this man, did she breathe a silent prayer, "Jesus, I cannot forgive him. Give me your forgiveness."

At that moment a current of love sprang into her heart that almost overwhelmed her. Then she could forgive. Then she felt free.

Only with Jesus' forgiving spirit in us can we forgive and be free.

His forgiving love is stronger than any human hatred. One of the reasons Jesus was to be called Wonderful (Isaiah 9:6) could well be because of the wonderful freedom His forgiveness gives. He gives a wonderful opportunity for a new beginning if we forsake our sins and accept His forgiveness.

Then if we forgive others their actions toward us, we can experience a wonderful freedom from our own unforgiving nature. A grudge in the heart produces a venom which is poisonous, most of all to ourselves. That old inner nature cannot be changed, but it can be replaced with the forgiving spirit of Jesus.

God wants us to forgive. Anything He asks us to do, He will also help us to do. We are to pass on to others the same kind of love we daily receive from God.

And that love includes forgiving.

The Work of the 29 Carpenter

"For we are His workmanship, created in Christ Jesus unto good works, which God hath before ordained that we should walk in them."
Ephesians 2:10

"It is well-known that Joseph, who lived in the town of Nazareth with his family, was a carpenter"
Matthew 13:55

As was the general practice in those days, the boys in a family usually learned a business or handcraft from their father, and after growing into manhood, worked at their father's trade to make a living. The Jews even had a saying, "He who does not teach his son a useful trade is bringing him up to be a thief."

In this respect the boy Jesus was no exception. Like his legal father, Joseph, He also became a carpenter (Mark 6:3).

The Bible does not tell us what Jesus made or what He built as a carpenter. The Greek word which is translated as "carpenter" in the English New Testament and "Zimmerman" in the German, could have meant a craftsman, not only in wood, but also in iron, brass or copper. However, in the Old Testament, carpenters and masons (as in 2 Kings 22:6 and I Chronicles 14:1) and carpenters and smiths (as in Jeremiah 24:1 and 29:2) were usually mentioned separately. So it is perhaps reasonable to assume that if a carpenter is mentioned in the Bible, his work was probably in wood.

We should remember that wood was a rather scarce item in that country of very few large trees. Most of the buildings were of stone or sun-dried bricks. It is therefore very doubtful that the people in those days who wanted a house built depended on a carpenter to do much of the work. Perhaps about all

a carpenter was needed for, was for wooden ceiling beams on their flat-topped housed or for making the wooden doors.

So if we go by what is known of the customs of that country in those days, we can take for granted that like most of the carpenters in that rather poor country, Jesus did not build houses. Instead He probably made some of the wooden articles that His neighbors needed and used.

Let us form a picture in our minds of Jesus making wooden doors, ox yokes, ox carts with wooden wheels, and wooden plows and harrows. This should give us a fairly accurate idea of the type of work Jesus did with His skilled hands while He was here on earth.

Wouldn't it be a spectacular discovery if sometime in our days, something like an ox yoke with Jesus' name carved on it would be unearthed in the vicinity of the city of Nazareth?

We can only imagine the excitement such a find would cause. A team of scientists would soon be looking all over it with microscopes in hopes of proving it to be an actual work of Jesus' own hands. If it could be proven that the yoke really dated back to Bible times and was really a genuine piece of Jesus' carpenter work, it would probably be displayed only in a glass case with controlled humidity to preserve it from further deterioration. That piece of wood would be deemed too priceless to leave in an unguarded and unlocked place.

Visitors would stream by and marvel to really see an actual example of Jesus' craftsmanship. His workmanship would be studied. People would comment on how He had the yoke smoothed and curved just the right way so as not to chafe the necks of the oxen.

Finding an article like that would cause as much speculation and debate as that piece of cloth called the Shroud of Turin. That piece of linen is believed by many people to be that actual clothes of Jesus (John 19:40). It is going to be impossible, more than 1900 years later, to ever fully prove it was the same linen shroud, even though there are so many things that cannot be explained otherwise. It does seem it could well be an actual relic of Bible days which has somehow survived down to our time, but we cannot be sure.

But, sorry to say, it is highly unlikely that a wooden article actually made by Jesus as a carpenter will ever be found, and if found, could ever be proved to be authentic. People in those days just didn't save things for their antique value. Then also, very few wooden articles in that country could have survived all the years that have gone by since Jesus was on earth. Wood decays from moisture. Wooden articles were either taken along or burned to ashes by the plundering armies that have gone through the Holy Land throughout the years.

So we might as well forget ever hoping to see a work which Jesus made with His hands while He was in human form. Maybe it is just as well, because God knows that such an object would not help, but would actually hinder people from becoming what they should be as Christians. Many of the people going thousands of miles to see such an object would revere and venerate it to the point of nearly worshiping it. The object would become more sacred than the Creator (Romans 1:25).

It would be a little like the brass serpent that Moses put on an uplifted pole to help the dying Israelites (Numbers 21:9) (John 3:14). We read that the same article was worshiped as an idol some seven hundred years later (2 Kings 18:4) until King Hezekiah broke it to pieces and called it what it really was, only a piece of brass. God probably had good reasons for not permitting pieces of Jesus' handwork to exist down to our day.

No, we will never see a work in wood which Jesus made while He was on earth. Those works are long since gone. But Jesus also worked in something far more lasting and durable than wood.

He worked in people's lives. He worked in human hearts.

He worked in the changed and better lives and character of people—men and women, boys and girls.

He met the tax collector, Zaccheus, who in one day was changed from a wealthy, cheating and greedy man to one for whom material possessions were no longer his first and only interest (Luke 19:8). Zaccheus, by receiving Jesus joyfully, (Luke 19:6) was any one of the thousands of people who have learned how true Jesus' words were when He said, "A man's life consisteth not in the abundance of the things which he possesseth" (Luke 12:15).

There was Mary Magdalene, tormented by seven devils, (Mark 16:9 and Luke 8:2). But Jesus healed her (very probably the second time, Matt. 12:45), and changed her from a woman with a terrible fear, guilt, and mental struggle to a devoted disciple – the person whom He appeared first after His resurrection.

She is only one of the countless people who have found out that it is not necessary to stay in a mental confusion and torment, because there is help available through the healing power of Jesus. Those people have found a lasting inner peace and joy which has replaced the fear and guilt lived with day in and day out. They have learned what Jesus meant when He said, "Peace I leave with you, my peace I give unto you; not as the world giveth, give I unto you. Let not your heart be troubled, neither let it be afraid" (John 14:27).

Another of Jesus' works while on earth was the miracle which healed the boy who often fell into fire and into water (Matthew 17:14-21, Mark 9:14-29, Luke 9:37-43). Not knowing what else to do, the boy's father brought the lad, his only son, to Jesus and asked for help.

That boy, deaf and possessed of a spirit which worked the direct opposite of what the Holy Spirit works, has his counterparts in the boys of today who do things that are harmful to themselves and will not hear parents who are trying to help them. What better can those parents do but to bring them to Jesus and let Him do the healing?

The boy had first been brought to Jesus' disciples, but they failed to heal the boy. After Jesus came upon the scene, He healed the boy. He rebuked them for not having more faith and told them that only by prayer and fasting is a cure possible in a case such as this one. That fasting does not necessarily mean to go without a meal, but could mean to go without some other things we have an appetite and desire for, and would be better off without. Is Jesus telling us if we would do without some of the material things we think we must have, He could easier heal our sons and daughters? If that is the kind of healing Jesus can do if we help Him with our faith, fasting and prayer, shouldn't we want to learn more and do more of what we can do to help?

Jesus sometimes even brought back life when it had fled. One such incident was the only daughter of a man named Jairus. This girl was very near death when her father went to Jesus for help, and was stilled in death when Jesus came to his house (Matthew 9:18-26, Mark 5:21-43, Luke 8:41-56).

Had Jairus waited too long to ask for help?

After sending the people out of the rooms, Jesus took the dead girl by the hand and speaking to her in the Aramaic language said, "Damsel, I say unto thee, arise." Immediately the unbelievable happened. To the astonishment of her parents the girl arose from the dead. Some Bible scholars think the words could be translated, "You sweet little girl, arise," showing the feeling Jesus had for her.

Again that girls' counterparts of today could be those girls who are obsessed, or have most of their thoughts centered on their own vanity, or girls who have gone astray and are dead to the Christian life. What better can their parents do than to ask Jesus to come right into their homes to help them in their sorrow?

But Jesus then as now, needed people to help Him with His work. He could easily have done the rest that needed to be done, and by doing another miracle could have supplied the food the awakened girl now needed, but He did not. He did not do what the parents of the girl could do for her. He gave them the work of bringing her something to eat.

The people in Jesus' day did not save any wooden pieces of Jesus' handwork. That part of Jesus' work was unimportant to them when they saw what He could do with the lives of people.

The spirit of the risen Jesus, the Holy Spirit, is still doing the same kind of work in our times. Far better than seeing a work that Jesus made as a carpenter is knowing that if we permit Him to do so, He will work and change and better the lives of ourselves and other people. There is nothing else like it anywhere.

Hateful and spiteful people becoming loving. People with pride, thinking only of themselves, become humble people, thinking first of others. People with a "big I" and a "little you" reversing that order. Envious, bitter and jealous people becoming people of Christian good-will. People forsaking the world's pleasures, lusts and luxurious living, becoming contented to fellowship with people walking the narrow way. People accepting the miracle of contentment that makes possible living in today's world, but not going along with it. Unforgiving people catching some of Jesus' forgiving spirit and dropping their desire for revenge.

The list could go on and on. Things that make life more livable as we walk our pilgrim way together are the work of Jesus. Anything that makes the kingdom of heaven happen, not only in some faraway place in the future, but right in the here and now is a work of the spirit of Jesus. Really there is lots and lots of Jesus' work around, but still not enough. Let us prayerfully be doing our part in helping Him with His work, first of all at the place right at hand; that is in ourselves.

The work of Jesus is giving a new nature, (called the New Birth) to people who want it. He then helps them with the growth of that nature, which makes a new way of life possible. The Apostle Paul has described that new nature for us. Paul should know, if we compare that man he was with the man he became after he had seen Jesus, "Therefore if any man be in Christ, he is a new creature old things are passed away, behold all things are become new" (2 Corinthians 5:17).

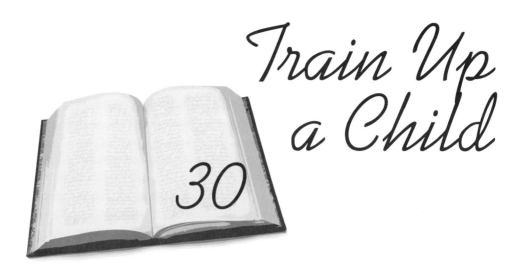

Train Up a Child

30

"Train up a child in the way he should go; and when he is old, he will not depart from it."
Proverbs 22:6

There is probably no verse anywhere else in the Bible that has been more misunderstood by parents than this verse has been.

This verse makes it seem so sure that what parents do will guarantee their children staying in everything that they teach them. It makes it sound like, given the right kind of training, it is positive that children will always do what their parents want them to.

But time and time again there are weeping parents wringing their hands in heartbreak, "We did everything for him we knew to do. Why didn't he stay with what we taught him?"

Then some parents who have been spared such experiences will have no sympathy for the parents of erring children. "It was the way they raised him and spoiled him that made him do what he did," they think. "The Bible says a child will not depart from the training of his parents."

Why then does this verse make it sound so sure that a child will not depart from his parents' teachings when he gets old, when all of us can think of dozens of instances that didn't work out that way?

First of all, this verse gives us parents a sobering thought on our awesome responsibility. Our actions, much more than our words, influence what our children will become in their later years. We are training our children even when we are not aware of it. This training received while at home does stick, whether it is good or bad.

Here we put those clothes with a little style on our innocent little children. They are still too young to care what we put on them. We do it only because of our own pride.

Then in later years we wonder why it is so hard to get them to lay off some of the ways of dressing that look so much like the world. We wonder where that pride came from.

Really all that happened was that the children did not depart from the training they got while they were very young.

Here we joke a little now and then on that sacred subject of God's wonderful way of bringing new life into the world. Then when our children get older we are shocked and wonder how they got led into saying some things and doing things we thought they knew were wrong.

We wonder where that impurity had its roots.

Here we make ourselves so busy. We all know it is sometimes necessary to hurry and cut corners. We know if people can't get themselves out of slow gear they will fall behind.

So after awhile we have this habit of constant hurrying formed so deeply in our lives that we can't ever slow down. We then have precious little time with those who should be closest to us–those in our own families.

Then in later years we wonder why our children never shared their deep inner feelings and joys with us. We wonder why they never talked to us about their concerns and problems. We wonder when the generation gap got to be beyond bridging.

We want our children to do their best. After all, other people will notice how we raised our children. To get them to do what we want them to do, we criticize them. We shout at them and drive them like many an overseer of a southern cotton plantation used to drive his colored slaves back in the time of slavery.

Then when the children get older we wonder why their interests and values are altogether different from what ours are. We wonder why their outbursts of temper, sometimes even directed at us, are not kept under better control.

We do reap what we have sowed. So much of what we did in our younger years comes back and haunts us in our later years. For example, did Jacob's deception of his old father Isaac (Genesis 27:19) have anything to do with his own sons' deceiving him in his old years? (Genesis 37:32). We know King David deeply regretted his sin (2 Samuel 11, Psalm 51), but he had a fresh grief coming to him when the same type of sin later occurred in his own family (Samuel 13:31).

But let's not just dwell only in the wrong way to train and to be an example to the next generation. Thanks be to God, a good influence can also be catching and will stay with our children. Seeing their parents living a sincere Christian life is worth more than thousands of do's and don'ts to them.

It might not be a proper way to compare the training of children to the training of horses, but in many ways it is somewhat similar. It is very true, as many good horse trainers say, "If you want to train a

horse, you have to train his owner first."

The Hebrew word which has been translated as "train" in this verse in Proverbs means both to give instructions and to dedicate.

That dedication might even mean much more than the instructions. We have the example in the Bible of the woman, Hannah, who prayed her son, Samuel, into the world. She promised to dedicate, to give him back to the Lord, all the days of his life (I Samuel 1:11), and she kept that promise.

But then, as we know there are no mistakes in the Bible, how can we explain the fact that some children do stray away from the good teaching of their parents and never come back? How can we explain that and make it harmonize with this verse that says that children will not depart when they are old from the training they received from their parents in their younger days?

Let's put it this way. A child who gets good Christian training with both instruction and example, will never forget that training as long as he lives. He will never forget what his humble God-fearing father and mother taught him. His parents may someday no longer be here, but still he will choose whether to make good use of what he was taught or he will choose to reject it.

If he follows their good precepts he will be eternally grateful for the upbringing God has provided for him. If he rejects it he may wish he could forget some of the things they said, so he could ease the guilt he carries. He knows what they said was right and what he is doing is wrong.

Such a man or woman will never be able to erase that memory. As much as they may want it to, that influence will never leave them and they can never get away from it. They will have to live with the guilt of turning it down as long as they live.

They may wish they could, but they will never depart or get away from the memory of that training.

The Commandment 31 for Youth

"Remember now thy Creator in the days of thy youth, while the evil days come not, nor the years draw nigh, when thou shalt say, I have no pleasure in them."

Ecclesiastes 12:1

It is always heartening to hear of young people who want to make something of their lives. There is still so much good to be thankful for, and we do want to be grateful to God for all the good that is still among us. One thing to be thankful for is surely that we still have many, many young people among us who seem to realize that living a life full of gratitude for what God does for them starts with being decent and obedient while still in their young days.

But then sometimes things that we all have to hear can be so discouraging.

Some of the things that you have to hear that are being done by some of the young people that come out of the homes of our plain people are one example.

Here are young people of teen-age or older who were raised in the homes of lay members, bishops, deacons and ministers (there seems to be no difference), who in their younger days went to church in the back seats of their parents' carriages. They probably got their formal education at a parochial school supported by the church. They had the opportunity that millions of children in this world do not have to find out in their young days what it takes to live a holy Christian life that leads to joy, contentment, and peace.

Then the time comes when they turn sixteen and start "running around."

Some of the reports coming out as to what goes on when these young people get together are pretty bad. We have to hear that some of these young people, who just a few years before were of the pure, innocent bloom of the church, are doing things that puts a blight on our plain churches and a shame on all of us.

We hear of disrespect to parents, people and property. We have to hear of the muddled condition of drunkenness among them and of dancing and going to ball parks and movies. We see them trying to dress more like movie stars than like a follower of the teachings of Christ. We hear of them getting a craving for worldly music and songs and getting radios and recorders to try to satisfy that evil appetite.

Here we have parents who in their wish to keep the church from drifting into the world, and in their contentment with less of the luxuries of our times, are limiting the use of cars and modern machinery. Then along come their children who "burn up the rubber" on the public highways with their cars. This has come to be so bad that more than one of the non-Amish living among us has said that they have a fear of going on the road on Saturday nights and Sundays.

Of course nobody would like to believe that all that we hear is true, but sadly too much of what we hear proves later to be true. We even hear of some of them knowingly abusing God's wonderful gift of a sound mind with drugs. We hear of the shameful misuse of Gods miraculous gift of the creation of life by fornication and living together unmarried, and even of having abortions. Instead of being a light for the world, and an example of holy living for other people, the young people who do these things are making many people in a non-plain church say that they would not want their children to associate with any of us.

Such living is far, far from what God expects a new-born Christian to lead. There are many people, especially young fathers and mothers with school-age children with heavy, burdened hearts. What can be done to improve things before these children get to be teenagers? What, oh what, can be done to make things better? Why doesn't somebody start something that works? If there is anybody anywhere who has an answer as to what can be done, stand up and let yourself be heard. Surely there must be a way to improve the behavior of our young people.

What are us older people and parents doing about it? It doesn't make things any better if we are so unconcerned about it that we don't believe that we have a problem to be worked on and are not even alarmed about it. Neither does it make things any better if we don't want to know what is going on or if we don't care to find out where our young people are spending their time. Nor do we want to continue to harbor a secret wish to have our children looked up to in a popular crowd. The young people will sense that pride in their parents pretty quickly and will soon be out of control.

Neither will it work if we get so demanding that our children be well behaved that we provoke them to anger. That will only widen the generation gap, or more accurately the communication or "talk things over" gap.

Shaking our heads in despair and saying that things will always be this way, and there is nothing that we can do about it, is also surely no way to help to better things. Saddening to us all is what some parents are doing about it, in that they will start to question and even ridicule our way of life, leave our churches and take their families along. By some unknown way of reasoning they seem to think that

getting more of the world's luxuries will make them better followers of the examples and teachings of Christ.

What is then the answer? Well, one answer that would also not work, even if it were practical, would be for all of us to move out to some remote island, far out in the ocean, far away from all evil influence, and expect to live a life free from all temptation there. Satan would be there, even before we would ever set a foot on the shore. Joining a church where plain and simple living are ignored and not required for membership is also not the answer. By what reasoning could we hope to lessen the worldly influences around us by walking closer to them?

But thanks be to God, there is an answer. There is something for us to do that worked a thousand and more years ago, and will still work in our time. It will also work for any of the people living on this earth after us. One of the many verses in the Bible that tells us what to do is found in 2 Corinthians 6:17 – "Wherefore come out from among them, and ye separate, saith the Lord." Another verse, in telling us about that city of Babylon, or the world, says the same thing in a different, but in a powerful way: "Come out of her, my people, that ye be not partakers of her sins, that ye receive not of her plagues" (Revelation 18:4). So the answer to the young people and to us all us to stay away from the things of sin.

There is one pretty good example for us in the world of nature. That is the barn swallows, a bird many of us are familiar with. They don't build their nests to raise their families away out in the woods somewhere. God has put an instinct in them that they build their nests in our barns, just a few feet away from the cats, their mortal enemies. But they stay away from the cats, and thus can not be harmed by them. They build their nests; they spend the long days sitting on their eggs to hatch them; they raise their families and bring food to their young till they are old enough to go for it themselves, all just a short distance above the cats who are just watching and waiting for one of them to make a mismove that will put them within the reach of their claws. As long as the birds stay away, they are safe. But just let one of them fly too close, or let one of the small birds leave the security of the nest before it can fly, and it is doomed.

So the answer to living a better Christian life is taking your stand and not associating with those who want to keep on doing evil things and with those who go along with sinful worldly doings. Even if it is one who is now your best "buddy" but still wants to continue to live a life that leads to destruction, you owe it to your own soul to drop him and turn around and go the other way. Even if you will have to stand alone it will be eternally better than drowning your soul in sins.

This is not to deprive you of joy. You will have to go through some heart-rending to make the change, but later you will have a peace and contentment that you never before have thought possible. We will always be exposed to the evil around us, but that will not be harmful to us until we go along with it. The Bible says, "My son, when sinners (bad boys or "bösen Buben" in German) entice thee, consent thou not" (Proverbs 1:10).

Thanks be to God, there are still many young people in our churches who are decent company to associate with. There are still many who find a satisfying answer by obeying the teachings and examples of the One who has redeemed them from their sins. That they do not keep company with those who continue to live in sins is not because they think themselves better than the others, but because they know that one rotten apple in a barrel will spoil the whole bunch.

More of God's power to them! The churches all need more of their kind. The churches need everyone to help, every single one of us. If there would be anybody among us who has never done a single wrong act, we surely would need that person for an example for the rest of us. Since we don't have any like that among us, we need people who, whatever their past, have repented and started all over again. We need people like the Apostle Paul who was such a help to the early church when he made a change in his life and with it started associating with a different kind of people. Such ones will help to make the light to the world shine more brightly again.

If we allow Him to do so, God will make it easier for us to live a better life by having good companions for us as we travel on our pilgrim way. In return for what He does for us, let us seek to better our lives so that we can be better company for all the others that we may travel with. Our journey through this life on the way to a better land is a pleasant walk if we help each other to make it so. Our stay here is too short and eternity is too long to have it any other way.

When Children Ask 32 Questions

"And it shall come to pass when your children shall say unto you, what mean ye by this service? That ye shall say, It is the sacrifice of the Lord's Passover who passed over the houses of the children of Israel in Egypt, when He smote the Egyptians, and delivered our houses. And the people bowed their heads and worshipped."

Exodus 12:26-27

Those little boys and girls wandering through the wilderness and living in the tent homes with their fathers and mothers must have been very much like the children of today.

They wondered. They were curious to know. So they asked questions.

God knew those Israelite children would ask questions, so He commanded their parents to give them satisfactory answers to their questions.

As any parent or teacher of today knows, that is one thing that has not changed one bit in the several thousand years that have passed by since the nation of Israel was saved from their cruel bondage in the land of Egypt. Children will still ask questions.

Questions and more questions. The typical child starts asking questions as soon as he starts to talk. Those questions, hundreds and hundreds of them, will be the child's way of learning about the interesting world that he or she has been placed in. Those young children are new in this world and are just beginning to learn things we older people at one time didn't know either and had to learn. Each and every one of those questions is really a little one-time opportunity to plant yet another kind of good seed into that tender, easily-impressed heart.

So it is very important to get ready to listen to and to supply those questions with answers that are satisfactory and understandable to the child. God is using that stage of a child's life to give us a golden opportunity to help those children become what He has planned them to be.

Never shrug off or brush off those questions as being too unimportant to listen to. It is a hundred times better to take the time when a question is asked to do a little explaining right there than it is to sometime later try to tell a child what you think he needs to know.

And what then happens is that good interesting answers to their questions will promote still more questions! At the time those questions are asked is when their interest is at its keenest. They will believe every word you say as being the gospel truth. Whatever gets planted and cultivated in their tender hearts at that age will grow, whether it be good or bad. If no good seeds are planted, those tender hearts will be like a fertile field which is soon covered with weeds.

When the child starts to talk and ask questions, he will not stop wondering and questioning until some adult, usually one or both of the parents, begins to suppress those questions. Such a child will then soon be conditioned to seek his answers elsewhere, or which can be just as bad, he will withdraw into a shell of his own. Those questions may be stalled and squelched, but their wondering, curiosity and thinking will not be stopped. At that time the seeds can be sowed for a wide generation gap between the child and the adult which later cannot be bridged.

What is this that will quench and throw a wet blanket on that interchange of questions and answers between child and adult? What is it that helps to ruin those conversations which are such an important beginning in the building up of a good healthy relationship later when the child is growing up?

One is the attitude like that of the lady who was overheard in a supermarket talking about her small son, "That kid asks enough questions to drive me up the wall. If I were to answer all his little questions I would get nothing else done."

Lady, you do not realize the small joys you are missing by not being understanding enough to listen to your small son's questions. Your son will too soon be seeking his answers elsewhere. Your number one job right now is to be a mother to your son. Your frazzled nerves are not the result of your son's questions, but are coming from the too many other things that could wait or are not necessary. You better forget trying to impress others with you loud talk and your vain way of dressing yourself and start thinking about the boy God has placed under your care and teaching.

You are a housekeeper; but first of all, you are to be a homemaker. The quiet little "small talk" which you could be having with your little son could be remembered by him until his dying day; which could be long after you are gone.

It could be a little like a man who was talking to a friend about the rough days he had in his childhood. His father, a drunkard, abused him and his mother until his death in a drunken stupor. After his mother abandoned him he was put in a Catholic orphanage. He had nothing but bitter memories of both his father and mother.

But he was flooded with fond memories of his grandmother, who often came to visit him.

His grandmother was the only friend he ever really had in his young days, even though he was surrounded by boys his own age. "We used to talk and talk," he said.

When he was asked what they talked about he said, "You could talk to her about anything." With his eyes overflowing he added, "We used to talk about just anything at all. I still really miss her." The biggest tragedy in the memory of his childhood was the day when his grandmother died.

It is time for us parents to re-examine what we think to be most important. If we are always too busy or if we are too short-tempered all the time to give satisfactory answers to the questions of our children, we should not be too surprised if they will clam up to us in their later years. They will just be copying what we did to them in their younger years. Being short-tempered or being moody is contagious.

It is time we show enough interest in what our children are saying and asking to sometimes pause in what we are doing and look into their eyes when they talk. That interest expressed by what is called "eye contact" between adult and child can be worth more than a thousand words. Usually a child doesn't desire be rebellious to an adult who is loving and understanding enough to be a good listener to what he asks or says.

Of course, children's questions can soon become too much a way to get attention to themselves. They can become too frequent or simple enough that they should be thinking out the answers themselves. If such is the case, perhaps we can sometimes ask them questions to find out if they are listening to our answers and remembering them, or if they are simply thinking up a new question at the time.

If for any reason you can't answer a question properly right at the time, tell your questioning child you will explain later, and when. And don't forget to keep that promise! You can read to your youngster on subjects you know too little about or feel unable to explain and answer in your own words. If you make it a point to explain and answer questions as you read, you will both be learning.

Sooner or later questions will come up about God and about those deep questions of why we are here, and how we came—those questions which are mysteries even to us. They will question us about their little problems which seem to them to be too big to ever see a way out.

The Israelites were to tell their children of the

first passover of the Lord when they were saved from their cruel and unmerciful masters in the land they used to live in; which in a spiritual way is very much like God still saving people today from the slavery of sin to which they are being bound. We can just imagine the tears flowing in their eyes and their helplessness in answering their questioning children. It is no wonder that they "bowed their heads and worshipped."

Yes, heathen indeed is the home where God and His wonderful works of grace, hope and love are never mentioned, or His marvelous works of nature are never discussed. Pagan and unchristian is the home where God's miraculous way of creating new life is never mentioned except in highly improper jokes. Such a subject is always much too sacred to talk about lightly, but it must be talked about when the children start asking questions about it.

Like the Israelite children, our children will also grow up and start becoming aware that we live different from many people around us. They will sometime ask us questions similar to the "What mean ye by this service?" Who can then blame them for later becoming discontented or even rebellious if we shrug off the question, or if the best answer we can give them is to tell them that is what the preachers want us to do?

This brings to mind the story that has been told of the small boy who asked his father questions about life and questions about God.

"I am sorry, son, I am busy now," the father said. "We will talk about such things later when I have the time. Anyway by then you will be able to understand it better."

So the boy went back to play in the sandbox. The father went on with the cares and concerns he had. After all, wasn't there only one opportunity in life to accumulate a fortune for himself and for his son?

Later the boy grew up, and by then the father was old and no longer able to work. But he had now made a fortune.

One day when the son was getting ready to go away the father called him to his side.

"Now, my son, come and I will answer your questions abut life and your questions about God," he said.

"I am sorry, Dad, I am busy now. We will talk about such things later when I have the time. Anyway, I know as much about such things as I am interested in knowing," the boy said as he walked away out the door.

Lighting a cigarette, zipping up his leather jacket, he jumped on his motorcycle and roared away.

Watching him until his son was out of sight down the road, the father bowed his head. He bowed his head not to worship, but in remorse for an opportunity that was now lost and forever gone.

94

Be Still and Listen

33

Then Samuel answered, "Speak, for thy servant heareth."
I Samuel 3:10

The verse quoted above is a part of the well-known story in the Bible when Eli was the priest in the tabernacle, the place where the people met to worship God. The young boy, Samuel, who was a helper in that holy place, was taught by the old priest that when he heard the Lord speaking to him, he was to be quiet and listen to what He had to say to him.

This story also has a valuable lesson for us in our day. We can also have two-way communication with our Lord and Creator. Prayer is when we speak to the Lord. Then He speaks to us through the reading of the Bible and Bible-based literature, through the sermons we hear in church, through the words of the good songs we sing, and often through the conversation that we have with other people. He also uses our conscience when He wants us to know what His will is for us.

When God speaks, we are to stay quiet and listen. If we want God to listen to us when we talk to him, that is when we pray, we will have to listen to Him when He speaks to us. His voice comes to us, not always in loud words of thunder such as the children of Israel heard when they were camped around Mount Sinai, but often in a "still, small voice" such as the prophet Elijah heard when he was hiding in the same wilderness some six hundred years later (I Kings 19:12).

Listening is not only necessary in our relationship with our God and Master, but with each other in our daily lives. You, as a teacher, can probably not do much about parents who are too busy or too unconcerned to communicate (talk to and listen) with their children, but you can be an understanding friend and by taking a little time now and then to listen to their problems, you can nip many future problems in the bud.

Good listeners are a rare type of people. Being a good listener is really more important than a good talker. Conversation with other people is really a game of give and take. If you don't play the game, you will find yourself without a listener. If we do a lot more talking than listening, we are likely to become what is called a bore—someone who becomes tiresome to other people. Even the Scriptures say, "Let thy words be few" (Ecclesiastes 5:2).

The children in your classroom have many problems that you help them with. They get stuck with an arithmetic problem, so they raise their hand and ask for your help with it. They know that you will know what steps to take to solve that problem, and will not hesitate to ask you for help. But there are problems that will come up in life that go a lot deeper than the problems out of a school book. To us older people these problems may seem to be very minor, and we have to watch out that we do not

95

brush the children aside when they come to us for help. The problems are very real to them. They need someone to help them unravel their difficulties. They need to be assured that when something turns up they can come to someone who will be concerned with what they have to say. If they can't find anyone to confide in, they are likely to keep their feelings bottled up, which can lead to depression and to rebellion against the parents, the teacher, and the other authorities over them.

Listen, Teacher. You can be a great help to your scholars in this way. You can read it in a child's face and see it in his actions if he has a problem that he is struggling with. Here is where the full measure of Christian sympathy (not pity) and understanding is needed. Feelings are more important than exams and corrected papers. Have a warm, human interest in all your pupils. Human interest has always been a winning quality.

Children are very sensitive. Take the time to ask a few questions that will require a response on the pupil's part. Gently encourage a two-way conversation. This will take a prayerful and loving attitude on your part. Your reward will be when their eyes and their face light up with a smile. You don't have all the answers; you don't need to act as if you did. Just being a sympathetic and prayerful listener is often all that is required.

Discipline in a school also requires a lot of listening. So often if we would only listen we wouldn't have to say half as much. Usually a child won't try to outsmart someone who is loving and understanding enough to listen tho his problems. Ignoring or neglecting a problem that a child has will often lead to an attitude of resistance. Many of our problems with children prove to us how little we listen to what is going on and to what they say. They will have things to confide to someone, but if they know that we won't listen anyhow, or if they know that we'll only shrug or laugh them off, they won't approach us for help with their personal problems. The result is a rebellious child.

We know that Jesus was never too busy doing other important things when a child came and had something to offer. When that unnamed boy brought to Him all the lunch that he had, and offered it to feed the multitude of people, Jesus didn't brush him away or tell him to run along. He used that small offering to perform a mighty miracle (John 6:9-14).

This is a gripping lesson for all of us. It is often the little things from little people that still work miracles in our times. By just doing a little more listening we might be able to find out what some of these little things are. Jesus warns us, "Take heed that ye despise not one of these little ones" (Matthew 18:10).

34 Sowing and Reaping

"And he that reapeth receiveth wages and gathereth fruit unto life eternal; that both he that soweth and he that reapeth may rejoice together"
John 4:36

A teacher could be likened to a sower. A farmer knows that he has to sow good seeds if he wants to expect a harvest. Parents and teachers, the first adults to have an influence on a child's life, will also have to sow good seeds if they want to expect any good to come out of the lives of the children they are in charge of.

We could think of ourselves as grown-up children and the children as future adults. If the Lord tarries they will have the positions of responsibility in later years. Each of us, as a Christian, should consider himself called into full-time service, being an example to the younger generation coming after us. Teaching is more than instructing and correcting a child's actions; you must be a good example.

Talk to anyone you will, even to very old people, and they will remember the teachers they had back in their school days. They will remember the ones that were strict and the ones who let the pupils run the school. In the same way you will be remembered in the minds of your pupils long after you are gone. Within a week after you started teaching school, your pupils (and their parents!) had sized you up and put you into some category or another. If we think about it this way, it is really important that we do our job in a Christian way. Our influence, whether good or bad, will long outlive us.

Your attitude can not remain hidden. There was once a teacher who said that he really liked teaching school, but it was the students who bothered him. Then there was the young girl who was asked to teach. Although she didn't always have high marks in her school days, she had a firm, loving way around her pupils that she taught. We will let you guess which of the two was a successful teacher.

God works through us humans. He has given us parents the job of raising and has given you teachers the job of teaching His dear precious children. He Himself is not here to do it, but with His spirit He will supply the strength, love, and wisdom for you to do the work that He has for you. When Jesus was here on the earth in person, He helped people with their material needs, as when He fed the multitudes, but His main work was ministering to the needs of the spirit. The Great Teacher is the perfect example of how we are to work with our children and pupils. As the different situations and problems come up, let us ask ourselves what we think Jesus would do if He were in our place.

Teaching is going to require the touching of some of the soft spots in the hearts of your pupils. Only God knows where those tender spots are. That is why you will need His help. You can help your pupils learn to control some of their immediate desires to gain the rewards of longer-term satisfactions and achievements. You will have to do a lot of reminding, but remember that talking can be overdone. At a certain point, the more you say, the less your pupils will remember.

It didn't just happen that you got this task of teaching. You can be sure that circumstances in your life controlled by God have led you into the work that you now have. Your work is a job of helping a generation younger than yourself to understand the subjects you have in your textbooks, and to learn some of the songs in the songbooks. They will also need your help in learning how to get along with other people. When things go wrong, don't despair. You can get all the help you need for all the duties that you are to do. Our Heavenly Father is always more willing to give us help than we are to ask for and receive it. Some of the helplessness that you feel may be God's way to get you to ask for a power beyond your own.

The parents of Moses are an example to us teachers and parents in the sowing (teaching) that we are to do. They must have done a lot of sowing in the short time that they had the child in their home and care. Their teaching must have had a goal and a purpose. They were slaves in the land where they lived. Even if the father came home, tired at the end of a long hard day's work in the brickyards, the young boy's spiritual training was not neglected. If his parents were still living when Moses forsook the Egyptian court and came back to his people, we can believe they rejoiced. In the same way Moses, who later reaped the blessings of God upon his life because he harkened to their influence, teaching, and training, could also rejoice with them.

In the same way, the teachers and parents who do the sowing and the children who reap the harvest of a Christian training will someday rejoice together. May the time come for us all when, like that line in the well-known song, "We shall come rejoicing, bringing in the sheaves..."

The Great Harvest Field

35

Say not ye, there are yet four months and then cometh the harvest? Behold, I say unto you, Lift your eyes, and look on the fields; for they are white already to harvest"
John 4:35

This verse has often been thought to refer to the old people that we have among us. The white and gray heads that we have in our midst are like the grain standing ripe in the fields. That grain will soon be cut. Just as the farmer will decide that the grain is now ripe and will cut his crop, so will the All-knowing God above us decide when a person has finished his life's work and will send the angel of death, often known as the Grim Reaper, to take him out of this world into the next.

That could well be what Jesus had in mind when He said these words. But many Bible verses have more than one meaning. We can take many of the verses in the Bible and uncover one meaning after another. The depth of Scripture is fathomless and will never be fully understood.

This verse could also be written to teach us parents and teachers another great truth. When the grain is ripened and we harvest in our golden fields in the middle of the summer, we need everyone who can help out in the fields. When Jesus looked out over the fields four months before the time of the summer harvest, He did not see fields of ripe golden grain. He saw fields of young plants with little green blades just starting to grow. He saw the young shoots that were ready for the spring rains and the warming rays of the sun.

This is a lesson that we all need to learn. We don't have to wonder long about God's will for our lives. We don't have to go far to find out what our life's work is to be. If we will only "lift up our eyes" we will be able to see the great duties that are now here waiting for us to do. Those dear, precious children in our charge need help to make something out of their lives. They need that help in their early years when, like the green shoots of wheat, their hearts are tender and can easily be impressed. When they are young they do not easily forget the instructions that we give them. They are also not so likely to be resentful to those who instruct them. We are the ones hired by God to do the work. The work of the harvest is greatest when the heart is still young and easily influenced.

Jesus tells us at another place, "The harvest truly is plenteous, but the laborers are few" (Matthew 9:37). God needs more men and women dedicated to the great harvest that is right now waiting for us to work in. The fields are found in our homes and schools. The generations that have lived here before us have laid down their work and are now gone. The work is here for us to do now. "Other men labored, and ye are entered into their labors" (John 4:38).

Oh, dear teachers, don't let the boredom and the difficulties in your schoolroom blind you to the fact God needs your help in the great harvest field that is waiting to be worked in. Learning reading, writing, and arithmetic are very necessary, but they are not really the most important things for you to teach your scholars. Inspiring them to be aware of the beautiful and uplifting things in this life is really more important than textbooks and scores.

Your work, first of all, is to help mold and shape these young minds so that they can, with God's help, resist the forces of evil that they become exposed to as they grow older. Let your prayers be that the Lord can help you to see beyond today's problems and frustrations and be an example to your pupils so that they can, in turn, be a help in the harvest that tomorrow will bring.

May God grant you the wisdom, strength, love, and knowledge that you need for your daily duties in helping to shape the lives of those little ones whom Jesus blessed, saying, "For of such is the kingdom of heaven" (Matthew 19:14).

What Is in a 36 Language?

When the church services are over in our plain churches, the hymn books that were used that day are gathered together and put back into a box to be kept there until the next church service.

In more than just a few of those book boxes somebody thought it necessary to write a line of instruction for the packing of the books, "Please lay the books flat."

It is unknown who the first person was who marked a song book box with that line. Whoever he was, he evidently felt that the books should be laid down flat for the jostling over rough roads on a steel-wheeled wagon to the next house. And he was right – the books do stand the rough trip much better packed flat than they do standing on edge.

Now someone could come along and say that those lines penciled or painted on the inside of the book boxes are a contradiction. The line is printed in the English language and yet those song books are printed in the German language.

But it is not a contradiction at all. We are bilingual – a people of two languages. We use both languages with about equal ease. As such we are like the familiar Puerto Ricans who use both Spanish and English, or like some of Canada's people who are as much at home with the French language as with the English.

English is the language of our country. But we, the descendants of immigrants from the German speaking parts of Europe, have clung to a language which has become largely our own. Over the years that our people have lived alongside our English-speaking neighbors, we have without even trying, gradually accepted numerous English words into our German dialect. The Pennsylvania Dutch we speak is really a slowly-changing language. It is somewhat different now from a hundred yeas ago, and is not even exactly the same in different parts of the country.

Our case is very much like that of the Jews in New Testament times.

The Old Testament was first written almost entirely in the old Hebrew language. Hebrew was the language of Abraham, Isaac and Jacob. It was the language of the Jews on down through the times of Moses and King David until the time of their captivity in the far-off land of Babylon.

Those years of living among the strange people in Babylon who talked a different dialect did something to the language of the Jews. In that land they kept their faith better than they did in any other time in their history, but by the time they returned to their homeland again most of the people talked a different dialect called Aramaic. This was then the language of the Jewish people when Jesus was on earth some five or six hundred years later, even though they still used the ancient Hebrew in their temple worship. We know that Jesus talked the Aramaic language because several of His statements are recorded for us exactly as He pronounced them. Some of these are the "Talitha kumi" of Mark 5:41, the "Ephrata" of Mark 7:34 and the "Eli, Eli, lama asabthani" of Matthew 27:46 and Mark 15:34; all words which language scholars recognize as being Aramaic words.

Then later, by the time the books were written which now make up the New Testament, roughly between the years 50 A.D. and 100 A.D., another language had worked its way up to become the chief language of commerce in the land of the Jews and in most of the lands in that part of the world. That language was Greek.

Then instead of writing in the Hebrew of the Old Testament or in Aramaic, the language that was spoken by Jesus and His apostles, the New Testament writers used the Greek in nearly all that they wrote. The four Gospel writers were like interpreters of Jesus' words into the Greek before they wrote down the words He has spoken, The letters of Paul and the other apostles to the churches, and the rest of the New Testament, were also written and then read in Greek.

Thus the case of the people at that time was very much like ours today. They had the traditional Hebrew for their worship just like we use the German Bible in our homes and churches. They had the Aramaic, a language that was spoken in their homes, but hardly very popular as a written language at that time; very much like we use our everyday Pennsylvania Dutch. Then they had the Greek, the easy-to-write language of world commerce and business, for their writings and correspondence, somewhat similar to the way we use the English language in our day.

Now why do we keep on using more than one language? Couldn't we find out if there is a language more holy or sacred than the other languages and use only that language?

To begin, we do not even know what the original language was. We have no way of finding out what language God used to speak to Adam and Eve in the Garden of Eden. It could have been any one of the hundreds of languages now used throughout the world, or it could have been altogether different from any of those.

Neither do we know what language was spoken by Noah and his descendants. They lived before the Tower of Babel, when God changed the speech of the different families so they could not understand each other anymore, and thus couldn't work together anymore (Genesis 11:7).

Nor do we know which language will be used in heaven. If we would know, we probably would want to learn it here on earth. Even though we read in Acts 26:14 that the voice from heaven to Saul was in the Hebrew tongue, that still does not tell us that Hebrew is the language spoken in heaven. Jesus was just speaking to Saul (later called Paul) in a language that could be understood.

Are then the original Hebrew and Greek, as they were used by the holy writers, the holy languages? If they are, we should put away our translated German and English Bibles and get a copy of the Bible in Greek. Then we should learn to read the pure, unadulterated text in the exact words in which it was written.

But that would not be as easy as it may sound.

Before we could ever get any meaning out of reading the Bible we would first have to spend a long time studying those languages. And it would take a lot more than learning the meanings of the thousands of Hebrew and Greek words used in the original text. We would have to learn what those words meant at the time they were written thousands of years ago. Word usages change. Some words used in the Hebrew and Greek of today have different meanings than they used to have at that time. Then there are some words no longer in use.

We would also have to learn to read the Hebrew words from right to left on the pages, just the opposite of the left to right we are used to. We would have to get used to a very different sentence structure. For one instance, the first part of Genesis 50:2 translated word for word would read something like, "And commanded he Joseph servants his, physicians his to embalm father his."

If you ever do get the idea it would be better to

read the original Greek of the New Testament exactly as it was written, ask to see a Greek New Testament the next time you are in a public library. Some libraries do have them. Those ink marks on paper mean nothing until they can be read. Just seeing pages of those strange-looking letters which you do not understand should cause you to appreciate those translators who labored long years to make God's Word available to us in a speech we can understand. We do find it hard to believe that God wants us all to have a college education in order to read the Bible.

Before the Reformation in the sixteenth century, the Roman Catholic church objected to the Bible being translated into the language of the ordinary people. Only those highly-learned scholars having a university education were supposed to be able to read the Bible. If you were one of the unlearned common people you were supposed to accept the Bible as the learned scholars explained it to you. You were not supposed to worry about learning to read it yourself.

But the people wanted to read and to know the Bible for themselves. There were people who were versed in the different languages who were willing to make the Bible available to them in their everyday language. Some of those translators were cruelly persecuted, and for some it cost them their lives. But they were determined to put the Good Book out in languages the common people could read and understand.

But even then, some of the translations were not accepted right away by all the people. One example is the now-familiar King James version of 1611 which was translated into the everyday English of that time. The "thee" and "thou" of that version, by the way, show us a little how much the English language has changed since then. The Pilgrims, a group of the Puritans, who came over here to Plymouth Rock in 1620, never fully accepted this version. They considered it a modern version. They used an older English translation, called the Geneva Bible. They did not trust the King James version, since it was approved by the powerful Church of England which persecuted the Pilgrims.

Even our Anabaptist forefathers did not at first accept the Luther German version, which we now use in our homes and churches. The Anabaptists could hardly be blamed for not using Martin Luther's work, preferring instead Christopher Froschauer's German printing. Luther was a bitter enemy of those who did not share his beliefs. He believed in baptizing babies into the church soon after they were born. Plus he believed so strongly in salvation by faith only, that he was not afraid to say that he thought very little of the New Testament book of James, which teaches a balance of both works and faith. Like most of the other Reformation leaders he also did not believe in nonresistance. He and his followers were bitter persecutors of the Anabaptists, many of whom gave up their lives rather than accept the faith of their persecutors.

But for all his failures, Luther was a genius who knew his languages. It was not that his translation was perfect and the others were not, but his version was somewhat easier to read than the Froschauer. Many thought he brought out the original meanings more accurately and clearly, even in the book of James that he didn't like. The result was that the Luther version was gradually accepted over the Froschauer.

Luther's version was even considered such an accurate translation of the original Hebrew and Greek that some of the men who later worked on different English translations used his German version as one of their sources. At any rate, it has stood the test of time, as there has not been another German version for these 450 years that has become better known, or even some close to taking its place.

But there is no doubt about it, the translators did have a difficult and formidable task to bring out the exact meanings that the original words contained.

For one example, the writers of the New Testament had several Greek words, all of which in the English are translated as "love" (or "charity"), and for which the German has only one word "Liebe". One of the Greek words could be defined as a self love, such as liking people only because they like us or are interested in what we like. Another meant physical love, the same word that is often used in a shallow way in many romance stories. Then there was the Greek word that stood for the selfless love such as Christians should have for other people, or such as God has for man, a love which gives even when others have not earned it or do not deserve it.

Another interesting example of the difficulties the translators had in getting the exact meaning is that it was not always clear if a verb was meant to be in a past, present or future tense. As in Matthew 25:8 the German translation says of the lamps the foolish virgins were carrying, "Unsere Lampen verlöschen." One English translation gives it as "gone out" (King James), one as "are going out," (Revised Standard), while one gives it as "have almost gone out."

Taking everything into consideration, it is amazing how the translators did get God's message transferred into other languages as well as they did. It is not always the exact word that is most important and which gives God's Word power. It is really the wonderful meanings and insights that those words stand for. The Apostle Paul in I Corinthians 4:20 says, "For the kingdom of God is not in word, but in power." The best translation of the Bible is when those living words get translated into the changed and bettered lives of people.

So it could really be said there is no language more holy than another. Nor is any language more worldly than any other language. Really, we should not value one language over the other, or condemn one more than another. When the people left the unfinished tower of Babel, some could talk only one language, some only another–probably some of the languages in Acts 2:9, 10, 11.

It was God who made all the different languages and tongues. There will be people in heaven from all over the world, "Out of every kindred and tongue and people and nation (Revelation 5:9).

Therefore, just as there is no one holy or sacred language, there is also no one holy version of the Bible. Not all new and revised translations are bad, nor are all old translations good. It is the accuracy to the original that counts, so that no words give us a thought that should not be there. It is my feeling that some of the old versions have an air of reverence about them which some of the newer do not have.

If a translation would come out in which the translator would have tampered with the words to make them say what he wanted them to say, there would be many scholars who would detect such errors and the translation would never have wide acceptance.

We do want to remember when we select what we read that there is much Bible-based reading around, but there is only one holy, inspired and sacred Bible. No other writings can be depended to be 100% free from parts that could be misleading. But not so with God's Word; "They are spirit and life (John 6:63).

Now we come back to the use that we, as Pennsylvania Dutch-speaking people make of both the English and the German languages.

If you have a family circle letter, or if you wish to write to a married son or daughter living in another community, in what language do you choose to write your letter? If you wish to write to some of your friends to let them know to come to your home when you are planning to have a German worship service, do you write that letter in German? If you write to the "Botshaft, or to the "Diary" or to Pathway Publishers, in which language do you do that writing? If you are like most of our plain people, you use the English to do most of that writing, although many people do appreciate some German in their letters and in the reading material that gets mailed to their homes. It helps to keep them brushed up in their German, and there are often words or whole lines which can best be expressed in the German or in the Pennsylvania Dutch. But even so, there is no denying that the biggest percentage of the letters written and the books and magazines put out by the Old Order Plain people are in the English language.

English is the language that our government requires to be taught even in our church-supported schools. We are allowed to teach other languages, but we must teach English. Really, it is good that English is compulsory. How else would we talk with and do business with our English-speaking neighbors if we did not learn their language?

Because we can read both the German and English, we have an opportunity to learn the meaning of some Bible passages better than if we would know only one language. Some verses are clearer in one language than the other. By comparing different versions in the two languages we can sometimes get a better idea of the exact meanings of the original text. In some passages we can even discover that the original might have had several different shades of meaning.

One such example is that of the Hebrew word "menuchah", which is defined as a place of rest. This word as used in Psalms 23:2 is translated by Luther as "frischen", by Froshauer and King James as "stillen" and "still", and by some of the other translations as "restful water" (Modern Language) and "quiet stream" (Living Bible).

All of these shades of meaning add to the riches that we find when we dig deep for the full meaning of a Bible verse. Those versions which bring out the meanings as being by still waters make us think of a shepherd leading his tired and fearful sheep to a place of peace, rest and calm. We can just see the shepherd and his sheep resting beside a still pond with the evening moonlight reflected in the still waters. Those versions which bring out the meaning as being by a fresh water give us a picture of a fresh, unpolluted, gushing spring of water to which a shepherd leads his thirsty flock on a hot and tiring day.

In some versions then, we get the understanding that if we let Him, the Good Shepherd will lead us to places of peace and calm where we can rest from the confusion and the strain and tension, most of which is of our own making. But as Luther's version also brings out, He can also show us the way to a renewal of life where we can get a new and refreshing start when we are discouraged and about ready to give up. Both insights are helpful and both meanings are accurate.

Still another passage in which the German and the English bring out a slightly different thought is in Numbers 11:21 where Moses speaks of "the people among whom I am". The German, which is translated in both the Luther and Froschauer as "darunder ich bin" (under whom I am) gives us an insight into the humble nature of the man Moses who felt himself as being of a lower rank than the people God wanted him to lead into the Promised Land.

It has been said that the German has more words for the different shades of meaning than many other languages have. One English-speaking pastor of a large church says he has spent a long time learning to read the German. He thinks its expressions are more beautiful and likes it because of its different shades of meaning. Here he has spent a lot of time and effort to learn what we too often take for granted. Knowing two languages is a privilege God has provided for us that we can put to good use.

Although we have a knowledge of two languages, it would be wrong not to make an effort to express ourselves better in the English language. But it would be just as wrong to fail to keep and pass on the German to our children – that rich heritage our forefathers left for us.

This is one thing that is threatening to get lost in some of our homes. Our forefathers kept the German language alive for us down to our time by daily using it. We should all appreciate that we have been left richer because of their efforts. Let us pass it on to the next generations.

So often when the mother tongue gets dropped, many other good things get dropped with it. It is not the German language in itself that will keep us from drifting into the world. Yet it is a well-known fact that losing our mother tongue and drifting into the world usually go together.

It would be good for any one of us to become even better acquainted with the German than we are now. Using an English-German edition of the New Testament or of the Bible is a little like having a German and English dictionary on facing pages. If you come across a word you do not know the meaning of, make it a habit to look up that word right away in a good dictionary. If you do so, you will recognize that word the next time you read it. When parents talk to their children, when a teacher talks to her school, and when a minister of the church talks to the people are good times to include the definition of a hard-to-understand word.

Some people who are ready to drop the German say they can't understand the German anyway. It wold be more accurate if they were to say they have no appreciation for the heritage passed on to them and thus are not interested in making the efforts that it takes to understand it. Nobody was ever born knowing a language. It has to be learned.

Our German will become a dead language to us unless we use it. There is no other way. The inspiring reading in some of our old German books will be lost if we don't appreciate what we have. The singing out of our German songbooks, and especially in the slow tunes, will be but relics of the past, unless we have convictions that we want to keep them alive. Many of those songs come from our persecuted forefathers, who were living out their last days in prison. Here some people go to hear what is called "inspired and talented gospel singing and playing" to get "rich spiritual experiences." They do not realize that such is only a weak counterfeit when compared to what we can get out of a church service, or a young peoples' gathering with everybody there singing together from their hearts, each to his or her own ability.

Those school board members who insist that our parochial schools have some sessions to teach German are doing our churches and schools an immense favor. Those teachers who supplement the German being taught at home by parents, with German lessons and singing in their schools are helping to slow the drift of the churches into the world.

Those parents who have convictions on keeping the mother tongue alive and who insist that their children talk Pennsylvania Dutch at home, and those young people who talk the dialect while they visit and work together are doing their descendants a favor. Of course there are times when the Pennsylvania Dutch is proper and there are also times when it is improper; and also so with the English. If you were to have the men of the neighborhood in to help build a machinery shed some day, and several of your English-speaking neighbors come with the others to help, it would be highly out-of-place and discourteous to them if you were to speak Pennsylvania Dutch when giving explanations or while visiting among them.

But if all the neighbors who showed up were your Pennsylvania Dutch-speaking neighbors it would be just as out of place to be speaking English. Useful as the English is to us, we have to keep English speaking in its proper place. That place is not in our homes nor in our church services.

There are two extremes. One is to think of English as being too worldly to learn and to read. The other is the sad case of too many of our people who come along and think it is demeaning or beneath them to use the German to talk Pennsylvania Dutch. Really, nobody seems to be able to explain why it is more proper and smart to talk English.

We now have some teenage groups who talk very little Pennsylvania Dutch when they are together and do very little German singing at their singings. As can be expected, the result could soon be whole families who will be talking English in their homes. There will soon be a generation of people who will have lost the German altogether.

Anybody who speaks English around home when just family members are around, or while working or visiting with others who know Pennsylvania Dutch is putting in a vote to drop a rich heritage that will never again be brought back if we lose it.

The value of that heritage is so great that we can't afford to lose it.

Going About Doing Good

37

"God appointed Jesus of Nazareth with the Holy Ghost and with power; who went about doing good."
Acts 10:38

Back in the time of Moses when God set up a system of laws for the new nation of Israel, He wanted the people to live differently from their heathen, idol-worshipping neighbors. He wanted all the people to be "a kingdom of priests and a holy nation" (Exodus 19:6). He said to them, "Ye shall therefore be holy, for I am holy" (Leviticus 11:45).

However, the people of the tribe of Levi were appointed to do most of the work connected with the worship of God. In those days, before Christ's death on the cross made all the other blood sacrifices unnecessary, the people brought animals to the place of worship to be slain and offered to God.

The Priests had a long list of things to be done at the movable tabernacle, and later at the temple of Jerusalem. This was where the sacrifices were to be offered and where the people went to worship.

The priests were to keep the lamps burning at the place of worship (Exodus 27:20 and 21). They were to keep the fire at the altar burning so that it would never go out (Leviticus 6:13).

They were to teach the laws to the children of Israel (Leviticus 10:11). They were the messengers of God to the people (Malachi 2:7). They were to blow the trumpets to warn the Israelites if an enemy was coming near or to herald a day of

gladness or the beginning of a holiday that they held (Numbers 10:8-10).

And, as if all that were not enough, they were also to judge the matters of controversy that should happen to come up between the people (Deuteronomy 17:8-13).

But still their main work was to help with the rites of sacrifice when the people brought their offerings to God. Every day they themselves were to make an offering for the sins of the people and then cleanse the altar after each sacrifice (Exodus 29:36).

And then there was one night of each year, the Passover night, that was always the busiest time of the whole year. That was the night that the people celebrated the remembrance of the release of their people from the cruel slavery in the land of Egypt.

One Passover night, hundreds of years after their forefathers had made that memorable flight out of the land of Egypt, a happening occurred that must have nearly disrupted the sacrifice that was being done at the temple that night.

There had been a teacher going around in the land preaching of a way of life of love and humility that did not appeal to these priests. The priesthood at that time had drifted pretty far away from what it was first intended to be. The priests did not like to hear what He had to say. The pride and arrogance of their hearts did not have any use for the denial of self that He preached.

Instead of changing their way of life by seeking a new nature (which this teacher, Jesus, claimed anybody could have if they wanted it and asked for it) these priests sought to have Him killed. They even got one of His group of close friends to accept a bribe to watch for a good chance to capture Him. However, they did not intend to carry out their evil intentions until after the crowd of people, who had gathered to celebrate the Passover, had dispersed and gone home (Matthew 26:5).

It happened that this disciple, who had turned traitor, probably thought he had a good chance to betray Him on that Passover night, for late that evening he gathered a group of armed men together to capture Jesus. The ex-disciple, Judas, must have feared that Jesus might leave Jerusalem the next day and then his chance to keep the bribe of money might be gone.

We can only imagine the scene at the temple and the stir that it raised when news came that Jesus was in custody and in bonds. The priests, even the chief priests and the high priest left what they were doing and at once tried to find false witnesses who would charge Jesus with something serious enough to get the Roman governor, Pilate, to condemn Jesus to death. Their envy and jealousy of Him had turned into a fierce anger and hate.

It is almost unbelievable that these priests would have left what they should have been doing, and what God had appointed them to do, to lead a crowd that had gathered to demand the death penalty for Jesus. Right there they were breaking several of the ten commandments that they held as the sacred law of their religion.

Did they forget the charge made to the first priests hundreds of years before to sanctify, (make themselves holy) or the Lord would "break forth upon them" (Exodus 19:22)? The priesthood was not set up so that they should be honored above the other people, but that they should "bear the iniquity of the sanctuary... and the iniquity of the priesthood" (Numbers 18:1). In other words, they had the grave responsibility of bearing the blame if they abused their office by their lack of righteousness or justice.

And that night, the priests were not doing what they must have known they should have been doing. They were doing something else. The result was that Jesus, who "went about doing good" was crucified as though He were the worst of criminals. By three o'clock the next afternoon, this Jesus, with blood and dried-up spittle on His kind face cried, "It is finished" and bowed His head and died.

The ex-disciple, Judas, who turned traitor to his master, was also doing far from what he should have been doing that night. Here he had walked with Jesus for three years, heard His life-giving teachings, and saw His wonderful miracles. Judas had even been given at one time, along with the other disciples, the power to heal the sick and to drive out devils (Matthew 10:1).

What a wonderful opportunity Judas had! Here God had given Judas the opportunity to be one of Jesus' twelve disciples, but in the end he had not only betrayed Jesus, but had also been traitor to God's plan for his life and for the saving of his own soul.

Even though we know that their evil motives drove the priests and Judas to do what they did, it is hard for us to understand how they could do some of the things they did. But it is even harder to understand some of the things the rest of the disciples did. Peter, claiming he would stay with Jesus even if it cost him his life, then denying Him with a sworn lie just a short time later; the quarrel the disciples had about who would be called the greatest (Luke 22:24). And to think that this quarrel took place at the very same place Jesus did a humble servant's duty in washing their feet! These incidents show that having been with Jesus for three years did not seem to have changed their natures.

But now let us come a little closer home. Why are we, as today's disciples of Jesus, so often doing directly the opposite of what we already know that is best for us to be doing?

In His last instructions to His disciples, Jesus gave them four places in which they were to be witnesses for Him (Acts 1:8). These four places run parallel to where we are to be witnesses in our day.

The Jerusalem and the Judea in our times could well mean we are to be witnesses or good examples to others right in our own homes, communities and churches. That is the place to start. If we are not Christians there, we will not be Christians anywhere else.

The disciples were also to be witnesses in the neighboring land of Samaria. The people there had adopted some of the Jewish religion alongside of their idol worshipping. They "feared the Lord" but "served their own gods" (2 Kings 17:24-41). They had a mixture of the good and the worldly, just like some of the churches in the world today. How can we be better witnesses to the "Samaritans" of our day than by quietly living our lives in a simple and humble lifestyle which our forefathers felt was their mission to live up to and to pass on?

Then being a witness "unto the uttermost part of the earth" could well mean to the evil and materialistic world around us. There are many around us who see only godless pleasure, wealth and comfort as the only goals in this life. Some of those see only our failings and are hostile to us, but then there are also others who look upon our ideals and have a secret longing for something better than only the empty values which the people of the world have a craving for.

There was once a tourist who, after seeing the plain people, made the remark, "I feel that is the way life should be lived, but I know few of us on the outside could stay contented to live that way for long, because we are now so used to our affluent way of life."

He was right. The ideals received from the teachings of Jesus and the examples of our God-fearing humble forefathers is the way life should be lived. Why should we ever have a desire for anything else or why should we ever do something else?

We are to be a witness to the world, but at the same time we are to be separate from it (2 Corinthians 6:17). How could we be doing both better than by living in a quiet and simple way? How can we better be the "salt of the earth" and a "light to the world" than by contentedly living a plain life and by giving up the idols which the world holds dear?

Only after the Holy Spirit came upon the disciples, did they witness with power. It is still the same for us today. With the grace of God to release the shackles of sin which bind us, with the teachings and examples of Jesus to shape and deepen our convictions and with the power of the Holy Spirit to guide us, we should not want to be doing anything else.

A man could retire comfortably in his old age if he could sell his experience for what it cost him.

I Need to Change

38

In Jeremiah 26 we read,

"Therefore now amend your ways and your doings, and obey the voice of the Lord your God; and the Lord will repent him of the evil that he hath pronounced against you."

(Editor's Note: One of our readers, a minister, sent us the following letter, with this explanation, "The article, 'I Need a Change', on page 18 of the June issue, was a good one and gave me a lot to think about. I have put some of my thoughts in writing and am sending them to you.")

The word amend means to make a change for the better. All of us are always changing . We do not stay exactly as we are. We are not now what we were five years ago, and five years hence we will not be what we are now. To make a change in the right direction takes a power and strength higher than ourselves, which can come only from God.

"I need to change," said the hired girl. "I sometimes feel so overwhelmed with all this work, but really, when I think of the people who are bedfast and cannot work, I know that I should be more thankful to God who has given me the health and strength to work. Also, when I think of the many young people in today's world who grow up and never really learn to work, I know that I should be more appreciative for having been taught to work. I know it is up to me whether my job becomes demanding and a drudgery, or whether it is satisfying and rewarding work – one of God's most inexpensive tonics for body and soul."

"I need to change," said a father. "There are many days when everything seems to go wrong. When I think of the awesome responsibility as the head of a household, I know that I have to have help. Seeing to it that my family is clothed and fed will take up much of my time, but I know I must not let it take so much of my time that there is none left to be with my family as a loving husband and a concerned father. I also know my children need the feeling of security which they will lose if I become too permissive. For that I will need courage and love – to set a good example, and to expect their obedience. I know I need God's help for my duties, and so many times when I do not know what is best, there is nothing else to do but fall on my knees in prayer for help. But when I get up from my knees, I must remember that, weak as I am, God will use me and give me a new wisdom and strength for what I am to do, even though it is only measured out to me in small portions a day at a time."

"I need to change," said a weary mother. "I sometimes forget that these years when the children are small and take so much care will soon be gone forever. The time will be here all too soon when I will be amazed at how fleeting was the opportunity to plant good seed in the fertile soil of my children's hearts. I know it is the same as planting seeds in the garden. The time comes each year when it is too late to plant, and expect a crop. My prayer is that, with God's help, I can plant some good seed in their young lives – seeds that will grow and yield useful and fruitful lives, and a home in heaven at their end."

"I need to change," said a church member. "I so often have doubts. Sometimes I despair and feel there is no use any more to try living the simple, quiet, plain life. These thoughts come to me when I see so many people forsaking the churches to do as they please, to have what they want, and to live as they will. Then so often, it seems they are convinced they are doing the right thing. I need to think more often of the blessings that are ours, and how our forefathers worked to keep the church pure and free from worldly influences. I must keep in mind how they labored to teach their children the beauty, satisfaction, and contentment of simplicity and humility in a plain church. I want to do more than I ever have before, and live up to all this and pass it on to those younger than myself, as well as to unborn generations yet to come. I must never again think of my church as a religion of 'don'ts' – Don't get this, or Don't do that. My religion is not that. It is a quiet spot of true peace and contentment in a troubled world. I know the most powerful sermons that can be preached in any church are the living examples of holy living among the members. I want to be one of those, even if I have to change some things in my life that are now dear to my carnal nature."

"I need to change," said the teacher. "There are days when the boredom of the classroom gets me down. I have often felt other lines of work would pay better, and perhaps be more rewarding. I sometimes nearly despair when I think of all the different children coming here out of different homes, brought up in different ways. What I need is a vision of the influence I can leave in their easily-impressioned hearts. I know the perfect example is that of the Master Teacher. When He was on this earth, He loved all the children who came to Him. He was never too busy to spend time with them. I know if I would really love children as He did, my work would be one of the most inspiring and rewarding undertakings of any on earth."

"I need to change," said the deacon. "Sometimes I get the idea that nothing I say is heeded. I must remember that my duties, which God himself has laid on me, are not to be taken as a chore. I must also be concerned enough about the future of the church and its people, to warn and admonish the member who is doing wrong. I must do this in the spirit of firm, but kind love. That is often all that is needed to start a person to make a change for the better. Truely the church should be a fellowship of people who are willing to change and amend their ways for the better."

"I need to change," said the minister. "So often I get the feeling my hearers know much more about the subject I am talking about than I myself do. Which is true, they do know more. But I must not let these thoughts discourage me. I must remember this could be God's way of keeping me humble. I need to depend more on prayer to God, and on the reading of God's Word. I must remember that the cup that I hold up to the Lord to be filled, to pass on to others, must first be completely emptied of self. That is the only way I can give God all the glory, and keep none for myself. I must also remember that the silent sermon that is preached by my way of life has more power than anything I can ever say. My prayers to God and my efforts should be channeled more to changing that one person over whom I have more power to change than anyone else – that is myself."

"I need to change," said the bishop. "So often I feel that the people in the church where I am placed do not want to be led. I will have to change my way of teaching and remember that this is not my church, but it is God's church and I am only a servant of the church. When Jesus was on earth, He said, 'I am among you as he that serveth.' So who am I, that I should ever think of myself as being the 'boss'. I am not placed in this position because I am better or more special than anyone else. (Really, one of the most special people in church right now is the little child, not more than a month or two old, who was in the church for the first time last Sunday. The retarded boy who is almost blind and will be a care to his family as long as he lives – he is another of the special ones in church. The rebellious teenager who is making a wreck of his young days with drinking and love for the world is also special. And still another is the father who is raising his family in a way which has never made trouble in the church, even though he has been called 'a little different'. Then there is a single girl in the church who has had several pretty hard knocks in her life, but has accepted her lot and is happy in spite of it all.) So the church is full of special people. Let me then think more of those special ones, and less of myself. Let me do more praying for them. Let me seek for help to make the changes I ought to make – yes, I must seek that help from our Perfect Creator, who has said, 'For I am the Lord, I change not.' Malachi 3:6."

More Inspirational Writings

This section contains letters and other articles that Benuel Blank wrote throughout his life.

39

That Ye May Know

These things have I written unto you that believe on the name of the Son of God; that ye may know that ye have eternal life, and that ye may believe on the name of the Son of God."

I John 5:13

Down through the centuries since this verse was written by one of Jesus' own disciples, on down to our time, there is a question that has become rather controversial, or much argued over. The question has bothered the thinking of many Christians; those people who "believe on the name of the Son of God", as the above verse puts it.

That question is: How sure can we be of our salvation?

That topic has often been called the question of assurance versus non-assurance. In other words, is it possible that we can know while we are still in this life that we are saved and thus are sure of a home in heaven after our life here on earth is over, or does God want to leave us in the dark all our lives and then spring a complete surprise on us when we stand before Him on the Judgement Day?

Surely the Bible, as God's message to us, would contain some verses that would tell us what we need to know on that subject.

Of course, right away, we will have many in our time who will say that the verse quoted alone settles that argument; for once and for all. There are many tracts printed and sermons preached which try to tell others that they may know that they have eternal life, "the Bible has a verse that says that we may know," they say. But then some will go further and

say that we can be sure that we are saved. Adding to that, they say if a Christian is not sure that he will go to heaven when he dies there is something very much wrong somewhere with his faith.

But that is making the verse say more than it was ever intended to say. The verse does not really say that we are to be sure that we are saved. If you think that it does, go back and read it again carefully for yourself. There are at least several verses in John's same epistle that give us a somewhat different thought on being so sure.

The Apostle John, in his young days, had the wonderful privilege of walking with Jesus when He was here on earth. He had the opportunity to listen to His teachings, which were unlike those ever heard before. (Matthew 7:29 and John 7:41), He was there when Jesus was crucified, when He arose from the dead, and when He ascended to Heaven. He was also with the group of about one hundred and twenty people at Pentecost who received the Holy Spirit. Such a man would surely have been qualified to write about some questions that came up among the believers of the early church. If only John would have written down some of the things that he had heard and learned, wouldn't that be interesting reading to us in our days?

That is exactly what he did. The same Apostle

John who wrote the Gospel of John and the book of Revelation also did some more writing which has been preserved for us to read. In his old age he wrote a few letters to some Christians who were scattered throughout the Roman Empire at that time. The people to whom these letters were sent, then read and re-copied these letters for others to read. Thanks be to God, they have thus survived down to our time. John's letters are now "books" in the New Testament which we use in our homes and churches.

The young churches in those days were made up of people who believed that Jesus was the long-awaited Messiah, which is defined as "one who is anointed to save His people." The people of the early churches often needed some instructions and advice on some of the questions that presented themselves as time went on. The letters which John and the other apostles wrote were intended to help the people understand what Jesus would want them to do when different situations came up. In other words, they helped them to know what God's will was for their lives.

Satan, that deceiver who sometimes comes as a dangerous, roaring lion (I Peter 5:8), and sometimes as a helpful angel of light (2 Corinthians 11:14), was also very busy in those days. Then, as also in our days, if he could not get people to go to one extreme, he did his best to get them to go to the other. As has often been said, "If Satan can't push you into one ditch, he will try the one on the other side." He was right there trying to destroy sound teaching right from the start.

We do not know what John was thinking while he was writing those letters that are now a part of our Holy Bible. But we can read between the lines that he was very much concerned about those Christians who went to extremes. Some were deceived by Satan to go to one extreme and some to another.

The Christian churches of those days, as well as all those ever since, had members very much like the patients which nearly any doctor has to deal with.

Talk to almost any doctor and he will tell you that, basically, he has two kinds of patients who need his help. One kind will hardly own up to the fact that they are sick, and do not take good care of themselves or their health. The other kind is also

sick, but when they do get better, and could get up and go, they can hardly get themselves started again. If you are sick and a doctor comes to visit you, he is not only trying to find out what your illness is, but he is also studying you to find out what type you are likely to be.

Then, although it may not sound consistent at all to do so, the same doctor, on the same day, will give two of his patients with the same sickness, two altogether different kinds of advice. If the first patient would only admit that he is sick, slow down and take care of his health until his sick body has a chance to recuperate, he would soon be well. On the other hand if the second patient, who has the same illness, but who now is better, would get up on his feet and start to use his muscles, which are now weak from lack of exercise, he would soon be back to his work and feel much better at the same time.

Now to get back to our subject. The contents of one of John's letters to the churches, which is now I John in our Bible, is very much like the different advice which a doctor gives to his different types of patients who have the same illness.

When John wrote the verse quoted at the beginning of this article he must have been thinking of those Christians who were always fearful and depressed instead of claiming and practicing the peace and joy which belongs in a Christian life. They needed some hope and reassurance. When he wrote "that ye may know that ye have eternal life" he wanted to tell those that they were not to live as though they had no hope. The promises in the Bible to those who live a Christian life, as best as they know how, gives to such a living hope that is real and can not be found anywhere else.

But then, John must also have had another kind of people in mind while he was writing what is now a permanent part of God-inspired Scripture. There must have been people in those days already who were saying that they had no sin. This could have been people who really thought that they had always lived good and upright lives without sinning, very much like the rich young man who we read about in Mark 10. Then also John could have been thinking of those people who didn't have enough cares about the living of a pure and holy life, but said in a bragging way that since they had accepted

Christ who washed away sin, it followed that they now had no sin.

For both of these kinds of people John had some rather sharp words of rebuke. In the same letter John wrote to those who went to the opposite extreme from that of the depressed Christians; those people who were always so sure that they were sinless and had eternal life. "If we say that we have no sin, we deceive ourselves and the truth is not in us" (I John 1:8). We have two altogether different thoughts from John's pen just a few pages apart.

Yes, there is something like "the full assurance of hope unto the end" (Hebrews 6:11). "The work of righteousness shall be peace, and the effect of righteousness, quietness and assurance forever", says the Bible (Isaiah 32:17). There is an assurance and a hope in the Bible of the saving which will take place in the future. That will be when the righteous shall be saved just before God will kindle the fire that will light "the earth also and the works that are therein will be burned up" (2 Peter 3:10). That saving in the future will take place "when the righteous will be caught up with them (meaning the righteous who have died) in the clouds, to meet the Lord in the air; and so shall we ever be with the Lord" (I Thessalonians 4:17). Another verse which gives us something to do, but with it a promise of that saving after our life here on earth, is in Matthew 24:13 which says, "he that shall endure to the end, the same shall be saved."

The saving of God's righteous people on that day will be much like the saving of Noah and his family when the first world perished in the flood. Only those who believed and did something about their belief were saved. Belief alone was not enough. They had a work to do and probably were ridiculed by those who didn't believe. The first time that the Lord's grace is mentioned in the Bible is when it is giving us the story of that event (Genesis 6:8). We can believe that those eight people were ever thankful for that grace which saved them by warning them of what was coming and for letting them know what they could do to be saved when it came.

We know there is a saving which will take place in the future, and we want to prepare for it, but the Bible makes clear to us that there is also a saving that does take place right here in this life. In I

Corinthian 1:18 the Apostle Paul writes "Unto us which are saved it is the power of God." Paul knew that it was the power and grace of God that saved him from the wicked life that he had led, and the punishment that should have followed the sins which he had done.

Talk to one who used to be a a drunkard, but has now through the grace of God turned over a new leaf, and does not have a desire for strong drink anymore. He knows what it is to be saved from that evil habit. He knows that God has saved him because he knows that by his own strength and willpower he could never have broken the chains of the habit that enslaved him. He knows that it is through the grace of God that he is no longer in the miserable condition that he used to be in.

Let someone who has been saved from the desire of loving the world tell you his story. It is only through the saving grace of God that he is now able to have the strength to no longer have a longing and a wishing for the things of the world, but is contented and happy to fellowship with others who walk a narrow and self-crucifying way. The grace of God is saving and freeing him from being a slave to the ever-increasing discontent which the love of the world brings with it.

Then there is jealousy, lust, bitterness, envy, pride, greed, the loving of riches and luxury and a hundred or more other shackles that Satan uses to keep us from being more Christ-like; any of which can not be conquered by any other power than through the saving grace of God. Those who are finding victory over such sins are living examples of God's saving grace; not in some far-away future, but in the here and now.

It is even when we are doing good and living a Christian life that we need to be saved with God's loving grace. Even those who have never been in gross sins have reason to thank God that they were saved from the temptation from doing such things. If there would be nothing else, we would all need to be saved from the sin of being self-righteous, that "Pharisee" sin which was denounced by Jesus more than almost any other sin. That sin is so subtle because it causes a person to condemn others and makes him feel that he needs no help from God or from others to better his life. We are all nearly blind to our own faults, so we need others to remind us of our weaknesses and we need God's help to correct them. In other words, we are all going to need God's saving grace every day for the rest of our lives. It is not just a once in a lifetime experience.

Yes, God does save here in this life. We can sing songs like, "Amazing grace, how sweet the sound, that saved a wretch like me," — and mean it. One prophecy which the angel of the Lord made to Joseph before Jesus was born was that he shall save his people from their sins" (Matthew 1:21).

One example of the saving in this life is the adulteress who was saved from being stoned to death for her sins, the account of which John wrote in his gospel in chapter eight. But she was saved from a lot more than the pains of being stoned. She had her sins forgiven, thus she was saved from the struggle with the terrible load of guilt which she was carrying with her day and night. She was now free. She had the freedom to start all over again without the fear of punishment hanging over her, without the shame of still living in such sin, without the burden of guilt, and without the desire to live in such sin again. She was cleansed of her past. When Jesus told her to go and sin no more, we can believe that she was glad to obey His word out of gratitude for the unloading of her burdens.

What would our life here be like without some measure of assurance, or a living hope? Talk to those who have known what it is like to be in the depths of depression and despair, but through grace have now received help from others and from God, and have now overcome it. When they talk about a living hope, they know what they are talking about, because they know what it is like to go through days which seemed to them at the time as having no sunshine and no hope. They have learned that grace is receiving what we don't deserve.

Then again, what would our life here on earth be like if we did not have some measure of hope when our dying hour approaches? Only God knows how many people have been comforted in their final hours by the simple reassurance of the many verses in the Bible about hope, or by the comforting words of such as the twenty-third Psalm. There have been many who have known the trust in Jesus in their everyday life, who, when their end came had no doubts when thinking on that first verse, "the Lord is my shepherd; I shall not want." When they come to that door that no human friend could go through with them, how reassuring was the thought of those words; "Yea, though I walk through the valley of the shadow of death, I will fear no evil, for thou art with me." They knew that the grace of God would take their life's work and even though it was incomplete and imperfect, would accept and bless it.

When Jacob was blessing his sons while on his death bed the Scriptures record that when he was about halfway through be suddenly exclaimed, "I have waited on thy salvation, O Lord" (Genesis 49:18). He then lived just long enough to finish blessing his sons and to tell them where he wanted to be buried before he pulled his feet into his bed and died.

How different were the deaths of some that history record for us. One instance is that of Voltaire, a French non-believer who had made some rather boastful remarks in his lifetime about the Bible being on the way out. When he lay on his death bed, he exclaimed to the doctor at his bedside, "I am abandoned by God and man. I will give you half of what I am worth if you will give me six more month's life." His doctor told him that he could not do that. "Then I shall die and go to hell," he said just before he took his last breath and passed from time to eternity.

The last words of Sir Thomas Scott who died in 1878 were just as sad and hopeless. In his lifetime he had written over two hundred books and pamphlets attacking the religion of Christianity. "Until this moment I thought there was neither a God nor a hell," he said. "Now I know and feel that there are both, and I am doomed to perdition (hell) by the just judgement of the Almighty." He was not a believer while he lived, and died without hope. What a miserable and fearful way to die!

Then compare these men's last words with those of the Apostle Paul. When he was closing the second letter to his young friend, Timothy, which could have been one of the last letters that Paul wrote; he had a reassuring hope. "I am now ready to be offered, and the time of my departure is at hand. I have fought a good fight. I have finished my course. I have kept the faith." In the next verse he tells of the assurance that he has from receiving the crown of righteousness that is laid up for him. At the same time he does not brag that he is sure that he will get the crown; and does not say that he already has it, but has the living hope for himself and for others when he writes "that the Lord, the righteous judge shall give me at that day, and not to me only, but unto all of them also that love his appearing" (2 Timothy 4:8).

Our Anabaptist forefathers did not think it was wrong or out of place to express their thoughts of having the hope and assurance of a reward in heaven after their life was over. Many of their letters in the "Martyr's Mirror" and their songs in the "Ausbund" were written when they knew that they were living out their final days here on earth. One typical thought is that in Leid No. 103 which is a favorite song in many Old Order churches. The closing verse contains a prayer asking God to not let that small divine spark in their hearts be extinguished so that they could prepare themselves for that blessedness of life on the other side.

But be ever on the watch for extremes. There is something like having a false hope when really we have no ground for it. Our way of life should surely be showing that we are trying to follow Christ's examples. Also in John's letter is a verse that makes that clear. "He that saith he abideth in Him ought himself also to walk, even as He walked" (I John 2:6). In his young days John had seen for himself the perfect example of a blameless Christian walk of life when he was with Jesus. He knew if anyone would follow all of the example that he had seen, such a man would have no sin, for he says that "Whosoever abideth in Him sinneth not" (I John 3:6). John really is saying that no one has a right to say that he is a Christian follower of Christ if he is not following all of Christ's examples. That is a big order to fill. That is something that none of us will ever be able to make more than a weak attempt at doing, so why should anyone ever brag about it?

That is where that comforting verse at the beginning of the Sermon on the Mount comes in. "Blessed are the poor in spirit, for theirs is the kingdom of heaven" (Matthew 5:3). What Paul writes in Romans 8:24 should also make us think before we brag that we are sure. "For we are saved by hope, but hope that is seen is not hope, for what a man seeth, why doeth he yet hope for?"

There is yet another thing to be said about being so sure. "Pride goeth before destruction, and an haughty spirit before a fall" (Proverbs 16:18). "Wherefore let him that thinketh he standeth take heed lest he fall" (I Corinthians 10:12), is another verse that we had better not be too sure about ourselves. The outspoken Apostle Peter did not believe Jesus when He told him that he would deny Him even before the next morning came. He did not know his own weaknesses, and as it was he did deny Jesus three times in that same night. He fell, but he repented and came back.

Then there are too many instances in Scripture times, and since, of people falling away who we have no record of coming back, that we just better forget about bragging that we are born-again and are sure of heaven when we die. There was, for one example, the downfall of King Saul, who Scripture records as having been humble at one time (I Samuel 9:21). Let us mark, — there are also at least two times that tell us that Saul was "filled with the Spirit of God" (I Samuel 10:10 and 11:6), but it did not last till the end of his life. When he was no longer little in his own sight (I Samuel 15:17), the Lord rejected him.

Then take Solomon, that king who was commissioned to build the first temple of the Lord. He felt small when he became king (I Kings 3:7) and the Lord gave him much more than he had asked for in wisdom and riches.

But he fell. The Scriptures are silent as to whether he ever repented or not, so we do not know. It is very hard to believe that a man with such a wisdom and knowledge such as he had written in Proverbs and in some of the other parts of the Bible could ever fall. When we read his prayer that he offered at the dedication of the temple (I Kings 8:22-53) it is very hard to believe that such a man could later forget God and His commandments. The sad story of his life shows us again that man can fall, even after he has been exceedingly righteous.

Judas is another example. He was one of the original twelve disciples, those twelve men who we could think had an opportunity that no group of men had before that; nor ever since. Judas was there when Jesus "called his twelve disciples together and gave them power and authority over all devils and to cure diseases" (Luke 9:1). But for all the wonderful opportunities that he had, Judas fell; one of the reasons being that he started being dishonest (John 12:6). He probably never had the least bit of an idea how things would turn out when he started playing with sin or he would not have done so.

A man named Demas is another example of one who was at one time a Christian worker (Philemon 24), until he started to love the world and gave in to its' temptations (II Timothy 4:10).

Yes, God "is able to keep you from falling, and to present you faultless before the presence of His glory with exceeding joy (Jude 24), but at the same time it is possible to become a backslider; very much so. It is possible to have the great debt that was forgiven us loaded onto us again by our sinful actions and unthankfulness (Matthew 18:34). All the verses in Scripture that warn us to be on our guard and all those which instruct us in the betterment of our lives would be unnecessary if there were nothing like falling away.

The persecuted people in our days in other lands must also be aware that there is something like falling away. Many of their letters that they send to their Christian brethren in other lands ask that they be remembered in their prayers. They ask us not to pray that the persecution will cease, but to pray for them that they will be able to hold out while they are under the pressure of government persecution. If they are so concerned about falling away under the stress of persecution how much more should we be concerned about falling away in our land of freedom and plenty? The prosperity of our times and the drift into the world are much more dangerous than persecution.

Let us never again say that we are sure of heaven. The Bible tells us that there will be some surprises on Judgement Day. Jesus gave us several examples of some people who will be disappointed at that time. In Matthew 25:31 to 46 we read of some who will be turned away who did not expect to be rejected. Those who felt that they were not worthy were the ones able to inherit eternal life. In Luke 13:25 to 30 we also have some who thought that they would go with Jesus who were turned back. They did not expect to be told that "I know you not whence you

are." The sobering part of it all is that when that time comes all the opportunity to have another chance to change things will be gone forever. Only while we are still in this life can we still do something to change all that.

God's word makes it plain that it is possible for those who hear, and even those who gladly accept God's Word, to later fall away again. The parable of the seed sown in stony places (Matthew 13:20) and the seed sown among thorns (13:22) teaches that to us. Some of the good seed did start to sprout, (very much like a person having the new-birth) but the soil of the heart was not cleaned of the stony self-will and the thorn bushes of the deceitfulness of riches and the cares of the world, so it was choked and did not grow up and yield fruit. That new fruit would have contained more seed for planting again the next year, either again in the same field or at another place. When those new-born sprouts were dead all hopes for an increase in that year or in future years was gone.

Becoming a Christian, or a child of God, does not ever mean that the battles are all over. It is only a start. The dangers of being enslaved by Satan are as real as they ever were before. He will soon find out that there are some kinds of bait that you will not even be interested in, but he has so many different kinds available that he will soon bring out the kind that you will like. That is then the kind that he will use and he is ready to snap the trap anytime that we are not on our guard.

Our spiritual life is a little like a field planted with a crop. Even with good seed and good soil and the sunshine and the rains that God sends, any hoping for a good crop would only be wishful thinking if we neglected the field and left the weeds take over.

God gave us our abilities to use. Salvation was never meant to take no effort or sacrifice on our part. God never expects us to let Him do it all. He did the part that we could not do, but that does not excuse us from doing our part.

All summer and especially when harvest time comes close, we can look over the field that we have planted and taken care of. We still know that our effort would have helped nothing without God's miracle of the seeds sprouting and growing and without God's sunshine and rain. If we like the work, there is nothing else that we would rather do than work with the crop that we have planted. Such is also the part that we are to do for our salvation; we can find contentment and fulfillment in what we are to do for that. The toil will not always be easy because anything that we will ever get of any worth will have to be worked for. Those who do God's work will get God's pay.

Really this argument that has too often come up in times past about assurance versus non-assurance has not always been necessary. The term "assurance" and the term "a living hope" really mean very much the same thing. It is really very much like the name of the place where Jacob and Laban met and made peace with each other. Laban called it one name; Jacob called it another, (Genesis 31:47) even though it was one and the same place.

Just so that nobody uses this argument as a handle to leave a church that is non-conforming to the world to go to one that has drifted further into the world. It is hard to understand how anybody could leave such a church and say that he was in the dark about his salvation before this, but now he is sure of heaven. On the other hand, just so that nobody uses that argument to condemn others who see that having a living hope is as necessary a part of the Christian life as it is to follow Christ's humble walk of life. Let us not feel that it is wrong to have a living hope and let us not feel that it is unnecessary to brace ourselves against the drift to the world. Like in everything else, there are still two extremes.

One is to be so depressed and ever so fearful that we will do something that will make God angry at us and send us to eternal torment. That is where Christ's redemption and forgiveness of sins come in, and that is also where faith and hope and the joy of a Christian life comes in. The other extreme is if we are so certain and sure that we will not miss getting to Heaven that we brag to others that we are new-born Christians and are saved and in the meantime forget, or are not willing, to put away our idols and make some of the changes in our lives so as to be more pure, holy and humble. That is where Christ's teachings of non-pride and the non-exalting of our own lives comes in. That is where love and God's power for the ever-bettering of our lives comes in. That is where our own effort and the sacrifice of our own wills comes in.

Finally, let's all take as an example from the two men who went to the temple to pray. We don't want to be like the one who bragged about the good life that he was leading (Luke 18:11), and trusted himself that he was righteous and despised others. Luke 18:9).

The one to whom the Scriptures give record as going back to his house justified was the one who smote upon his breast saying, "God be merciful to me, a sinner." He knew that he was unworthy of it, but he knew that he daily needed God's grace to forgive his sins and to change his life.

Let us all live a closer walk with God and be ready to do the same.

The Cares of This Life

40

"Casting all your care upon Him, for He careth for you."
I Peter 5:7

The sun came out nice and bright that spring morning. The weather was perfect. The skies could not have been more nice and clear on that day long ago in the week of creation when God first caused light to appear on earth.

Today was church Sunday, and as church was going to be held at the neighbors' not quite a mile away, the whole family walked.

The group consisted of the father, the mother, the nineteen-year-old son, the sixteen-year-old daughter and the three boys of grade school age. They made their way along the side of the road that led over the hill to where the people in that district would gather together to hold a worship service.

As they passed their field which was still unplanted the father could not help but to think of how he had the field just about ready to plant on Saturday a week ago when the rain came up. Now most of last week it had rained and he still did not have his corn planted. If it kept on drying today like it did yesterday he would be able to start working his fields again early tomorrow morning. Then if the weather held he would be able to start planting on Tuesday.

If the weather held. Would the weather hold? The feed man who always talked weather told him on Friday afternoon that the long range forecast called for only two, or at the most three days, of clear weather. Then it was possible that they would have another rainy week like last week.

And here he was. He knew he had the neighborhood reputation of always being one of the first to get his corn in. Now it was this late and he didn't have any in yet. It could get late enough yet till he got it planted.

He wondered if any of the other farmers in the district might have gotten any corn in before the rains started last Saturday. It would secretly give him a feeling of satisfaction to find out today that there was no other corn planted in the neighborhood as of yet.

So the head of the family that walked up the road that nice spring morning did not notice the spring flowers that grew along the banks by the side of the road. He did not hear the happy birds singing. He did not notice the nice growth that the rains had made in the neighbor's alfalfa field on the other side of the road as they passed. He did not think of the blessing which had been shared with him in that his family walking along with him were all healthy enough to go to church with him.

There was one thought uppermost in his mind. Will the weather hold?

The mother had other thoughts on her mind.

She took a look at "Miss Sixteen" who was walking a short distance ahead of her. She took a critical look at the dress that she had just finished for her daughter the day before her birthday only a month ago. She had spent a lot of time on that dress for her only girl. But as she looked over the dress worn by her daughter she could not quite figure out what it was that did not look right.

Last week she had found out from one of the other mothers that the small bunch of the supposedly most popular girls in the young people's group had dropped her daughter from their circle. No wonder her daughter had seemed so blue last week. The mother had wondered what had happened and what was wrong, but she thought it was best to figure it out herself without asking.

It must have been that dress. The mother was already figuring out how to make the next dress a little different so that it would look a little more like those which the popular girls wore.

The nineteen-year-old boy had thoughts of his own. Today his best friend, John, would be at church again after being laid up for a few weeks. They had missed John at the singing last Sunday evening. Well, they called it a singing because singing did go on at the place where they were, even if John and his three best chums rarely got in to sing.

He could hardly wait to get to church to tell John what he got when he was in town last week. Even more exciting, he could hardly wait till this evening to show him. When he thought about the fun they could now have he could hardly wait.

Still in the back of his mind he knew he was doing things that he should not be doing. His parents did talk to him sometimes about such things, but very few were the times that he had a heart-to-heart talk with any of his parents. They were the busy kind. But still he knew that his parents would be deeply disappointed if they did find out about some of the "fun" that his gang had been into the last while. He secretly hoped that his smaller brothers would somehow stay away from living a life like he was living when they grew up.

His sister, the sixteen year old, was again rehashing the same thoughts that had plagued her most of all last week. Her thoughts were still on the let-down that she had last Sunday evening. She would show those girls. The only thing she could think of to do was to show those girls that she could also fix up her hair and get a dress made that would make their eyes pop.

She had fixed up her hair and her devotional covering a little extra that morning and had been surprised that Mom didn't object. But the younger brothers had been a little slow in getting themselves ready for church this morning, and in hurrying them along Mom probably hadn't noticed her. At least, till now she had said nothing about it.

There were hardly any words exchanged among the family that was walking toward the church service, so of course the three school-aged boys were also left to think their own thoughts. Everything had been hurry-hurry all morning so none of the three were in the best of moods.

So – how many of those seven people in that family going to church that bright spring morning on the Lord's Day were carrying what could be called really happy thoughts?

If you guessed that all seven of the family were unhappy, you are right.

There was something wrong with that little group going up the road with the spring flowers blooming and the birds singing. What was it that was wrong? Why was it that what could have been a soul-satisfying walk to a place of God's words, was really nothing but an ache of unhappiness.

What would you say was wrong?

The answer could be summed up in two words — uncontrolled stress.

The whole family in one little true-to-life story had an inner stress and strain which had its root from what has often been called the "modern rat race to keep up with the Jones's." It is ironic, or directly opposite of what would be expected, that a plain, Christian family would have to do with such stress; and of all times, while going to a house of worship.

The definition of stress is a pressure from outside that can make us feel tense and strained inside. Of course, it is not necessary to tell anyone how this tension feels, because everybody living knows well enough how it feels. It comes in all degrees of severity, from the mild to that which seems to be unbearable and close to the breaking point. We will all have more or less of stress in our systems at all times as long as we are alive.

Not all stress is bad. We all have to have a certain amount of stress. If our systems were not able to work with a certain amount of the right kind of stress we wouldn't be able to get out of the way when danger comes toward us. We could do no work without stress. Stressing a muscle and then relaxing it is really what all the muscles in our body are for.

It is only when stress overflows from the times we need it to the times when we don't need it that it is bad.

Uncontrolled stress has been blamed by those who study the human body for nearly all of the illness, diseases and unhappiness that can occur to mankind. Everything from depression and nervous breakdowns, to arthritis, heart trouble, headaches, backaches, and shingles has been blamed on the upset which uncontrolled stress does to the fine balance which God has put into the human system. Some go as far as to say that even broken bones, from being accident prone, are often the aftermath of stressful living.

When we get a new piece of machinery we depend on the operators manual that comes along to tell us how to operate and take care of it. We know that there would be nobody who would know how to run and care for that piece of machinery better than the manufacturer who built it.

In the same way the Bible, besides telling us about God's grace and love, is like the "instruction manual" for our lives. There is nobody better able to tell us how to live than the One who created us. God has very wisely provided us with His Word to teach us how to live.

Now, if uncontrolled stress caused so much misery in human beings we would think that the Bible would tell us something about stress. But we find that, at least in the King James translation, the word "stress" is not even mentioned!

But the Bible goes one step further. Without even mentioning stress the Bible gives us priceless reading on how to live to escape the damage done by uncontrolled stress.

In an article of this size it would not be possible to mention more than a few of the hundreds and hundreds of verses which tell us how to live and find that inner contentment and peace without which life can become nearly unbearable.

We will mention only a few. You could probably easily find dozens of other Bible verses which to you are more important than these, but we will start with one, which if we would follow it, would cause much of our stress to come to an abrupt end.

"Let us not be desirous of vain glory, provoking one another, envying one another" (Galatians 5:26). The German translation makes it a little plainer and more forceful, "Lasset uns nicht eitler Ehre geizig sein, einander zu entrüsten, und zu hassen." The envy, jealousy, anger and hate which will follow the seeking of vain self-honor will work up a stress which can eventually destroy us, if not checked in time.

Isn't that what the father in our little story was doing when his aim was to keep the really vain honor of being the earliest in the neighborhood? If he got his crop in early, fine, but to always do so for the honor that he hoped to gain, was something else. It would have been more sensible if he would have waited until early Monday morning to get his stress up for the work he had to do.

The mother who was satisfied with nothing less than having her only daughter be what she thought was one of the "tops" was doing untold damage to herself and to her whole family. She unknowingly placed a heavy burden on her children who would grow up thinking that is the way life is to be lived. She could never be a mother in which her children would open up to and confide in unless she changed her ways of thinking.

By always living in this way, both the father and the mother could never set aside time to be a listening, understanding and concerned parent to the children which God placed in their home. They would grow up having too many interests outside of the home and would think that always making an impression on others was the important thing to do.

Even when they had time with their children, as on this Sunday morning walk to church, they had no idea of the priceless moments which passed, and were lost forever, in which they could have shared some worthwhile thoughts and feelings with each other and with their family. It would not necessarily take many words to do so, but it would take a change in thinking.

They were missing a golden opportunity for a short rewarding family relationships right then and there, and did not know it, because of their own "self" thoughts. If they missed out then they probably missed out on many more.

The ones to be pitied in this family were the three school-aged children. At that tender age they were really the innocent victims of the "competing-with-others" stress that had taken over in the family. Besides missing out on the loving concern and understanding from their busy parents they would grow up thinking it was the normal thing to do to ignore some of the modest and plain standards of dressing like their sister was doing (and even with the help of her mother). They would grow up thinking that the wild behavior of their big brother would be the smart thing to do when they grew up.

If we are to live together in our families and communities and worship together as Christians we do not have any time for desiring a vain, empty and useless honor for ourselves and for provoking and envying one another. Our relationships should not be based on the law of the jungle; on the survival of the strongest and fittest. Rather, we should take our living and working together as though we were fellow passengers on a pleasant voyage together through sunshine and storm.

Making a living and making the ends meet and making the meals and clothes for our families is going to take work and thus be a stress for all of us; both men and women. Only when that stress is uncontrolled is it going to be harmful.

Of course, somebody will say that we have to work harder than people used to long ago to pay off the bigger debts and bills that we have in our days. That is true, but most of the debts and bills that we have to pay off are usually debts that we willingly signed up for ourselves. Nobody ever twisted our arms to make us sign.

Too much of the money that we say we need is used to buy what we would not really need. Are we becoming slowly addicted to loving luxuries in this life which we would not have to have? Do we want to live in this life like the rich man but in the next we still want the reward of the poor man? Luke 16:24) It is possible for us to work and stress ourselves in our chase after money and the things that money can buy and forever lose the good things that money cannot buy.

The next reason for much of the stress in our lives is our misuse of rest and relaxation. The Bible gives us an example of a person who goes to sleep with all the tensions of the day loosened. Psalm 4:8 — "I will both lay me down in peace and sleep, for thou Lord, only makest me dwell in safety". Here again read the German version which adds a somewhat different thought when it says "dasz ich sicher wohne" which expresses an inner peace and calm which only God can help us to attain.

God knows we need rest. He Himself rested on the last day of the week of creation. Rest, relaxation and sleep are certainly one of God's gifts to all of His living creatures. If we would waken up in the morning and would have to start each day as tired as we were the evening before, we would wear out fast and would not last very long.

God has marvelously made our bodies with the muscles in our systems made so that they are strengthened by using them. Surely we are "fearfully and wonderfully made" (Psalm 139:14). But after a time our muscles become weakened and tired, but then God has made them so that they are self-renewing, but they have to be at rest to do so.

Even our heart muscles which have to keep going day and night as long as we live have a short period of complete rest between each beat. That is then when the muscle gets repaired and strengthened from the stress of the work that it did.

Uncontrolled stress, or a continuous and uninterrupted tension in any part of the body is a little like using a chain saw. If we would start it up and run it wide open all day it would soon run itself to pieces. Anybody who thinks anything of his saw will open up the throttle only when speed is needed. That is when the chain is working its way through a cut.

It has been said that the opening and closing of the throttle in the human body is one of the hardest things for people to learn to do. Either we can not learn to calm down our stress or we are too lazy to start it up the moment we need it. Nobody will ever be able to learn to govern stress perfectly, but we can very much improve the way we handle stress if we make an active effort to do so.

It can be learned to sit in a chair or to go to bed in the evening and to perfectly relax. Just thinking of action or work will cause the muscles to tense, so we will have to lay aside all the thoughts of what we could be doing or what we want to do when we get up. The time comes to get up again.

Some methods of relaxing that work for some do not work for others. There are many ways to do it, but one popular exercise to loosen a build-up of stress is to lie down and tense every muscle that you can think of, from head to toe. Hold the tension as long as you can; then let go. If you are still tense, do it again. You will relax immediately if you do it right. Working at loosening stress in this way is far better than taking pills and tranquilizers to sleep as they mostly have some undesirable side effects.

We could think of the stress in our systems as being like the tension on the bow that an Indian used. When a bow was used to shoot an arrow it was stressed, and stressed hard. But a bow would soon be bent out of shape or even broken if the Indian were to pull the bow back all day long without releasing it. Such a bow would soon be done for and would never again speed an arrow on its way.

The Indian kept the string on the bow during the day just taut enough or stressed enough to be ready if a quick chance came up to use it.

When the Indian came home in the evening from hunting he did a very wise thing. He would unwind and untie one end of the string from the bow. The bent piece of wood could then straighten out for the night. This way the bow would last much longer and would have full strength the next day when he needed it again. That is what relaxing and sleep do to our systems if we will but let them.

So let us loosen our "bowstrings" when we go to bed to sleep. It has been said that a clear conscience and honest labor are the best inducers of a good sleep. The Bible has verses to that effect. "He gives His beloved sleep" (Psalm 127:2) and "the sleep of a laboring man is sweet" (Ecclesiastes 5:12) are a few that picture the blessing of a good night's sleep. Another is in Proverbs 3:24 which says, "Thou shalt lie down and thy sleep shall be sweet."

The Apostle Peter must not have had a worry in the world on that night when he was almost sure that he would be executed the next day. (Acts 12:6). He was not lying there awake, but was sleeping soundly when God's angel came to rescue him.

We read at one place that Jesus was awake and prayed all night the night before He chose His twelve disciples (Luke 6:12). Then at another time He was so unworried and unafraid of what His disciples thought was a danger to their lives that He slept on while a storm was nearly swamping the boat He was in (Matthew 8:24). We are too often apt to have our values just the opposite from what He had. We sometimes say we didn't sleep well because of some worldly worry, but then we have no trouble sleeping in church; at the place of God's worship. Do we have our values mixed up that much?

Then, just like there is one extreme in not relaxing enough to get a refreshing night's sleep, so is there an extreme the other way in what could be called laziness. The Bible also tells us what that will lead to when it says in Proverbs 20:13, "Love not sleep, lest thou come to poverty" and in Proverbs 10:5, "He that sleepeth in harvest is a son that causeth shame."

What we want to do is not to eliminate all stress from our lives, but to govern and control it. The first step to governing stress is to loosen the stress when we do not need it. The next step is to turn on our stress when the time comes to do so.

It is when getting out of a chair or out of bed in which we have been resting that it is again like the Indian's bow. The sooner he stressed his bow part ways, wound the string around the bow and tied it, the sooner he was ready to go again. When getting awake in the morning, it is not necessary to do a lot of fancy exercise to get those repaired, and now stronger (and sometimes a little stiffer!) muscles limbered up and going again.

Most of us get enough of exercise during the day with our work. There is, however, one simple exercise which will help to get the muscles limbered up for a new day. That is the well-known touching of the toes then times without bending the knees and taking a deep breath each time. In fact, how limbered up we are could almost be measured in how easy or how hard it is to do that exercise.

Stress will work for us and not against us if we will learn to use it right. It is when we are highly tense and keyed up all over that we are irritable, easily annoyed and impatient and more apt to have digestive upsets and all that goes with it. There are many ways to upset the digestion, but a stressful mealtime is one of the quickest ways to do it. We get that run down, tired out feeling, even if we have not done much physical effort. A nerved up person will jump way off the floor at a sudden noise, while a person who has his stress controlled will calmly stop and find out where the noise came from.

Doing nothing would not stop the stress in our lives. It would only tend to make it worse, because thinking of the work we should be doing, but don't get done, can be more of a stress than the actual physical stress that it takes to do it. A person sitting still twiddling his thumbs or one lying down all nerved up can still be carrying a tremendous pressure of nearly unbearable stress, while another person who is working hard can truthfully say that he does not feel any stress.

In our days, many will tell us that the remedy for stress is to go on a long vacation at a resort of some kind to "get away from it all." This seldom works because most people will take their stress right along with them, and then they will still return to their stressful ways when they come back, even if they have done nothing but "play" while they were gone. It has been said already that if you see a man all tired out, don't tell him to go on a vacation. Chances are that he just came back from one.

Far better, and more stress-relieving is to make better use of the time that is given to us, which comes in short lengths at a time. The short time on which we are waiting on a late bus, for example, will seem like hours if we fume and fret about it, but it will seem like only a few moments if we will start up a conversation with a stranger, or watch a bird building a nest, or even just meditate on the wonderful works of God.

We do not have to go to a resort of some kind with our families to learn to know them better and to lose our stressful way of living. A relaxed atmosphere while we are at the table together (or walking to church together) will do in a short time

what could never be done elsewhere to relieve the unbalance of stressful living.

Our bad stress habits can be changed to habits which make good use of stress. We know it is possible to have an unworried and relaxing way to get hard work done instead of having the habit of always carrying along that mental stress that will tire us out even if we have done practically nothing.

The continuous tension which too many of us carry at all times did not all come in a day, but took years of stressful living habits to get out of hand. We know that we can not overcome such a habit in one day. But we know that it can leave much faster than it came if we work at it all the time.

So, just like all bridges have a safe load limit, so also does the human body have a limit in what it can stand. If we can learn to like the work that we are to do, and accept the conditions that God has willed for our lives; in other words, to bloom where we are planted, we will make it much easier for ourselves and all those around us. If we work at doing just what we can, and not feel that we have to do it all (Exodus 18:18) we can stay within our load limit, but still have a reserve to spare if we need it.

Governing our stress will not necessarily guarantee us healthier and longer lives, but it will make happier and more rewarding the years that we do have here.

Now comes another part of eliminating unneeded stress from our lives; the important part. This part should not take long to tell about. This is a part which occurs more unnecessary stress than anything else; in fact, includes everything that takes its toll in the damage that stress does to our lives. This is the stress which our anxieties, worries and uneasiness, in other words, our cares, bring into our lives.

It is astonishing as to how in a few words the Bible can tell us so much. "Casting all your care upon Him, for He careth for you" (I Peter 5:7). There is the secret of inner peace in a few words.

There are many cares and worries over which we have no control. If we were to start listing some of the cares which people worry about in our days there would be no end. We could worry about the weather over which we have no control. The uncertain economy of our times, the war clouds that seem to darken the horizon and the other vague fears that something bad is going to happen could well extinguish all happiness and peace from our lives if we would just dwell on such thoughts. If we were really atheists, or non-believers in God, we could well say "There is no hope."

But we know that our all-powerful God knows and controls it all. We know that whatever comes along, the Lord has planned it for us. He will give us what is best for us, if we will let Him make the choice. He will work out everything for good to those who love Him (Romans 8:28). He will ease our vague and nameless fears.

He will not come and tear our cares away from us. We will have to release them to Him. We will have to seek help for our problems and worries from a Power much greater than we are. We are to seek help from outside of ourselves. Whatever comes along, let us talk things over with those near and dear to us. And let us talk it over with God. And why wait any longer? He is ready to help us now.

There are still places in the world where camels are used. At the end of a day's journey the camels will kneel down for their master to unload the burdens from their backs.

Before starting out again the next morning they will kneel down again, and will wait for the burdens of the day, the work that they are to do, to be placed on them.

That is what our prayers to God should be like. Such is faith, which instead of dreading the next day and whatever it brings, we will be looking forward to what God has for us.

"Thou wilt keep him in perfect peace, whose mind is stayed on thee, because he trusteth in Thee" (Isaiah 26:3).

Dear Teacher

41

Dear Teacher:

I am taking this opportunity to let you know that I am thankful for what you do for our children. We send them to school, under your care and instruction, five days a week with the hope that they will pick up some of the things necessary for them to know in their later years.

The progress that they make in one day can hardly be measured, but the progress that they make in a month or a year can. I know that is why you teachers send them home from time to time with a report card. We are glad to find out how they are doing.

But I notice there is one space in your report cards that you do not fill out. My wife and I are very glad that you don't. That is the space on "Rank in Class".

You have some very easy learners at your school and you have others that have to be drilled time and time again. Even then you may think they do not make any progress. But, teacher, I am glad that you do not punish your slow learners by showing them time and time again on their report card that they are the slowest in the class.

That is enough to take the "wind out of their sails" as they say about something that causes a person to be discouraged and to give up. If we want to inspire a pupil to do better we should surely be thoughtful enough to know that it doesn't work to continually discourage him.

But then how about those "bright" scholars who are often in the top rank in their classes? We know that some of them already sense that they are "smarter" then some of the others, and we surely don't want to "feed" that feeling in them that they are more than the rest. There have been many instances where a child who was "smart" in school started to feel that he is more than others. This can be a real hindrance when he grows up with that feeling. It can lead to having no patience with anyone else, which is a character trait which can ruin many a friendship.

There is only one good thing which can be said about comparing one pupil with another and that is the spirit of competition. When two people or a group of people begin to have a contest for a top honor or for a prize of any kind they usually produce a lot more then they would if there would be nothing to work for. But the moment that competition or rivalry begins to make people look down on others or makes the ones on behind feel like giving up then it has gone too far.

Let me repeat. We are very glad that you don't fill out that space "Rank in Class". We are glad that you have better ways to reward those who do all they can and we are glad that you have better ways to prod those who could do better but need a little help to do so.

Best wishes from two of the Parents.

Why Mocking Looks So Black to Me

42

Since I am partly retired, I am spending a lot of my time in my small shop. The windows on the south side just above my workbench look out toward the road that leads past Pleasant Meeting School, about a quarter mile down the road. One of the highlights of my day is when the school children go past on their way to and from school.

I guess the scholars think I am an old man. They are partly right. The difference between my age and theirs is sixty years or more, a length of time that would seem like ages to a child who is just starting out in life and learning about the world around him.

But the scholars and I are friends. Not a day goes by that they don't remember to look in and wave as they go by. And then for a short while, even though the thinning hair on my head is almost all grey, I am young at heart. I think back to my own carefree school days. I think of the teachers I used to have who have now gone to their eternal reward. I think of the school chums I used to play with, some now scattered all over the country. Others I have not seen or heard of for years.

I think of some of the happy days we had together. I have memories of days when I can say we had good, clean fun. It warms my heart to see those school children, the future adults of the homes, churches, and communities of tomorrow, go past my window with their cheer and laughter and with what looks like the unhurried and unworried times of childhood.

However, the last while I am seeing something else—another kind of laughter—when the children are going past that causes me to have other thoughts. Painful thoughts, sad thoughts; thoughts about a part of my school days that I should not have allowed to happen, because I knew better. Memories come to me that I wish I could go back and erase, like an arithmetic mistake is erased from the blackboard.

I first noticed the change in the scholars last spring after the new family had moved into the community, onto that old Davis farm about a half mile beyond the sharp bend in the road on the other side of the bridge. I did have a feeling their three school-aged children might have a tough time getting accepted by the other children in the neighborhood. I've known these parents for a while, because at one time they lived next to my youngest brother's place about fifteen miles west of here. They are nice people, and very helpful. What they do, they do in a quiet way.

It could be said they are the kind of people who think there are things more important to do than keeping their buildings looking like a showplace. It is not that they are lazy; they just have the right combination of ambition and relaxedness that they can get along in life reasonably well, but they don't have the time or money to do those extra things that make a place look like some of the others in our community.

Evidently I'm not the only person in the community aware of this. Last spring at old Mr. Davis' sale I overheard two of the neighbors talking. One of them said, "This rundown place here probably won't look much better in the next years than it has in the past, if I know those people (meaning the new owners) right."

The other one laughed. "The place will just stay the same old eyesore in the neighborhood it's been all these years."

Knowing that parents' attitudes often rub off on the children, I may have been looking for the change in the children going past my shop. As far as I can tell the upper-grade girls have accepted the two oldest girls pretty well. But with their brother who is in the third or fourth grade, things are different. I notice that he usually walks a short distance behind the others, and at times he hurries on ahead. It seems he's trying to avoid walking with the others. It's no wonder, the way they've laughed at him and even pushed him around on the road.

What really is going on at Pleasant Meeting School and on the way to and from school, I really don't know. But I am afraid the same thing might be happening that happened when I went to school – the things that bring back those painful memories that I was telling you about.

To tell you about it, I must start back pretty far, before I went to school. But in my memory some of these things are as plain as if they had taken place yesterday.

I had a cousin named Amos. He was about half a year younger than I was. We didn't live far from each other, and when our parents got together, we went along whenever we had a chance. Amos and I spent a lot of time together. We explored every inch of the creek that flowed through their pasture. We knew every tree in the small woods in back of our barn. I will never forget those days. They were happy days.

But times changed, or maybe I should say we changed. It started soon after we went to school. Now I'm not saying this to brag, but I always had a lot of friends. With Amos, it was different. He was a little timid and unsure of himself, and often seemed to have a faraway look in his blue eyes. And on top of that, he was a little slow in grasping a lesson.

I hadn't noticed that Amos might be a little different until some of my friends started teasing him and poking fun at him. The teasing was mild in the start, but increased as time went on. The words "stupid" and "Porkey" and "Dunce" were often used to describe Amos.

I remember when Amos failed to pass into third grade with the rest of us. I pitied my cousin, because I felt he had tried hard. I really believe he worked harder in school than any of the rest of us that year. It hurt me to see the painful look that crossed Amos's face when he found out he would have to repeat the same grade, but I think he accepted it bravely.

Amos did pretty well the next year, but the following one he fell behind in his lessons again. I can well remember when the teacher in her disgust told him if he didn't wake up soon, she would flunk him again. She gave him a lecture in front of the school, and not just a short one. She was a little short of the virtue called patience, and especially so with slow learners.

As this was still the time of public school, we had all kinds of children in school. One kind we had were the teasers. Amos became the target for more and more of their teasing and mocking. Of course, the teacher's attitude didn't help matters any. I think at first I felt sorry for Amos, but out of fear of being mocked, too, I didn't stick up for him. Then there were times when I smiled at the remarks they made. What one of them didn't say, another one did. And as time went on, Amos's place in school became accepted, and more and more of us helped to tease him.

There is one instance I recall in particular. Amos was in sixth grade, and hopelessly far behind in his lessons. His life in school had become increasingly miserable. One evening as we were walking home, one of the boys asked, "Do you think Amos will still be in sixth grade with his grandchildren?"

The remark struck the rest of us as being really hilarious, and we simply roared with laughter. We laughed until we had tears in our eyes, but I stopped short when I happened to look into Amos's face as he was walking with his head down a little on the edge of the group. His eyes were damp, too, but his tears hadn't come from laughing. That hurt, hopeless look on his face was to haunt me in later years.

It was around this time that my parents asked me to stay up one evening when the others went to bed. They asked me about Amos, and what I knew about the mocking he had to endure at school. I didn't give them very good answers, because I felt guilty myself. I'm pretty sure my parents didn't know to what extent I was involved in the mockery myself, or they would not have let me off with just a talking-to. They did tell me that if I was around when the others mocked Amos, I was not to take part. They also told me to try to put myself into Amos's place, and try to feel how it must be to be laughed at all the time.

There is something else my parents told me about that evening that I've never forgotten. They said there was a boy who got mocked a lot when they went to school. When this boy grew up, it was the same among the young people. He was not accepted by the group. He left the church and went out into the world, probably to escape the mockery he had to put up with nearly all his life. My parents explained that the boy should not have done this, but they felt those who had mocked him might be partly to blame for it. That really gave me something to think about.

It was also about this time when the subject of mocking was brought to us in church. We were told of the forty-two children who mocked the prophet Elisha, but God put a stop to that in a short while. He sent two bears to tear the mockers to pieces.

All these things made an impression on me, and for a while I tried hard to keep quiet when Amos was teased. But as time went on, I forgot about these incidents. Besides, it gave me a feeling of importance if I was able to say something about Amos to make the others laugh.

Deep down in my heart I felt terrible about it. I liked Amos, and never had a single reason to hold anything against him. He was often lonely and eager for my friendship when the others weren't around. But did I stick up for him? Of course not.

My reasoning was that if I did, the other boys might even start mocking me, and I couldn't stand that, or so I thought. So in order to be one of the group, I went along with all these things, and sad to say, even added a joke or two of my own whenever the others had their fun with Amos.

By this time I was old enough to have a conscience, and it bothered me. I knew mocking was sin. I knew it was evil and cruel to trample someone down like we did Amos. I didn't forget the story about Elisha and the bears, but I remember thinking that nothing like that could ever happen to us. I knew that except for the bears caged up at the zoo, there weren't any for hundreds of miles.

But I was totally unprepared for what did happen.

One day in particular the teacher had read aloud some of the "stupid" answers Amos had given to questions on his health lesson. I think she probably did this in hopes of shaming him into doing better work in the future. But I truthfully think Amos had done his best, and all the teacher's method did was give us new ideas to taunt and jeer Amos with. On the way home from school we boys really had our fun about some of these ridiculous answers Amos had given. I helped, thinking I was smart whenever I said something that made the others laugh. It bothered me, as usual, but I remember comforting myself with the thought that I hadn't started the mocking. The others had started it, and I was just helping along.

That was the last time any of us mocked Amos. I distinctly remember where I was and what I was doing that evening when a neighbor came over. He asked for Dad. Dad came around just then and the neighbor said, "Your brother Andy's son got killed about half an hour ago. Andy'd like to have you come over right away."

"Which one?" Dad asked, his voice sounding unnatural.

"Amos."

It is impossible to describe my feelings. That evening we went over to the place where Amos had lived and again the next day. I couldn't believe it. Memories flooded over me when I was over there and saw the places Amos and I used to haunt in our younger, happier days. Who would have thought that Amos would not even live to be out of school? Who would have thought last evening when we teased him on the way home from school that we would regret our folly so deeply so soon? Oh, the lessons we learned through it all – painful, painful lessons!

I also remember when I took the last look at Amos's face just before the coffin lids were closed. Those deep blue eyes were now closed in death, and would never again have to look upon the cruel and ugly things he had seen in the past. My grief was bitter, especially when I thought of how I could have made many of the days in Amos's short life here on earth a little brighter simply by exposing the feeling of friendship I had in my heart for him. Not once had Amos done anything to deserve the cruel unkindness I had shown him, all because I was afraid of being ridiculed myself.

I went through what could be called a trauma for a while after Amos's death. But the experience did something to me. I knew I could never go back and undo what I had done. I had to seek forgiveness.

Amos was not longer here to forgive me for what I had done to him. I was old enough to know I had to have forgiveness to heal the remorse in my heart, and since Amos was no longer here, I sought it from God. I also knew I would have to stop the sin of mocking for once and for all, now and forever, if I wanted God to forgive me. I needed God's help to do this. In other words, I came to realize in a small way that of myself I was helpless, wicked, and condemned.

Time has mellowed the pain in my heart, and much has taken place since this happened, but I will never forget what I went through.

So now you understand why I am so concerned when I see things that tell me mockery might be creeping in at the school up the road. I know the teacher well enough to know that she will not want this evil to take root in her school. I know none of the parents will want their children to become mockers. If we want to keep that sin from leaving its ugly stains on the lives of the children, it is going to take all of us.

I keep wondering what my part might be in nipping this mockery in the bud. Seeing what I've seen, I think I should talk to the teacher. I don't think I'll make a special trip to the schoolhouse, because the pupils might wonder what I want there. But surely sometime soon the chance will come for me to speak to her about it. But what should I say? I don't know if she's aware of what's going on, or what steps she may have taken to correct it.

I wonder what her reaction will be. I hope she gets good and angry – not at the boys who are doing the mocking, but at the cruel and thoughtless things they are doing. It is a sin to become hot headed or angry at another person, but a righteous anger at an injustice is something else. That is sometimes what it takes to get started in the correct actions.

To tell you what I mean, I have to think of what I read in my history book a long time ago about Abraham Lincoln becoming angry. He had worked his way down the Mississippi River on a flatboat and while in New Orleans he saw something he had never seen before. He stopped in to see a slave auction in progress. He saw the young crying Negro children being torn away from their weeping mothers to be sold as slaves. Lincoln gritted his teeth together and said, "If I ever get the chance to hit that thing (slavery), I'm going to hit it hard!" Later when he was president, he did it, even though he made enemies by the thousands for doing so.

That's the way I hope the teacher feels about the sin of mocking. I don't think she should act while in anger. Anything done in the heat of anger is not a constructive or good thing to do. Nor is a prolonged anger any good. Something constructive has to be done to get these feelings out of the system. When I think of what the third grader is just starting to go through, I hope the teacher gets angry enough in the right way and will, with a prayer in her heart, do something about it.

Someone will have to tell the parents what is going on. I think it will have to be the teacher. That's part of her duty if we're really going to root out this sin. Supervising the activities on the play ground is going to be necessary, but it's going to take more than that. She can't be everywhere with the children, so they will have to learn how wicked mocking is, and learn to not do it when no grown-ups are around. For this she's going to need the help of the parents.

Then what should the parents of the school

children do? Here we have two kinds of parents – the parents of the mockers and the parents of the ones who are being mocked.

Let's take the parents of the mockers first. They will have to be made aware of what is going on. The teacher then has the right to expect the parents to do whatever homework it takes to stop the mocking. The parents know their own children, and it is up to them to decide what it takes to bring this cruelty to an end.

There is no better example of teachers and parents helping growing boys and girls to learn respect and obedience than to compare them to a grapevine. Those vines must be trimmed back, sometimes severely, or we soon have nothing more than a hopeless and tangles mass of unfruitful shoots. It is not just the teacher but also the parents who will have to do the trimming.

Another thing the parents must do is to change their own attitudes toward other people. Their attitudes and opinions of what people have and don't have will rub off on their children. Not only that, but when children pick up attitudes from their parents, they often get magnified. So those snobbish remarks, even if the parents try hard to keep them hidden from their children, must go. This is possible only when the proud spirit of better-than-thou is replaced with the Christian virtue of goodwill to all men.

Maybe these parents need to be reminded that even though some people are richer or poorer, bigger or smaller, thinner of fatter, we are all human beings. Just like God has made countless billions of leaves with no two exactly alike, and uncountable numbers of snowflakes, all somewhat similar but each with its own different unique features, so also has He made us humans. We are all somewhat different, but we are all here for a purpose and we are here to help each other. None of us is in a position where it is right to despise anyone else.

Next we come to a difficult question. What can the parents of the ridiculed boy do to correct the situation? I know parents hurt when they find out that their children are hurt, but it will not do any good for them to demand that their children get treated better, even when they are deserving it. And it will not work for these children or their parents to try to correct the matter by punishing the mockers. They must not let anger at others or self-pity for themselves get a start in their minds.

Another thing that won't work is if the parents try to elevate their child's importance by allowing him to have more things that he might want and they know he should not have. It is a well-known fact that a child who has anything he wants and is allowed to do everything is not necessarily a happy or popular child. Being allowed more things will only make him another discontented and proud human being. Such children have often turned around, and strange as it may seem, have become worse mockers than those who had mocked them.

What then can these parents do? One thing I hope they do is help their children with what is called self-esteem. This is not to be mixed up with pride, but a healthy feeling about ourselves and what we are able to achieve. It is recognizing that God has given us some talents He wants us to work with. The commandment to love our neighbor as ourselves means we are to esteem our fellow men, but it doesn't mean for us to have no self-esteem. The Bible also does not tell us to think nothing of ourselves when it teaches us not to think more highly of ourselves than we ought to (Romans 12:3). It is merely telling us to keep that opinion of ourselves within the proper perspective.

Those who get mocked again and again for the things they do and say, or merely for the person they are, can not be blamed for having a low opinion of themselves. We are all sensitive about how we think others feel about us. Those victims of mocking need friends to help them cope with the ridicule they are getting. For the school-aged children, there are no people on earth as eligible to be these friends as their parents and teacher. They need help in combatting the self-pity and depression that often comes with being mocked.

We will now return to the grapevine. It is necessary to cut off those surplus shoots at the proper time if we wish to have a fruitful vine. But we must not stop there. There is one more very important step to take. The healthy, growing shoots must be helped up and tied to a firm support.

That is what happens when the teacher and the parents help a child build up his self-esteem. They will not feed his pride by praising him all the time, but they will encourage him enough to let him know that what he does is worthwhile. He needs help, day in and day out, to become the kind of person God wants him to be. It takes a combination of trimming and supporting—sometimes one and sometimes the other.

When that self-esteem is built up, those mocking words of others will then just roll off instead of getting under his skin. He can laugh at himself more, and then he can laugh with others, but never at them.

That, in truth, is what it takes to be a well-adjusted, well-liked member of the group.

So Are You a Teacher?

43

Reading, writing, and arithmetic are often considered the three most important subjects you will be teaching. However, after you have read this article, you will realize there is more to teaching than merely using the textbooks.

Your pupils wend their way from their homes to your school in the morning, some from up the road, some from the others side of the woods, and some from down the road. All of them are coming to school to see what you will teach them today. We hope the parents had a prayer in their heart when they sent them off; we hope you breathe a silent prayer when you see them come.

You have undertaken a great responsibility. These children are just in their years when they are forming opinions and learning about the world around them. They have eager eyes and open minds, anxious to learn more. You are in a position to guide their thoughts and attitudes.

You have arithmetic classes. From the one-plus-one problems in the first grade to the finding of an unknown number in an equation problem in the eighth grade, you are teaching something which your pupils will use many times in later years.

You have other subjects, too. Your pupils are learning the reading, writing, and spelling that they will need to know in order to make a living when

they grow up. You probably have health classes to teach your pupils how to take care of their bodies.

There is another subject you should also be teaching. "Oh, no," you say, "I wouldn't have time for something else. I am busy all day the way it is!" This "something else" that needs to be taught is not an extra subject; it blends with the subjects you are already teaching. Since you are studying nature, studying our bodies in health class, studying the marvelous ways in which the laws of numbers work out, and studying the thousands of other interesting and awe-inspiring things God has put here for us to use and ponder over, shouldn't you also teach those pliable young minds about the One who made all this?

You know well enough how these things are taught in public school. They study the same subjects, but they are still trying to figure out how these things have come into being. Modern professors are trying to find out how that force, called life, which they call "the most mysterious force in the universe", came into existence. They are searching for a solution to these questions without admitting that a Great God did it all. Yes, we know that the home is the place where the children should learn about God. The parents who are paying the taxes which make up your pay cheek at the end of the month are all believers and worshippers of the powerful God who called everything around us into existence with His Word. There is probably not a child in your school who has not at one time or another wondered about these things and was told by his parents that God made them. Your pupils also go to church and hear the ministers preach about how God created heaven and the earth and everything that is in it. This, however, does not give you an excuse to remain silent about it at school.

No, you are not supposed to conduct a Bible School. You will know better than to even mention points of doctrine which you know the parents of your pupils are not all agreed on. But to remain silent about the Great Power which made and rules over us will make your school very little better than the public schools which we thought were too worldly to let our children attend. You don't have to remain silent on religious matters like the public school teachers do; the parents of your children are not opposed to religion.

Teacher, you have a wonderful opportunity to plant something in your pupils' minds that they will never forget. When you have nature study class or when you are going on a walk in the woods with your pupils, there are hundreds of awe-inspiring things for you to notice and talk about. There can be nothing as effective to kill boredom as a discussion and research on the beauties of nature. What causes those tight little buds to open up when the warm days come in the spring, then produce such beautiful flowers and delicious fruits? What awakens the billions of little seeds that are lying in the dark brown earth, waiting for the warm spring rains? What causes the tiny seeds, some much smaller than the head of a pin, to increase and grow and finally produce thousands of seeds exactly like they themselves were? How can water lilies, with bulbs deep in the black mud in the bottom of the pond suddenly send a shoot out of the water and produce such a perfect, beautiful, and fragrant flower?

How can birds fly? It is so common to see birds flying that we hardly think anything of it. But men who have spent their whole lives studying the principles of flight and trying to design airplanes that can fly call it a "marvel of engineering". This is only one of the many marvels around us. The ability of a bee to fly out to honey-bearing flowers and then straight back to its hive; the ability of a bird to fly hundreds, even thousands of miles south and then return to the same nest year after year; the ability of fish to go downstream into the ocean, then find their way back up the same stream to where they were born; and the ability of the tiny eels, born out in the ocean to come up the same rivers and streams their parents had gone down the year before – all these are miracles the modern world can only marvel at. But we know that a great eternal God rules over His creatures and cares for them. You, as a teacher, have the opportunity to make your pupils aware of these wonders and also the Power which rules over them.

Most of our homes have reading material in the form of newspapers, magazines, and books which contain articles on the wonders of the earth and the universe, but are silent about the Great Designer who created and is controlling them. We must face facts; in less than ten years from now there will not be any pupils in our schools who will remember seeing the moon before men walked on it. We are living in an age where we are being flooded with reading material about man's great achievements, but the world remains silent about the indefinable works of God.

It is a sobering thought that most of the writers of the articles which find their way into our homes actually believe in evolution, the theory that everything came into existence and then was changed into different forms in the course of many millions of years. Some of your more avid readers in the upper grades will probably find it hard to understand when they read such literature. You, as their teacher, should have the answer to their questions. Just because monkeys and man are somewhat similar in appearance does not prove that they are related. You could explain to your pupils that it would be the same as trying to prove that all houses are related because they are similar in outside appearance.

Evolutionists also tell us that it took millions of years for the earth to form. They will probably tell you that it took that long for the Colorado River to wash out the Grand Canyon. They point out that the sea shells found on high mountains prove that the mountains were under water millions of years ago. We know that God could have created the earth with Grand Canyon already looking like it does, now and that at one time God unleashed the forces of nature and the whole earth was covered with water (during the Great Flood).

When we see a locomotive coming down the tracks, how could we say that it just came into being by itself? We know that some man's mind designed the locomotive and also the machinery which was used in building it; somebody's mind is guiding the muscles that push the levers that run the locomotive; somebody's thoughts ruled over the order of which the cars in the train are hooked together. Everything down to the smallest detail was planned out in the dim recesses of someone's mind. How, then, can we look at the great universe and not realize what a great and wonderful Mind it took to create and govern it. Everything we see is here for a purpose and works together in perfect harmony, except when man, who was created with a power we call wisdom, interferes.

In order to get a deeper understanding of the great Power over us, stand outside on a clear, starry night. Look down at the small space of earth your two feet take up. Then look up into the starry sky and consider how vast the universe is and how great the God that created it all. You will probably feel like the Psalmist David when he said, "when I consider thy heavens, the work of thy fingers, the moon and the stars, which thou hast ordained; what is man, that thou art mindful of him? and the son of man that thou visitest him?" (Psalms 8:3, 4).

We know that the universe is vast, beyond the comprehension of the human mind. Scientists have not yet found the outer limits of the universe. On a clear, starry night the naked eye can see between 5,000 and 7,000 stars. Every time a bigger telescope is built, scientists are able to see more distant stars. It is now estimated (these estimations have changed many, many times) that there are at least 100 billion stars in the galaxy (or star group) our sun belongs to. They estimate that the Milky Way, the galaxy of stars we see, is 600 million billion miles across. That's a six with seventeen zeroes after it! This is not all; they claim there is an unknown number of galaxies in the universe, all having vast void spaces between them.

These are not facts which have to be taught to our pupils, just thoughts which might help us realize how small we are compared to God. We can also see what the Bible means when it compares the difference between God's thoughts and man's thoughts as being like the difference between heaven and the earth. (Isaiah 55:9).

When scientists talk about the laws of gravity that hold the earth, moon, and stars at their proper places, they call it an "unseen force". We can read in Job 26:7 what causes this "unseen force". It says "He (God) hangs the earth upon nothing." How can teachers explain such things without making reference to the almighty power of God?

One of God's greatest miracles of all is life itself. How can atoms of different kinds of matter be arranged into the countless living cells of which all human, animal, and plant life are composed of? Even now as you are reading these lines the muscles of your eyes are at work to enable you to read back and forth across the page. Your brain, composed of another kind of living cells, enable you to understand what you are reading. How can creatures, awakened out of dust, think, remember, understand, and reason like we do? The one and only answer is that an Almighty Father has imparted some of His own undying breath of life into our bodies. We call this life our soul. Because God's life is endless, so also is that inner life of ours endless and will be in existence somewhere ages after our bodies are again returned to dust.

I could go on and on. The variety of things to study and marvel at is endless. We know that the earth would soon be barren if we had no rainy days, but when we have windy days we should consider that they, too, are not without reason. Without the wind to move the clouds it would only rain on the oceans. How could we deny that all this was designed by One who thought of everything that life must have in order to exist?

There is yet another thing that teachers should be reminded of. The same God who "telleth the number of the stars; He calleth them all by name" (Psalms 147:4) and Who "dwelleth in the high and holy place" also dwells with those of a contrite and humble spirit (Isaiah 57:15). How can we worry and be anxious about the future when we know that we can have such a great Power helping us if we but humble ourselves so that His spirit can enter into our hearts?

If the Lord tarries, the pupils you are teaching will be the church members, the fathers and mothers, teachers and ministers of tomorrow. Your work and your influence in the classroom will do much to determine their character when they grow up. Here you need help. Humble your heart so that God's great power can enter and help you with the big task that you have undertaken. Take that difficult pupil of yours (and maybe his difficult parents, too). If you could exercise more of God's love in your heart, things might change so much that you would hardly be able to believe it.

We need soldiers to fight faithfully against the worldly and evil things that are trying to wreck our churches. Read the story about the vision Ezekiel had (Ezekiel 37). He found himself in a valley strewn with dry bones. When he prophesied or preached to the dead bones they grew sinews and flesh and bodies, but they were still dead. Only when he prophesied to the wind (prayed to the Spirit) did they all rise up and live, to be a great army. We can see by this that our teaching and preaching might help. But it is only God who can come into a person and make him a living soldier in His army, fighting on the battle ground of evil. We can learn by this story that we can do more by praying for a person than we can by reproof alone.

So, teacher, don't weary in your work. In all your dealings with your pupils and anyone else, try to keep God's perfect law of love, the Golden Rule. Be firm but loving in all discipline you may have to use. When clouds come, as they sometimes will, you can know that God has sent them so that you can learn from them and appreciate anew the sunny days when they come again.

Sing songs of God's praise, redemption, glory, and power in the schoolroom. After the Judgement Day all singing here on earth will be stilled forever. The humans heard here now are but a faint whisper of the great Hallelujah chorus which will some day sound in a fairer land. As you help your pupils enjoy the great beauties of nature about them, remind them from time to time that these beauties are but a faint shadow of the beauties in the Promised Land.

In closing I wish to thank you, Teacher, for what you are doing in helping the parents and ministers build up the churches. When the time comes when you have closed the last school book, corrected your last school paper, sung you last song here on earth, may your Maker welcome you with the words, "Well done, thou faithful servant; enter into the joy of the Lord."

Keeping Your Thoughts Pure

44

I have a story that I hope may help you.

There was once a young man happily married to a wonderful young wife. One day he was walking down the road near his home by himself. Somebody had thrown a paperback book in the grass along the side of the road, and as this man walked along, the book caught his eye. Out of curiosity, the man picked it up and thumbed through it. As he read a few sentences here and there, he knew right away that the book was much worse than trash and that it should be destroyed immediately.

But such is temptation that he put the book in his pocket and thought it might not do any harm to read some of it before destroying it. Well, the book got read all the way through before it was destroyed. The story was about a married man who was living an immoral life with other women and it was intended to arouse the sinful passions of lust and whet the appetites of sensuality in whoever read it. It made the acts of adultery appear as a common occurrence among married couples and made sin appear as pleasurable and exciting.

Of course, the man could not easily forget the evil thoughts that the reading to the book put into his mind. No actual actions of sin came from the reading of the book, but a battle raged in that man's mind for a long time afterward in trying to keep out impure thoughts.

I know about that terrible battle because I was the man in the story. I was in a deep sin by daily entertaining those thoughts of sin. I knew all along that it was very wrong to harbor such thoughts that could so easily have resulted in an immoral act. I knew "that whosoever looketh on a woman to lust after her hath committed adultery with her already in his heart." (Matthew 5:28); and I knew that "whosoever toucheth his neighbor's wife shall not be innocent." (Proverbs 6:29) I also knew that "whoremongers and adulterers God will judge." (Hebrews 13:4) and I was familiar with Ephesians 5:5 where it says that "For this ye know, that no whoremonger, nor unclean person... hath any inheritance in the kingdom of Christ and of God."

I now shudder to think of the scandal that I would have been in if my thoughts would have had a chance to become actions. I tremble to think of what my loving wife and my dear children would have gone through. How easily I could have started enjoying such a life and never have come back. I really didn't fully realize at the time the fire I was playing with by giving such thoughts a home.

You know that Satan in his great power is longing for your soul, but remember that God in His infinitely greater power and love is also wanting you to have that peace, contentment, joy and salvation that He offers to you. All this can be ours by turning away when evil appears. Only by again and again, over a long period of time, going to my knees in helplessness to God did I finally receive victory over the temptation that I had put myself in by reading that book. Oh, it would have been a thousand times easier to destroy that book without reading it than it was later going through the struggle of desiring things that I knew were wrong. Here we say, "Lead us not into temptation," but when the Lord told me in my conscience to destroy that book without reading it, I didn't obey. I feel that is why I had to go through what I did.

But winning one battle still does not win the whole war. I am now older, but I still have other temptations to battle against. There will be a struggle with Satan as long as you and I may live. Don't stop by merely dismissing the thoughts that now plague you. Do something to fill your mind with other thoughts, or your condition will be like that of the man described in Matthew 12:43-45—it will be worse than before. I feel that is what I still have to work on, to let the Lord fill the empty spaces of my mind with good things (Philippians 4:8) so that the evil thoughts do not have room.

When you wrote and asked for help among the family readers of this paper, you made a good start. We have to begin by admitting that we can't win in our struggle against evil without a power outside of ourselves. When we are ready, God will supply that.

Even though you are unknown to me, I will pray for you.

Christian Youth

45

An answer to Young Companion's problem corner, December 8, 1978

To My Dear Concerned Christian Young Friend:

The situation that you have described in your letter to the editor of "The Young Companion" is indeed a serious epidemic among our plain (or should be plain) churches.

We will give the answer, as we see it, to your question in three parts a little along the lines as suggested in the "Young Companion."

First, we will think about normal youth. We do have many young people who do want to do what is right, who still have high, uplifting, ideals for their lives and who would rather endure being laughed at than compromise with their conscience and do some of the things that are so popular with some of the young people. We have many young people who have made a change.

That they are what they are comes through the help that they got from their parents, their friends, the ministers and their church, the good and uplifting things that they read, their own prayers and many other things, all of which come from God, the Giver of all good gifts.

They were not born with a better will to live a Christian life than anyone else. They have chosen to live in a God-fearing way even if it might not always be the popular thing to do. They sometimes fail in choosing the right thing and they often fail in doing

the right thing; nobody is perfect, it is in the having the will and in the trying to be a good Christian that really counts. The ones that truly do want to live a life in the ordung of the church and in the principles taught in the Bible will have many joys and pleasures that the one with the guilty consciences will never have.

Thank God there are young people like you who do want to make a change and live a better life and who help to make us aware of the extremity of the problem.

There are people in every generation who are a living example of God-fearing lives for other people. Of course it is like being humble, the minute that we think we are humble, then we no longer are. We read of many people who the Scriptures say were filled with the Holy Spirit, and we read of the much good that was done through such people, but I don't believe I have ever read that a human who was filled with the Holy Spirit said so himself. I often think of the words in 2 Corinthians 12:9 where it says that God's strength is made perfect in weakness. In other words God can work mightily through a weak person, but that person is, through it all, still only a mortal, subject to making many mistakes and failures.

When the time comes for us to leave this world

and we will find out that we have failed to gain salvation, we will not be able to make an excuse for our wrongdoings by saying that we did not have some good examples in other lives to copy after and we can't say that we did not have a chance to make the choice ourselves. We won't be able to excuse ourselves and say that we did not have enough time to make repentance and we will not be able to say that we weren't warned as to what our way of living would bring to us, and with the power of God available through prayer, we surely won't be able to say that there was not help available to live a better life. God is waiting and wanting to help anyone who wants to make a change whenever they are ready to give up the forbidden pleasures of sin and ask for help to do so.

The part that we parents and ministers could have to make things better, to come up with a remedy for this disease, might be more than we realize. We, all of us, might have to make a change in our attitude about the way of living among our young people. We have heard say already that "they will soon settle down when they want to get married," but until then a lot of damage is done, some of it beyond repair. Their way of sinful living has then been passed on to the younger ones, many of who will think that this is the way to do; "everybody has done it for a long time."

Another thought that we would better not have among us is that raising a child is like breaking a colt; the harder he is to break, the better a horse he will be. Small wonder that the children do what they do when they know that their parents hold such an attitude. Let's not make it all sound so harmless and think that they are just sowing some "wild oats", lets take it for all the seriousness and gravity that it really is; they are living a life of sin. They are living in a life of sin that will have to be repented of before they can be a help in the battle that the church is having with unrighteousness and the things of the world.

The sad part is that many will not get the change made before they are called from this world. It is also sad that many do not get the change made before they start raising children of their own. The unrighteous that they were in then gets to be multiplied fast.

We parents and ministers have a narrow way to walk. We all have at times had a disobedient child or a disobedient church member and on the other hand we have also had time when they were obedient. Let us not, when they are obedient, say that we were the ones that have caused them to be so, but on the other hand if they are not obedient we are not to say that we can't do anything about it.

Some people seem to think that their children have more energy and pep than other people's. They will say that if they had mild-mannered children like so and so had they could also easily have raised them up to be obedient. Here again those with obedient children are not to think that they have done it themselves and on the other hand those with disobedient children are not to say that it was impossible for them to do anything about it.

The attitudes of the parents rub off on their children. A very small child will soon know what he can get away with. A child will quickly sense if the parents aren't really against some of the things that shouldn't be found in our churches. He will see it before his parents realize it if they will only obey church regulations only if it suits.

Discipline is something that will have to be used in raising children. Parents will have to be firm but loving. Just being firm doesn't work out the best nor does it work to be loving but not firm. Both have to be used. Are we as parents afraid of our children that we sometimes permit them to bring home or get away with things that we know is not good for them or for the others that may be looking to them for an example.

One of the places that we parents have failed the most is that we have not taken the time to be a caring, understanding friend to our children If we don't watch out our biggest interest will be our work and "velt and gelt" (world and money). If children are not treated like the small adults that they really are, they are apt to seek all their interests and company outside of the family. Really, we would not let our livestock run out of control like we sometimes let our children go for themselves.

We can be pretty sure that the attitudes that we older people have in the line of our possessions is doing untold damage to our young people. There is nothing wrong in having the possessions that we really need in making a living and in living a comfortable life if the Lord has so willed it, but there are probably many times that we really don't need as much in material possessions that we think we do. There is the great danger in these times of affluence that we keep getting new things all the time to boost our own importance our own eyes. We do things that other people don't have the ability to do, in a show-off kind of way; we get through our work better than so and so does, and we don't hesitate to make it known, and in perhaps several of a hundred other small ways we do things to get a feeling of our own importance, and the feeling that we are better than the average. This feeling rubs off on our children and when they are then with the young folks they will enjoy doing things, or buying and having things that some of the others will not dare to do. It gives them the same feeling of importance that got rubbed off on them at home.

The story of the man who had the son who often fell into fire and into water might apply to us here. This man wanted his son healed and the disciples tried but could not do it. When Jesus came on the scene, He healed the boy. He also told His disciple that this sickness will not go out except through fasting and prayer (Matthew 17:21).

We also want our young people healed of a disease who we could say keep falling into sins that will hurt them even more than it did the boy who kept going into places where he got hurt in a bodily way. It takes prayer, but also fasting. We do not believe that Jesus just meant going without a meal at times, but He is trying to tell us that if we would deny ourselves more of the things that we have so much pleasure in, and that we are so proud of, we might have more help in curing this disease among our young people.

We could say that we have two kinds of young people who are living in these sinful ways that you mentioned in your question. One kind has been warned about it, but parents and minsters may say what they will, they still keep living in sins. They will have to answer for their own sins and serving the appetites of the flesh. They know better and have been warned. When they first did these things they did have a guilty conscience against it, although they then partly silenced that still small voice by refusing to listen to it. These young people will have to answer for their own misdeeds; their parents and ministers have done their duty.

The other kind never really had a conscience against doing such things because it was never pointed out to them enough, that living in such a way is a great sin. If there are any young people like this, they are innocent. It is then the parents and ministers who are responsible for the evil doings done by such people. In other words, we older folks might be more responsible for some of the unrighteous going on than we sometimes realize.

Now what can you do? There is always the choice of going with company who will spurn all advice of the Bible and of parents and ministers to live a better repented life, or of going with company who have fun in a good and wholesome way. There will always be some who will choose to live a life of sin and the so-called pleasures rather than live a life of self-denial and humbleness. If you cannot live a life like you know should be lived in the company you are now in, it is time to change your company.

In the end it is only those who will choose to take the small and narrow path and who will try with God's help to live a life pleasing to their Creator that are living a life that is a help and example to those other people who are also going through this world with us. Jesus told Peter that when he was converted he was to strengthen his brethren and that still works that way; (Luke 22:32) only when a person's actions are a help to his fellow travelers does it show that he himself is converted.

So my dear young friend, I take from your letter that you want to live a better life. That is the first step; the step that many never get made. I am thankful to God for any young person who comes to realize that a short season of worldly pleasures here will mean nothing to us anymore in that place where we will spend eternity. I am so thankful that there are still young people who are wanting to do something about that nagging, guilty conscience and that fresh feeling of remorse every Monday morning. The best help that you can be for your companions still living in unrepented sins is to pray for them and try with God's help to live a life that is a good example for others. A few words now and then may help, but if we do all the talking trying so hard to be the one to convert them, we can make ourselves so repulsive to them that they will turn the other way and thus are really the cause of them not coming back. Actions speak louder than words. A real Christian has a joy that cannot be hidden; it will show through that he has something that is worthwhile having.

Associate from now on with young people who do not think that they have to go along with everything to be popular. Your good intentions could again be lost by continually being with too many evil doings. Don't get your hopes too high, you will never convert the whole world, but if you, by your example, will help only one poor soul struggling in sin, your life here on earth will be worthwhile in the sight of God. You may never find out in this life the help you have been to others, but God will reward you for it in that life beyond the grave.

The help to do this comes only from God, you cannot do it by yourself, but it is you who must first have the will and desire to make the change. This help will come to you through prayer, through reading the Bible, through the advice and example of other people, through the joys that you will have that were before totally unknown to you, and through the many other ways that God has in helping those who want to live a better life. The same Power who called the heavens and earth into existence and who awakened you out of the dust and the same Almighty God who had everything in the past, has everything in the present and in the future that is still unknown to us, under His control, will help you to live a better life if you will only ask Him to do so. He sent His Son, Jesus, into the world that we might have life and that we might have it more abundantly (John 10:10) and that your joy might be full (John 15:11).

Even though you are unknown to me, I will pray for you. I also need your prayers. I can say that at times we parents and ministers feel that there is no improvement among the young people in the churches and at times we feel like giving in and letting everything ride, but a letter like yours does show that there are still young people who care. We need the prayers of you all to keep steadfast to the end.

Filling Your Lot in Life

46

A response to the "Can You Help Me?" in the Family Life.

Dear Friend,

I just got done reading those lines that you wrote and were printed in the January *"Family Life."*

Actually you are asking, "How can God be so unfair to us humans that some have it nice and some don't?" You are saying that some of us are somebodies and from popular families, and some of us aren't and that life is not as it should be; that God allows things to be so unjust.

I have a deep feeling of Christian sympathy in my heart for you. I wish I could do something for you. That is why I am taking the time to put some of the thoughts, that I had since reading your letter, on paper for you to read.

I don't know who you are out there and it is just as good I don't, for I am going to be frank. You can probably take frankness off of somebody you don't know better then if one of your friends told you.

Please get a hold of something solid and brace yourself. I won't give you pity. You expressed enough of self-pity in your letter that I don't want to encourage any more of that.

I believe that you are a Christian. I can't help but believe that you try to live like a Christian. But being a Christian does not guarantee that we will have all our problems solved automatically by God

as a reward for obeying His will. He gives us a mind and body and He gives us time, all of which is to be used to glorify and honor His name.

Now, even if outward circumstances do not change for you, you are still the one who has to make a change in your way of thinking. The sooner you do that, the sooner you will be happy in wherever the Lord puts you, and with whatever the Lord gives you.

Your letter shows that you think that some people are "somebodies", in other words some people are to be more highly esteemed than others. If you think that some people are "tops" it follows that you also think that other people are "nobodies"; people who really don't count. You are judging people by their looks and by what they have. You then carry that line of thinking on to yourself. You are thinking too much of yourself.

Now, what happens when you think too much of yourself? You search for something in yourself to be proud of and if you don't find it you are liable to get depressed and feel inferior, if you do find something you are apt to be proud. It is wrong to be either depressed or proud. You don't have to be either.

So grow up. The sooner that you stop putting people into different degrees between worthful and worthless, the sooner you will get over your self-pity. People are not to be sized and judged by us humans. (Judge not that ye be not judged (Matthew 7:1). Don't just sit there watching those, that in your opinion, are pretty and have charm and come from popular families, (I get those words out of your own letter) but get busy, forget yourself, and do something else.

You are like little Amos who is playing with his cousin, Andy. Andy has a toy and starts to play with it. Amos sees that he is having fun with the toy and then he wants it. As soon as he has it he doesn't play with it but holds on to it and looks over to see what Andy has by now. Andy has given up the first toy to Amos, but that is all right, he finds some other toy to have fun with.

I know I make it sound too simple. By now you are probably thinking that I do not understand your problem. What you are wishing for is a lot more than a toy. You are wishing for a happy married life, but what I am trying to get across to you is that if marriage is not God's will for your life, you can then accept it that way and have happiness, or you can go through the rest of your life pining for something that other people have, but you don't, and then if you are unhappy you will be so because you have made it so for yourself. The gifts and talents that God has already given you should bring you happiness. Look around yourself and find out what they are.

So start with yourself. Maybe you have been reading some romance stories and thus have put your thinking and yourself in a dream world of your own. You will never be what God wants you to be that way. It has been said that there are three kinds of people in this world: Those who do things; those who watch other people do things; and those who don't know that there is something going on. Be one of those who does things.

You say that you are thirty-one and still single. You are starting to worry that your dreams (as you have them) will never be realized. Well, let me tell you something that took me a long time to learn. I think I learned it the hard way. Don't ever worry. Worry is a trait that is repelling and not pleasing to others. You know what I mean. You, yourself would not chose someone for a life companion who always worries. You would want someone who is friendly and pleasant to have around. On the other hand,

don't try to put on a false front by always acting gay. As they say "just be yourself, there is no one else better qualified."

You make it sound as if marriage would solve all your problems. Well, a marriage that is built solely on charm and good looks can drag both partners down to the lowest levels of unhappiness. There has to be good, honest character in back of those good looks to make a happy marriage. Charm will not make a living, will not keep the house a comfortable place to go to and will not make it a good home. Good looks will not raise and properly discipline the children; in other words these would better be traits that are more durable and lasting in people than charm and good looks.

Whether you ever get married or not, you can still be working on improving yourself and on developing such traits that God intends us to have. You can make yourself so busy working on self-improvement that you will forget your self pity. Whether marriage is in your future or not, only God knows, but being happy or unhappy is in your own hands; married or not married.

I guess by now you are wondering, "Who are you and how do you know what to do about what I am worrying about?" Well, I went through some deep disappointments in my young days. I had some of the same thoughts that you now have. Some people I worshiped the ground they walked on and others I didn't want to even be seen talking to. Maybe that is stretched a little, but that is about the way it was. It was only when I started to make friends with those I could reach and forgot about trying to get in with those I couldn't reach that I started to relax and enjoy myself.

I also found out that God can help with all the problems that we have; every single one. I found out that God expects us to not just be nice to those who are nice to us and to those who we think are more than others. He expects us to be friendly and nice first of all to those in the family where he has placed us and to those who we happen to live and work with. He gives us help through other people but then He expects us to be a help to others as we ourselves have been helped. The reward is friends and happiness and a change in our way of thinking and doing. So don't waste time wishing for a change

147

in the looks that God has given you. Work and ask for God's help to change that part of you that can be changed, your personality.

With God's help your whole personality can be changed. Your depression can be changed to hope and joy. Your feelings of inferiority and self-pity can be changed to feelings of self-worth and confidence. Your distrust and being critical of others can be changed to Christian sympathy and understanding. Your pride can be changed to warm humility. Your worried thoughts can be changed to cheer, unconfused thinking. Your gloom can be changed to being outgoing and cheerful. Your relationships with other people can be changed from being stiff and formed to that of understanding and with enough of warm, easy humor to be pleasant, relaxed and fulfilling. And last, but not least, your rebellion and resentment against your lot in life can be changed to complete acceptance.

I found out for myself that such things can be changed. You will find that some of the changes can take place almost overnight, and then others are rooted so deep that they take years of work, and still then the change can hardly be noticed, but it is still hopefully going in the right direction. I am now middle-aged and I am still working on changes that I have to make. I know that it is a lifetime job and it is so interesting that I have no time left for worry. God has been very good to me and I am happy.

You are probably also wondering if the dreams that I had in my young days ever got fulfilled. I can say that my dreams were somewhat different from those that you have, but most of the "castles in the air" that I had in my young days never got to be that way, but I am now glad that they didn't. God had better joys for me. I now see that God could do a lot better job of planning my life than I ever could. Your life can turn out that way also. You have no way of knowing what is in your future, but your future is in good hands; it is in God's hands.

I will be praying for you,

From one of your fellow pilgrims.

FOR THE SINGLES

My Dearest Friend

Why must I live a single life
And face each day alone;
While all my friends are married,
And live in happy homes?
It seems they find completed joy,
While I, still empty, roam.

Together now they can face life,
Together plan each day;
They share together all their needs,
Together read and pray;
Life has for them fulfillment found
Throughout each passing day.

But with me though, its' different,
For with whom can I share
The things that mean so much to me?
And who my load will share
When sore trials press upon me
And the burden's hard to bear?

Oh I must look, beyond myself,
And to my God above;
Who's waiting now to undergird
Me in His arms of love;
How it must grieve His tender heart
That I should doubt His love.

Oh, would my Savior ask of me
More pain than I can bear?
For living now a single life,
Would I judge God unfair?
And is there really no one,
My burdens that will share?

Has Christ not promised in His Word
My earnest Friend to be?
And does He not desire the best,
In all of life for me?
He has a special plan for me,
Beyond what I can see.

So may I cast aside my pride,
And be content to live;
The life my Savior planned for me,
So He can surely give
His blessings rich and full and free,
And all my doubts forgive.

Help me, O Lord, to trust in Thee,
And in thy will to rest;
For you will make my life complete,
And give me what is best,
To draw me nearer to Thy side
Where I am truly blest.

(Submitted, poet unknown)

Meeting Houses

47

David Luthy was preparing a discussion on having church services in meetinghouses. Ben expressed his thoughts in this letter to David.

April, 1981

Dear friend David,

I received your request asking for reasons why I would not like to see our people meet for church services in a meetinghouse. I do not feel qualified to write on such a subject as this, but with God's help I will put down some of the thoughts that I had since I got your letter.

First, we will search for Scripture that may shed some light on the question.

First - Matthew 26:18 - "I will keep the Passover at thy house with my disciples." Jesus held the first communion service at a private home.

Second - Acts 2:46 - "And they, [the people of the first Christian church] continuing daily with one accord in the temple, and breaking bread from house to house, did eat their meat with gladness and singleness of heart." The first assembly of believers in Jesus just a few weeks after His ascension to Heaven held their gatherings in one house, then another.

Third - Acts 5:42 - "And daily in the temple, and in every house, they ceased not to teach and preach Jesus Christ." "In every house," means just what it says; every family had worship services sometime or other.

Fourth - Acts 20:20 - "I [Paul] kept back nothing

that was profitable unto you, but have shewed you, and have taught you publicly, and from house to house." Several years after the Christian church was started, they had discarded some of their first ways of doing things, such as meeting in the temple and such as having all things in common, but preaching from "house to house" was still kept up. The "upper chamber" (Acts 20:8) where the people met to have a church service was undoubtedly the upper rooms of a private home.

These four verses tell us a lot about how the first, original church held its meetings to worship the Lord. A careful search and study of the Scriptures would probably uncover more verses to strengthen our belief that it is Scriptural to have our church services in private homes, in our times nearly 2000 years later.

There was once a man who was a member of a church which had a building to worship in, who went over to his Amish neighbor to borrow a tool. He found the Amish neighbor and his boys busy sweeping down the cobwebs in a little used part of the barn. "I see you are busy," he said.

"Yes, we are getting ready to have church here on Sunday. We may have to tie some of the horses in this part of the barn," the Amish man replies. "We really should have cleaned out and swept up this corner before this, but it seems it doesn't get done till church comes around."

Thinking of the corners in his barn at home that hardly ever got cleaned out, the non-Amish man laughed. "My wife says she wishes we would take turns having church so that my corners would get cleaned out."

That may be one benefit of taking turns to have church in our homes; our corners get cleaned up and the weeds get mowed off in places that we otherwise might not get done.

But the real reasons go a lot deeper than that. It fits in so well with many other things that the plain churches stand for. Doesn't it just fit in with our beliefs of having our homes a sacred, holy place both when worship is held there and then also in the whole time in between? Doesn't it make sense with all the rest of Christianity's teachings to keep our worshipping group small (Luke 12:32), something that couldn't be done in a church large enough to seat a thousand or more people? How could we really help to bear one another's burdens (Galatians 6:2) if the group got so large that we would be almost complete strangers to each other? Doesn't our custom of staying for a light meal, after the church service is over, do so much to deepen the fellowship between the members? Wouldn't it really be a waste of money and time to build and keep up an expensive building to be used only for church services, especially when we think of the extremes in which cathedrals have been built costing millions of dollars? Doesn't it help to keep out some for the rather shallow arguments that have already split some churches such as, do we have church bells, or not? Should we put a steeple on top, or not? A hundred years ago there was a denomination that split because one group thought it was wrong to put stoves in the church building to heat it . The other group didn't think it mattered.

Yes, Jesus taught in buildings built expressively for the use of worship; in the synagogues (Matthew 4:25 and Luke 6:6) and in the temple (Matthew 21:23). But He also taught on the hillsides (Matthew 5:1) and by the shores of the sea (Matthew 13:1), but also in private homes (Luke 19:5 & 11) so we can believe that He did not mean that only certain places were holy and sacred enough to hold a worship to God. His words written for us in John 4:21 to 24 make that clear to us.

It is true that we can't really find a verse in the Bible that downright commands us to hold our worship services in our homes, and neither do we find one that forbids us to build a house just for church services, but having worship in our homes matches so beautifully with our other beliefs of living a simple, humble, unpretentious life, and being the quiet people of the land. I am sure that those of us who were brought up in the "Old Order" and who helped our parents "get ready for church" would find it way out of place to start holding services in a meetinghouse. Let's help to keep it that way for those who will pass this way after we are gone.

My letter is now long enough. I want to tell you that I enjoy reading your articles. I would also enjoy meeting you, so plan to come sometime. I am sure there are many interesting things we could visit about.

Remember us in your prayers,

Sincerely

Ben Blank

P.S. A quick thundershower came up and chased me in from the field while I was planting corn; that is the only reason I am at my desk in the middle of a busy Friday afternoon. The next project on the list is getting several more pages ready to send to Elmo Stoll. Thanks to you all for the work that you do in getting out the *Family Life*, *The Blackboard Bulletin* and *The Young Companion*.

Being a Witness to Tourists

48

The scene which we are now going to describe takes place just about every day, especially during the summer, and on the Memorial Day, Fourth of July and the Labor Day weekends. That section of Route 340 between the towns of Intercourse and Bird-in-Hand, Pennsylvania, is probably the most typical place for the scene.

Traffic is lined up behind a slow moving vehicle; there is plenty of room to pass, but the driver of the car with the out of state license seems to enjoy driving slowly behind the carriage with the two cute looking, differently dressed youngsters looking out the back. There are several chartered buses, a few mobile vacation homes and several campers in the line of traffic and more cars with out of state license than there are cars with Pennsylvania licences. The local drivers can easily be distinguished from the tourists by the bored and sometimes impatient looks on their faces and sometimes when their patience is tried out too much they will lean on their horns to try to get things moving faster.

Every spot on the earth that has tourists coming to it has some so called attractions that makes people want to come to see what makes that place so unusual from anywhere else.

Niagara Falls, the Grand Canyon, and a host of other places have some natural feature that is very unusual that makes people want to come to see it. There are many places of historical interest that have an attraction that historical minded people want to go and see. Lancaster County is one of the top ten tourists spots in the United States. The tourists that come to Lancaster County where the plain people live want to see the plain people.

Lancaster County, the county that has often been called the "Garden Spot of America" has had many motels, campgrounds, hotels and tourist homes built on it the last twenty-five years or so. We know that the advertising that these commercial places put out to promote tourism has a lot to do with bringing people into the areas where the plain people live. Many of the tourists will be here for a week or more and will still not get an authentic view of what the plain people are really like.

The tourists are here to learn about these peculiar people that they read about, but if we do a little thinking on the subject maybe we plain people can learn a good bit from the very people who would come to see first hand our way of life and living.

Some of these visitors are highly educated. They see that the complex civilization that has been developed in these modern times is not always working out. They will conclude that going back to the simple life that they read about among the plain people might be the solution to many of the problems that modern living has brought along with it.

Some of the more wealthy of these visitors have liked the area and have come back and built homes or have bought homes and even farms and thus are helping to make the price of land and homes even higher for the plain people who are hoping to help their children establish a home or a farm close to their "freindschaft." Many doctors, lawyers and other professional people have decided that the rising price of farm land makes farms a good investment for their money. This has pushed the price of land even higher.

We have had some of these city people who admired the self-sufficiency of the plain people, who grow a large percentage of their own food. Many of them have then tried it for themselves. Many a family from the city has started out with high hopes of eliminating that burden on the family budget; the grocery bill. After going through quite a few seed catalogs, ordering the seeds and getting the garden started they were in for a surprise when they found out that there was more work in a garden than they had imagined, with the weeding and all, they had imagined that after the planting was done the rest would be easy; all you had to do was to harvest the food as it got ready. Their social activities and sports, their two week vacation in the summer, and the television that had to be watched in the evening left little or no time for caring for the garden. Needless to say, many of these gardening ventures turned out to be a flop.

Here we should be thankful for the teaching that we got from our parents. We grew up helping our parents with the crops and animals on the farm and in the gardens and truck patches. We might have thought at times that life was somewhat of a grind with all this work. But when we see instances like the one just mentioned we can be thankful that our parents passed the know how that they had on to us. We learned that duty comes before pleasure. We want to be thankful enough for the privilege that we had in such ways that we surely want to pass it on to the generation that, if the Lord tarries, will be here after we are gone.

Some of our visitors have concluded that the modern way of living is the cause of all the pollution of the air, soil and water, and of the mountains of trash that cannot be gotten rid of and of the wasteful use of energy and natural resources and are hoping to find an answer in the plain peoples way of living. Many of them are then somewhat surprised that we do use gasoline engines, we do some spraying and use some fertilizer on our crops. We are not as self-sufficient as they had thought that we are.

Here we sometimes have to wonder if we shouldn't all try to help to keep our way of life from becoming even more materialistic then it is now. The trend in the world in farming or any other business has been to get by or get out. We plain people may have been following this trend more then we realize. We are all also guilty of being too extravagant and wasteful with the abundance that God has given us.

Many of our visitors want to know more about our religion. Many of them will tell us that their first opinion of the plain people after having seen them for the first time is that we are all dressed alike. They do not think that we have any problems trying to keep up to the latest styles. Some of them have seen how discouraging, hopeless and costly it is to try to keep homes and clothing in the latest styles that always keep changing, they will get plainness and sloppiness mixed up as we see how some of them will wear clothing purposely put together with patches or will wear purposely faded clothes with some of the parts torn off with a ragged edge.

Here we can be thankful for our church ordnung in clothing. We also will wear patched and faded clothing, but being clean and neat is not out of the ordnung. With our ordnung we do not have to get a complete new set of clothes every time the styles and fashions of the world changes. Some of our visitors have tasted all of the pleasures that the world has to offer, but they still have a secret longing for the simple life that they think that the plain dressed people must have. We have something that money cannot buy; let's try to take care of it and pass it on. The plain ordnung can be completely destroyed in just a generation or so if we insist on following the worldly styles in our way of dress. The clothes that we choose to wear tell what is in our hearts. Being contented with the ordnung of the church is really one of the helps we have in raising our children in a God-fearing and humble way.

Some of the people wishing to find out more about the plain people are still looking for a church that they think is based one hundred percent on the Bible and also lived up to. We can imagine their disappointment when they find out about the disrespect and disobedience of some of our members. Who is at fault if they then get disillusioned and come to the conclusion that all Christianity is just putting on a false front or that all religion is just a sham? Since our way of living is being so closely watched and studied we are more responsible than ever for the way we live. We should try with God's help to live according to Biblical principles. Our lives are the only Bible that many people may ever read.

Most of our visitors know that we are a nonresistant people and are opposed to war. We may not be going as far as to kill another person, but according to Christ's Sermon on the Mount, if we have hate or anything else that is the opposite of love among ourselves, in our neighborhoods, schools or churches, we are a murderer to our fellow man. If we insist on having something that causes another of our fellow members to stumble and fall and thus are the cause of his coming away from the ways of Love, Humility and Truth we are also a murderer to his soul. Our visitors will quickly sense if we are not in love and harmony among ourselves.

Some are surprised that we even own guns. Then imagine their astonishment when they find out that some our members will leave families and duties at home for sometimes a week or more to go to the mountains to hunt. This was different back in the days when the food supply of a family depended on daddy bringing home some meat for the winter, but in these days when it is only done for sport, shouldn't we ask ourselves if it is really necessary?

As we drive along the road we will meet many tourists who are armed with cameras to record the scenes that they happen to see in their travels. We all probably have a more or less cool feeling toward these intruders of our privacy because of this. We certainly don't want to pose for a photograph. We can be firm when we are asked to do so, but we also should show respect, some will snap a picture anyway, but most of them will return the respect that we show to them.

As our plain people drive on the roads they will often meet with a tourist family with everyone in smiles; they are actually seeing some of the Amish people that they have read and heard so much about; they drive slowly past the Amish family in the slow-moving wagon and wave and smile as they go past. The children in back of the carriage are looking the other way at something more interesting than a gawking tourist family; the father and mother of the plain family are having a more serious conversation up front, so the waves and smiles are not returned. This happens so frequently that the tourist family will take the idea along home that the plain people are all business and no joy. They will conclude that a child growing up in an Amish home is really a deprived youngster. They aren't allowed many of the things that are so dear to and such a pleasure to the people of the world. They get the ideas that there could be no fun or joy among the Amish people.

We know that such is not the case. Our ways of living may seem peculiar to an outsider, but we have deep joys that are totally unknown to the world. It behooves us all to be more content with the way of life handed down to us by our forefathers who denied themselves the pleasures of the world to be a good example to their descendents. Let us do the same for the stream of humanity that is coming after us, there is a pure joy in trying with God's help to live a little closer to the example of humbleness that Christ Himself has left for us.

Some of our visitors in the "Dutch Country" are also here to have a fling at some of the wild night life places and at some of the horse races, movies, fairs, theaters, ballparks and so forth that can be found within a short drive from the locality. We can imagine their astonishment when they also find some of our own people at such places, even on Sundays, the Lord's day of rest and holiness. Here they were reading that the plain people are contented with the simple joys at home and are not at all interested in the gay lifestyle that some of their non-amish neighbors are often running after so much. Many of them have often talked about their surprise and astonishment at seeing the plain people at such places.

Friends, has our light for the world burned out that we will stoop so low as to find our pleasure at such places? We surely belong to the class of hypocrites that Jesus so often strongly denounced, if we belong to or intend to some day become a member of a plain church and then frequent such places. When the great day comes that the Lord will take His bride, the church, to her eternal home you can be pretty sure that He will not go to those places to find His followers.

We should be thankful for what we have. We want to hold on to the good that is still with us. The prayers and examples of concerned God-fearing parents and older people does show up in that there are still many, many of our young people who try to live a christian life, and there are many people who have seen the error, of their ways and have made a change into their ways of living for the better. But it is still sad to think what a few disrespectful young people, often under the influence of strong drink, can do to ruin the witness of our churches to the world and to the innocent younger ones coming on. The *Readers Digest*, (Aug. 1978, page 76) a very widely read magazine, even carried a few "jokes" about the shady practices among some of our Amish young people. All of us have been, and still are, in some sins or other. Let us make amends and ask God for forgiveness, and then in appreciation to God for His forgiveness, resolve to live a better example than ever before and if, as parents, God has entrusted the care of any young, precious soul in our care, let us humbly ask Him for divine guidance for that awesome responsibility. Let us not be too proud to tell our children that we have made mistakes, and let us let our children know that we are praying for them; praying that God will help them in their trials and temptations.

A Christian can be a good witness in many ways. Living a good example has led more people to Christ than any amount of talking has ever done. Quite a few of us have probably had some of these tourists visit us in our homes. Here again many of these people have expressed their surprise at some of the things that we have around that are purely for show. We can read that in the time of our Anabaptist forefathers not only did they show changes in their ways of living, but we also read that the homes that they lived in were also different, thus an Anabaptist traveling in a strange town could see in which homes he would receive a warm welcome. Having our homes looking different and plainer

than the homes of our "gay" neighbors has always been a church ordnung in all of our plain churches. Will we be content in our humble homes or will we keep on going toward extravagance and luxury till we would have to be ashamed to invite Jesus in as a guest? There is nothing wrong in building sturdy and durable and to keep out the cold and rain, but we don't have to build as if we would want to live here forever. One generation's luxuries tend to become necessities for the next generation. One writer has said that the trend is to have larger and fancier kitchens and after that go for picnics at the mountains and the seashore and to eat out at restaurants. Mom's old fashioned cooking is no longer good enough.

Some of our animal-loving visitors who go to the areas where the plain people live will notice more than we realize how we treat our livestock; horses, cows and so forth. It has been said that after a man becomes a true Christian, his animals will feel the difference. It is no wonder that some of the "English" people among us have some times talked about the disgrace that they have seen among us in that an animal has been beaten without mercy or in that teams have been seen going down the road at breakneck speed with the horses in obvious distress. "Blessed are the merciful for they shall obtain mercy" also applies to us in situations like this. Let us not be so thoughtless that we forget that our animals also have feelings of pain, thirst, and hunger.

There is still another kind of visitor among the many tourists that frequent our area. Not all of our tourist visitors will rave about the nice buildings and the well-kept farms. Jealousy, greed and envy are in their hearts. Some of them know that the total amount of dollars that they will make in a lifetime will not even be as much as the amount that some of our people have given for a farm. Some have thought that the Amish are all very rich people with their own private chauffeurs when they see so many going by sitting next to the driver of a car. Our lawmakers in Washington D.C. Have already been approached by groups that would like to see all land being treated as a public utility. This means that nobody could own land; all the land would belong to the government, they believe that land should belong to everybody, not just to the rich or to people who happen to be born into families that were landowners. When King Ahab back in Bible times coveted his neighbors land, he eventually got it, even if he had to get Neboth, the rightful owner, killed to posses it. When the princes from far off Babylon came to the land of Judea, King Hezekiah showed them all his riches; there was nothing he did not show them. When they went home the rich little nation was not forgotten. When Babylon became a strong nation, some one hundred and ten or one hundred and twenty years later their king conquered the land of Judea and then helped himself to probably some of the very treasures that King Hezekiah had been so proud of . The people left in the land were poor but they had the hope expressed in Zephaniah 3:12; "I will also leave in the midst of thee an afflicted and poor people, and they shall trust in the name of the Lord." We want to take a lesson from this. We are only stewards, not owners of our possessions. The Lord can give but the Lord can also take away. We have many, many examples of both in the Bible. Most land-buyers today are pretty sure that the value of the land that they buy now will be even more in a few years. This is yet to be seen. All previous land booms in history have ended with disastrous results. And in history where decay of the true religion has set in fast when a people or a nation have become too prosperous. We so often forget to thank the Lord for His manifold blessings and abundance; will these things have to be taken away from us before we realize how we had it? If money and many possessions are our god, who will we have for our God when the hour comes that we will close our eyes for the last time to all things here below and be taken away from it all?

Land is becoming expensive. It is getting so that only the rich (or those intending to be rich someday) can afford to buy a good sized farm. Land is often costing more than it's ability to produce. Owning a farm is fast becoming a status symbol among many of the wealthy. There was nothing wrong in a father buying a farm or farms for himself or for his children back in times when there were only a few buyers at a farm sale, and if it can be afforded there is still nothing wrong with it. But like everything else there are extremes. Let us remember that the privilege of landownership is one of the privileges that could be taken away from us in a short time. Hard times or a famine in the land or the government becoming

bankrupt could be cause of our banks, belongings being taken from us, or as in Rome the cause that people were taken away from their belongings. It can be understood that parents want to see their children living close by. When several neighbors have had the same idea about a farm or home that was for sale in a neighborhood, it has often been the cause of it's bringing an exorbitant high price and often has been the cause of much ill feeling. We probably all think it would be nice to have the family together. Let us keep in mind that it could be that we are desiring something here in this life that we should wait to have in eternity. Perhaps we should be making more efforts to live this life so as to keep the family together in that better land beyond the grave.

Many of our people having a small business will expand until an outsider would not recognize it as being owned and run by one of our plain people.

The high prices of everything that we buy is making a mark on our plain churches that is not good. To meet the costs of what we did buy, or are intending to buy, makes many of us feel that we have to go at it in a bigger way. Herds and flocks get bigger. Then when the money comes in fast, we are apt to worship the golden calf of money. Our grandfathers would not have believed that our own people would have ever made themselves so busy. This also has its extremes. We want to earn money to pay our bills. We don't want to be idle; there is truth in the saying that idleness is the Devil's workshop. There is nothing like the good tired feeling after having accomplished an honest day's work. But on the other hand if we are so busy ever trying to make more and more our prayers and our thoughts on things eternal will be slowly crowded out by our cares and anxieties of our natural things. We will be too busy with our work to keep the Sabbath in a proper way and what will such living do to our life at home as a family? Dad will snap at Mom; tempers will flare, both will be too busy all the time to be a caring and understanding friend to the children coming on. When this goes on year after year the children will grow up and probably find their interests and friends somewhere else. Communication among the family; talking things over, that one thing necessary for family unity and happiness will become less and less all because we had more than enough in material things but still we wanted more. Before we wish for more riches or more things lets think of people who already have it so. Are they happier and more contented than those who don't? The more money we have the greater is the danger that we won't have some of the good things that cannot be bought with money. Oh, what we miss by forgetting the words of the Bible; having food and raiment let us be therewith content, (1 Timothy 6:8.)

The answer to the high cost of everything that we buy could be to stay contented with less. What will too much spending do to our giving both in time and money to those who are needy or to those who have had misfortune? Having too much to do and still we may not have everything that we want or desire if we live in a humble way, but the Lord will richly supply everything that He knows that we need for our salvation. Wanting to be ahead of other people will lead to more and more things being brought into our churches that our forefathers thought best to keep out. One of Satans false works is when he tells us that if we would have more things that we desired on this earth we would be contented. We have had ancestors who have shown us that this life can be lived in a humble way; led us by word and example do the same for those precious souls going through this world after us and for those strangers, both the curious and those seeking the Truth, who came to find out about our way of living. Let us not be like Elijah who thought he was the only one serving the Lord or like Jonah who was disappointed that God showed grace on a people other than his own, but let us try to live in a humble way so that the Lord,

not us, be given the honor, glory and praise. The great day is ever drawing nearer when our Lord, Redeemer and Friend will gather His elect from among all kindred, tongues, people and nations, as written in Revelation 5:9.

Our life on earth is short, that span of time from birth till the time of our long, last days is short. Our mission in life is not to some far- off foreign land but at home and in our churches and home neighborhoods. The words of many poems and songs say much in a few lines.

One such is found in *Church and Sunday School Hymnal*, No. 378.

The vineyard of their Lord
Before His laborers lies;
And lo! We see the vast reward
Reserved in Paradise.

There all our toils are o'er
Our suffering and our pain;
Who meet on that eternal shore
Shall never part again.

To gather home His own
God shall His angels send,
And bid our bliss on earth begun,
In deathless triumph end.

In the year of 1989, a group of young families in Lancaster County endeavored to start a youth group with written guidelines and adult supervision. After he was asked for an opinion, Ben sent the following letter to the group.

Dear Friends,

With a deep interest we read the thoughts put on paper by the parents concerned about the behavior of the very dear young folks growing up in the supposedly Christian homes of our plain churches here in Lancaster County.

The doings when our youth are with each other are so often a source of thankfulness to God for the good that is still among us. Satan has not defeated all that we should be keeping. However, far too often what we hear about and see among our young people makes an ache in the heart that cries out to God that He may give us a new strength and understanding to help to better the widely-known conditions among us that we well know are not as they should be.

After all, these young people will so soon be the adults in our homes and churches of tomorrow if the Lord tarries. It is hard to believe, but it is estimated that the half of all the people in our churches are 18 years old and under. It is urgent that we wake up and do something to help to make things better. If we keep on doing things as they have always been done, we can expect to get the same results that so far have always followed.

The next day after you shared the pages with us, I shared them at lunch time with our oldest son and

his 17 year old son, and with our youngest son, 26 years old; the three people I am presently working with five days of the week.

The two boys happen to be with two different youth groups, (I guess they should no longer be called gangs, because to the non-Amish they bring to mind the rebellious city street gangs.) The reading of the pages stimulated quite a discussion the rest of the afternoon.

Since then they have photocopied your sheets a number of times to share with their friends. I hope you don't mind that we infringed on your copyright; if there is any! Should I return your favor by making some comments on what you shared with me? If so, read on.

Where did this young peoples' behavior that is such a thorn in our sides get it's start in our today's Anabaptist churches? The Christian churches we go to are like links of a chain, or rather like the branches of a living tree, that includes the God-fearing Anabaptists of the 1500's, and goes back to it's roots in the first Spirit-filled church at Pentecost in Jerusalem, shortly after Jesus ascended to Heaven.

We don't believe that God intended Pentecost to be a one-time-only experience for the first church of nearly 2,000 years ago. It is to be an on-going pouring-out quietly going on until the end of times.

We believe that any un-Godly and un-Christian behavior among our young can be traced to young people in the past who were being influenced by what was not really good for them. The history of how our churches became involved is a long story of much that should never have been permitted to have taken place. Nevertheless, it is very interesting to me. Perhaps we can learn from it.

When our forefathers were still a persecuted people in Europe they had problems, but their problems were poles apart from what we are having now. Being persecuted for their religious convictions was a way of life for them.

This is documented in more places than we can count. One is in the minutes of the court hearings held when the Passau Anabaptists were arrested. These records, which the court clerk wrote in the Latin required by the Catholic church of that day, have since been found and translated.

The fifty or sixty Anabaptists, actually a whole church congregation, were then imprisoned for five long years in a dreary dungeon.

But they did not indulge in self-pity and they kept their spirits up. They held what was something like a five-year-long church service. Some were to die from the hunger and torture that they were to put through, but during these years they spent their long days in prayer and singing. During this time they composed over fifty of our *Ausbund* hymns.

What is also remarkable is that this group included several teenagers who said at their trial that they would not recant unless they were to be shown a belief that was more Scriptural than the one they had. How many of our teenagers would be willing to spend five years of their young years in jail for their religious convictions?

At other places young Anabaptists were not only imprisoned, but they were martyred for their beliefs. In the Martyr's Mirror there are accounts time after time of those being martyred for their faith being young people. Of the seven brethren who each composed a stanza of the *Ausbund* hymn on page 329, one was still a teenager. (We have to wonder which one of the seven verses is the one that he wrote.)

This boy was offered a huge amount of money by a wealthy man who had taken a liking to him if only he would recant. He was martyred with the six others because his choice was to stay steadfast and faithful to his Saviour. His story is recorded in the *Martyr's Mirror* on pages 433 and 434 in the English edition and on pages 17 and 18 in the back part of the German edition.

One young girl composed the well-known Ausbund hymn on page 411. The young people in those days had a vital and a living faith that nearly puts what we have to shame.

It seems that the New World here in America was providentially opened up for these oppressed people as a God-given relief and an escape from their religious persecution. There is no other way to explain how the title to the lands that are now Pennsylvania were given to a man of another persecuted religious faith; William Penn, a devout Quaker.

Even before Penn arrived to see the lands that had been considered being "owned" by the king of England, he drafted the laws for his proposed colony. He had spent some of his young years in "gaol" himself for his religious beliefs and had a longing for a land of freedom from religious persecution.

His laws included the freedom of the new settlers to worship as they pleased. Even those of the Anglican Episcopal church which had persecuted the Quakers in England were welcome, and many of them came.

This idea of freedom of religion was practically unheard of anywhere else in the world before this time. This was an idea that was considered so unworkable that the governments of the other New World colonies did not believe in it at first. Even the Puritans of Massachusetts, the same church of the well-known Pilgrims, were known to have executed Quakers, a faith heretical to them.

William Penn made a tour of mainland Europe and it is known that he had contact with the Anabaptists. He wrote and distributed many pamphlets inviting any religious oppressed people who were interested to settle on his lands.

Although they knew they had a perilous six or eight weeks ocean voyage ahead of them, many of the persecuted Anabaptists were willing to make the journey. This was a trip that very few children of under three years old were to survive. These children, and the many others who did not make it, were buried at sea after holding a short funeral service aboard the ship.

They had no way of knowing how things would turn out in this new land; then a wilderness populated only with the native Indians. However, because of the decision of our forefathers to come to the New World with their families and their Bibles is why we are now living here in America in a persecution-free environment for raising our children. Ahead of them was an unknown and uncertain future. They did not know what the future held for them, but they knew who held the future. They were a people with a faith and trust in God.

William Penn made a peace treaty with the Indians that was to last "as long as trees grow and water flows." Unlike the other colony proprietors, he paid the Indians for their lands, before he resold it to the settlers. The people who bought Penn's lands could say they were not buying stolen goods!

This settling of the first lands that Penn sold was to come around the same time of the unfortunate split of the Anabaptist church into the Mennonites and the Amish in Alsace in Europe.

In the religious tolerating climate of today in which we appreciate our Mennonite neighbors, it is hard to believe the bitter hostility that these two groups then had for each other. So hard and deep-rooted were the feelings between these two groups in those days that it is known that neither of the groups would step into a Rhine River boat if they knew some of the other group were already in the boat.

Boarding the boats going down the Rhine to the Atlantic Ocean seaports was the first leg of their long trip to America.

The Amish believed in shunning, and well they should, for there are at least five New Testament verses upholding the practice. They believed in it enough that they banned and avoided all the Mennonites.

The Mennonites, who had earlier said how opposed they were to a strict social shunning, now believed in it enough to shun their rival religious opponents; the Amish.

This Scripture-based practice of the bann and avoidance now went much beyond what had been agreed as being Scriptural by the Anabaptists in their eighteen articles of faith drawn up at Dortrecht in Holland in 1632. This confession of Faith, in addition to three others, were printed in the first *Martyr's Mirror* of 1659, and the articles on shunning (now on pages 32, 37, 43 and 405) were of course, well known to both the Mennonites and the Amish.

However, the bann and the shunning of apostles, which was in God's wisdom put into the Scriptures to bring about a realization of what they were missing by being on the outside, and as a motive for causing a deep shame for their misdeeds, now became an abused practice. It deteriorated into being merely an outlet for their hate for each other's religious beliefs. Instead of a love which brought them together again, the spirit in which shunning was practiced with hatred, drove them further away.

What followed went the way that most political and religious arguments usually go. It happened in the Catholic/Protestant split of some 170 years earlier, and it now came between the Amish and the Mennonites. However, because both the Mennonites and the Amish were a non-resistant people they did not go to war against each other as did the Catholics and the Protestants, but the separation was just as complete and final. What one side did was only to set the practice of the other in the very opposite direction.

Whatever the Amish did was opposed by the Mennonites; and whatever the Mennonites believed in was contradicted in the opposite direction by the Amish. At that time it seemed that whatever one side believed in was wrong with the other. Both parties, unfortunately, no longer believed they could learn anything good from the other.

One instance was the wearing of the beard. All Amish churches require it. An Amish man is expected to let his beard grow.

Among nearly all of the Mennonite churches it became expected that they would keep their beards shaved off. One reason given was that it was much more sanitary. In fact, there have been instances, even in recent times, when the Mennonite churches would censure those men who started having religious convictions that they should let their beards grow.

The Mennonites believed in an assurance of salvation, which to them was really committing their spirits in God's hands, such as Jesus did at His death.

The Amish misunderstood this word "assurance" and took the other extreme. They said they did not want any part of being sure of being saved. They said they hoped to be "saved," but in many cases it is doubtful of some if them really wanted to understand what a "living hope" really is. It is much more than just wishful thinking.

Over the years this difference in thinking about assurance has been a major topic in countless sermons in both of the churches. One side says they could have no inner peace and would always have a fear of death if they did not have this assurance, while the other side says that anyone still living in worldliness and having assurance is only having a false hope in which they will someday be eternally disappointed and rejected.

Some Mennonites seemed to really believe the only reason the Amish wore a distinctive and plain manner of clothing was "to earn their way to Heaven," and became critical of the Amish because of being "much plainer than is necessary."

The result was that over the years many of the mainstream Mennonite churches have slowly but surely lost the plain dress and the simplified living that shows a separation from the greater society around them. Many of them even no longer consider the prayer veiling and uncut hair for the women to be necessary.

The Mennonites over the years were always more open, and even eager for new changes. This has brought much into their churches that the Amish simply would not have.

Some Mennonite churches of today are even debating if divorce and remarriage are always wrong on the ground that "the previous marriage was a mistake and we as Christians should be willing to forgive all past mistakes."

The charter to Pennsylvania was given to Penn in 1681. The first Mennonites started to come a decade or so before 1700 and the first Amish a decade or two after that date.

The first Mennonites settled on the available farms outside of Philadelphia, such as at Germantown, and many were soon living in villages and small towns.

Till the first Amish came over, most of that land had been taken up, and as they did not even wish to live among the Mennonites anyway, they looked for land further inland. Here also, the land was cheaper and could be had for only several dollars an acre.

After leaving the port at Philadelphia, they started up the Schuylhill River to what is now the city of Reading. Here they followed the Tupelehocken River to the Northhill Creek. It was in this area of Berks County, laying just south of the Blue Mountains, that the first Amish immigrants started to hold worship services in the New World.

Exactly when and where this first worship service was held is lost in the mists of time. We don't know which songs they sang out of their *Ausbunds*, or who had the sermons or what they heard in the message, but there are some things we can be pretty sure about.

They probably choked up with tears in their thankfulness to God for His protecting hand over them in their long and weary ocean journey. This group, close to each other in heart, were grateful to God for a land free from the tension of being driven from one place to another for their religious convictions.

Of course, our pioneer forefathers, living in their log cabins in what was then a dense forest, were glad for any neighbors living close by and made friends with them. It was Christian, and it was good and proper that they did. They needed each other.

They had to eat and game was plentiful in the woods. After the summer growing season ended the men and boys went into the forests to bring home food for the winter. They could have used bows and arrows, but something better was now available. The first rifles, somewhat similar to those of today except that they were muzzle loading, had been invented only decades before this.

Guns were then also used in war, and these non-resistant people probably never before had a gun in their hands, but they had to have something to eat to live.

However, this was to evolve into our today's mania among some of our men and boys leaving work and families to go hunting, sometimes for days on end, simply for the sport of it.

Here in hinderlands the first Amish had very few, if at all any Mennonite neighbors, but they had the friendly Indians and the people who were later called the Pennsylvania Germans.

The young Amish boys associated with the young Indian braves who taught them something they probably had never before seen being done. They taught them to smoke tobacco.

As tobacco was, of course as addictive then as it still is now, these Amish were probably soon growing a small patch of tobacco for their own use. The powerful addiction of nicotine took hold of them — some became as slaves chained to it — and from then on the Amish became known as a tobacco growing and using people.

This influence to smoke tobacco was something the earlier Mennonites living in the less rural areas away from the Indians probably did not have.

This also, was to become an Amish and Mennonite difference. It is not that tobacco was never used by the early Mennonites in America because it is known that some of them spoke out on the chewing of tobacco when their church houses had only dirt or rough wooden floors. Can you believe it that some started to object to "the spitting of tobacco juice on the floor in church which is an offense to the worshippers when they went to their knees in prayer"? There is an article in an old Mennonite paper about this.

However, the Mennonites were one of the first groups to develop religious convictions and promote a complete abstinence to all tobacco using; even in moderation.

When the Mennonites started to condemn the use of tobacco as a defilement of God's temple, the human body, many of the Amish defended it's use as an old custom that should not be talked against.

Unfortunately, this even went beyond the 1960s when health researchers made it quite clear that tobacco is very injurious to health. Some of them were even to use tobacco to openly show to all that "they were of the humble ones" who did not go along with the "worldly Mennonite" ways of thinking. It is indeed ironic that a habit started solely by one attitude — a boy wanting to be smart — should be declared as a humble habit.

Here in the backwoods wilderness the boys and girls of the first Amish pioneer settlers would, of course, be more or less associating with the sons and daughters of the neighboring immigrants from Germany. These German people had also been attracted to this low priced land and were also populating this very same part of Pennsylvania at the same time of this first Amish congregation along the Northhill Creek in Berks County.

These people called "The Pennsylvania Germans" did not come to America, "the land of opportunity," to avoid religious persecution, but to better their economic lot.

They had been brought to poverty by the effects of the devastating thirty years war in their mother country which took well over a hundred years to rebuild. In some places this war had swept back and forth over twenty times. It had desolated the land and reduced the population to a small fraction of what it once had been.

It is no wonder that these hard-working people did not then have much for religion, because the religious wars between the religious Catholics and the religious German Lutherans was what had destroyed almost all they had ever worked for.

These Pennsylvania Germans spoke the same language the Amish did, but their religious life was probably only secondary to them. They loved dancing games and social drinking, and it is known that back in Germany they practiced manners of courtship that the Anabaptists back in the old country would have never indulged in. That this way of courtship would have been nothing but revolting to them is simply an understatement.

These Pennsylvania Germans were also a superstitious people who believed in such things as planting only when the moon signs were right and in pow-wow ways of treating an illness.

161

After a time of being exposed to these influences the Amish people were doing things their God-fearing forebears in persecution days would never even have thought of doing. As is usually the case, two groups with a wide difference will usually socialize better with each other than will two groups who only recently had a fall out over a relatively minor difference.

This was the case with the relationship between the Amish and the Pennsylvania Germans and with the Amish/Mennonite relationship. Some of the Pennsylvania German practices wore off on the Amish.

The Northhill Amish congregation was destined to become scattered after only a generation or two. The Indians who had made a peace treaty with William Penn, and who had always before this been paid the price they had asked for their lands in trinkets they had thought were valuable, now became angry when that peace treaty was broken. Greedy land-grabbing settlers spread still further west and ignored the treaty of peace. They built their homes and cleared land the Indians thought was still theirs. The friendliness of the Indians waned.

Urged on by the French who were at odds with the English anyway, the Indians swooped back over the Blue Mountains and many of the settlers on the frontier were killed and their log cabins burned to the ground.

The well-known Hosteler Massacre of 1757 of an Amish family was the result of one of these raids. In the course of about twenty years most of the Amish who had not joined the religions of the other backwoods settlers moved out. Instead of fighting the Indians they quietly moved to more peaceful locations.

Some of these were the first Amish in Lancaster County, about sixty or so miles southward. The lands further to the west were shortly after this opened to white settlers, and many Amish joined the westward movement to Mifflin and Somerset Counties. From these many later went on to states further west, such as Ohio, Indiana and Iowa.

These Amish were to take their religious convictions with them; very few abrupt changes ever being made. But they also took along the practices

that had been picked up during their first years in America. After several generations the Amish parents didn't want to say much about things they themselves had indulged in when they were young.

It started to be said that, "this is the way things were always done," and "We don't want to have anything new in our churches." What the church was by then, both what was good, and what was not so good, now had deep roots.

They saw the drift of their Mennonite cousins who were generally more open to changes, and we can well understand why they did not want such to happen in their churches.

They also usually reacted negatively to the openness that the Mennonites had in talking about religious matters, believing it did not show the Sermon on the Mount "poor in spirit" attitude. It became embarrassing to mention things during their visiting with each other, and even in their families, about religious subjects. The insights that could be learned from the Bible and about prayer were generally avoided in their visiting hours and often even around the kitchen table to their families.

It seems they thought such was only to be talked about in a Sunday church sermon. Avoiding such talking while they visited each other surely did not start a religious argument; something they didn't want to happen.

Right there they were losing out in the best method of Bible study there is; talking over it while visiting with friends or with the family at the kitchen table over mealtimes. Where else did the Anabaptist in the old country, even teenagers, get such an amazing insight and knowledge of the Scriptures that can be seen in the answers they had for their questions at their court hearings?

Would our young people have such ready answers on what they believe if they were to be questioned on their convictions? Would our way of life be evidence enough for a court of law to convict us as being followers of Christ?

Really, the strength of the first Anabaptists was in their interest in things of the spirit in the days when the state - churches forbade the reading of the Bible by the common people. The authorities of the state - churches feared that Bible study would be a threat to their control of the religion of the masses and "would make heretics of them all."

What follows is not in any way to look down upon those gone before us who joined our faith in their young years and remained steadfast to it till God released them from the struggle of this life.

However, facts are facts. Probably none of our Amish forefathers ever owned land in the old country where they had been driven from one place to another. Here it was possible that they could own their own farms and homes. They worked hard and prospered. And with prosperity nearly always comes a dullness to the senses of religion.

In the course of several generations changes did come about in the Amish church. What happened was that most of their visiting with each other became to be about material things. Even making jokes about such sacred subjects as God's miracles of holy marriage and about birthing became acceptable. Such things became a common and loose talk and a popular way to entertain each other.

The inevitable happened. The morals of the church as a whole went on a downward decline.

With this shallowness of and a lack of deep-down Christianity also came a decline of talking about the fascinating and interesting things that God has put into the Bible for us. Reading the Bible for daily guidance and for a comfort and inner strength became neglected and became put on the back burner.

The Amish may have kept that necessary tenet of Christianity, non-conformity to the world, somewhat better than many Mennonite churches have, but something else very important became lost in many of our circles.

Today's epidemic of "wild oats sowing" among our young people is not getting any better. This term of "a season of wild oats sowing" is a much used way of excusing the bad behavior of our young people, and it is also often said that, "Don't worry, they will settle down after they get it out of their system and get married."

One writer who wrote to me of the deteriorating of the moral standards of the young in Holmes County, Ohio, tells of a great-aunt of his who remembered and told him of the first time she knew of a boy coming to a singing drunk. She said, "We

girls all cried that evening." By 1920, or thirty years later, the girls were also drinking.

Although it might not be quite that bad, some Amish settlements have been called "nothing but houses of prostitution" with their "open door courtship practice" among the young.

Just in this last year, headlines in newspapers the world over shocked the people who always thought the plain people were "a people living according to the Bible." They were to read that some of the youth raised in Amish homes associated with a pagan motorcycle gang and sold drugs to other young people; a high crime in the laws of our land.

Some van drivers have told how they are tired of having to nearly drag drunken Amish young people into and out of their vans when they are to pick them up late at night. One said that he will no longer play the rock music tapes on his tape deck that some Amish girls send up front to him to be played while on the road. Many of our public ball parks are crowded with Amish youth on Sundays and on our religious holidays.

Our major problem is really not that people from the world are a temptation to us. The person offering a sixteen-year-old his first drink is not an alcoholic from the world. It is someone raised in an Old Order home who is handing that first drink to him. Just as sad, if he does not have conviction enough to refuse it, his God-given gift of sound and clear thinking that he needs to resist temptations is then temporarily lost. He may have a deep remorse for what he did by the next day, but till the next weekend he is in it deeper than ever.

Our situation is serious enough. Evidentially someone is going through our Amish directories and getting the addresses to write letters to many of our fifteen and sixteen-year-old boys and girls. They are urging them not to join the fallen church of your parents."

Up to now, some of the attempts to better our conditions, especially among our youth, did have a degree of success. There are many God-fearing and decent boys and girls out there. We have many concerned parents.

However, every single attempt at improvement had been found fault with and was always met with a stiff and unyielding opposition. Why it has to always be that way is very difficult to understand unless we recognize that it is really Satan behind the opposition. Whenever something good comes up, he will without fail somehow start up an opposition.

One example was the work of a group of dedicated publishing house workers trying to put better reading materials into our schools and homes.

This work was actually soon to be called "the greatest deception our plain churches ever had," even in Sunday church sermons, simply because these publishers crusaded against the dangers and sin of two widely accepted practices among us; courtship in bed and on the use and growing of tobacco.

Because their school readers at different places contained Scripture verses they were soundly condemned at many school meetings because, "Scripture is like a two-edged sword, and it would be dangerous to put a sword in the hands of school-aged children"!

Many parents and teachers at these school meetings quietly disagreed with what was being said, but were too timid to openly disagree. They knew too well what happens when a ruling made by a higher-up is questioned. Some were to say later that it is about time that the two-edged sword of the Scriptures is being put in the hands of our young people to protect them from the evils of the day. Doesn't the Bible ask the question, "Wherewithal shall a young man cleanse his way?" (Psalm 119:9) It then answers it's own question right after — "By taking heed thereto according to thy Word."

It soon became clear that in the back of all this opposition was the fear that the sale of these new readers could be a threat to the big profits that had been made before this by the "School Supply Room", which at the beginning of the nationwide Amish parochial school movement did not have any competition and had the school textbook market to itself.

Another of the objections made was to the martyr stories in the readers because, "Our children could get nervous reading about the terrible sufferings the martyrs were put through." We have to wonder if our young children should then not be told of the crucified Christ suffering on a cross because of the

danger of becoming nervous on hearing about it.

Really, before the Pathway readers came out the school-aged children in our schools had very little, or nothing at all, in their curriculums about the history of the plain churches that were sponsoring the parochial schools they went to. Many of our people probably grew up, very little aware of the history of the sacrifice and sufferings their forefathers in faith went through to pass on this priceless heritage that we all enjoy today.

Another instance of opposition to "something new" was when homeschooling came along. It was condemned because it was said to be illegal to the laws of the land. A church rule was made that no one was to homeschool.

One family, who had started schooling at home because they could no longer take the mockery that the other Amish pupils at school put their children through, ended up being excommunicated.

Later on it was found out that homeschooling was perfectly legal. Unfortunately, no apologies were made to the homeschooling parents. Why they then later became bitter against the Amish Church and all that it stands for can easily be understood, because they really were the victims of an abuse of authority.

Also unfortunate in that it was through this ruling of the church that was to be the start of several other families becoming disillusioned by all Amish church rules whatsoever.

They were later to leave to find a church home somewhere else. They were people we needed, but through all this their choice was not to stay with us.

What is now interesting about this church rule on homeschooling is what is now happening at the present time. One example is the new settlement at Cecilton, Maryland. Here there are at present not enough families to build a school and to have a teacher.

The parents are temporarily homeschooling. They are doing the same thing that we were led to believe not long ago was an evil thing to do.

Is all this telling us to investigate something thoroughly before we start to condemn it?

Several years ago we visited the deacon, John

Y. Schlabach of Holmes County, Ohio, who just recently passed on at the age of one hundred and two. Before we left I asked him if he could sum up in a few words a highlight of something he had learned from his many experiences over the years.

He thought over it a lot before he answered. "Keep yourself from helping to make a ruling if you at all think you may not be able to help to carry it through later," he said.

If that wise advice were to be followed everywhere, we would have rules only for the basics, and none would be made only for a show of authority. Continually adding new rules and ordinances is not the answer to the betterment of our fallen natures.

One of the first serious attempts to start a youth group with a better behavior here in Lancaster County was probably the one made in mid-century by a small circle of close friends who called themselves "the Group"

They were a serious and likable group of young people who saw the folly and shallowness and evils of "wild" and rebellious behavior. This group was an offshoot of what was then the most liberal of the only two or three different Lancaster County youth groups of that time.

However, this movement did not catch fire among most of the young people of that day. They were soon to mockingly become called "the Goodies" by too many in the other youth groups, and later on even by the parents of other young people.

They were known to have a very decent behavior, but it seemed they didn't have too many cares in abiding by the accepted church standards in their mode of dress and in their ways of traveling. This seemed to make them lose the support of those in the church who felt that the way we look on the outside does show what is inside.

However, the fact that they knew their Bibles may have been the seed from which grew the "opp glauben" hysteria in the Lancaster and Franklin County Amish churches of only a few years back. As is now well known, this label started to be stuck on anyone who found the study of the Scriptures to be an extremely interesting way to apply the good mind and thinking that God has given to all responsible human beings.

I don't remember too much about "the Group", except that I do remember seeing a bunch of them playing "Scrabble" one Sunday afternoon rather than playing one of the "ball sports", such as baseball, which some of the other young people thought had to be one of their Sunday pastimes.

It is known that many of these young people belonging to "the Group" attended the revival tent meetings that the Mennonites held throughout the East at that time.

One of the girls of "the Group" once fell on her knees in the middle of a "hoe-down", or band-playing barn dance. She prayed aloud and wept over the godless sinning that was taking place right around her, but needless to say, it all provoked a mocking and laughter among the dancers who thought they were having "a merry good time"; some of who obviously had too much to drink, and very probably at least 99% of the boys were cigarette smokers. It was the smart thing to be doing.

Most, if not all, of these members of the Group were sooner or later in other churches. Their excuse was that none of the Amish youth were fit to associate with anyway.

I knew some of them. We are now of grandparent age and I would like to tell you that in the churches they were later to join "they lived happily ever after". However, I know some of them later met up with some things in their churches and even in their own families in which they experienced things that were not at all pleasant, and happenings occurred which were not at all Christian.

Going to other churches for a betterment for their children was not the answer. Rejecting and deserting the church of their parents, as though the ones before them had no enlightenment, very rarely stopped the cycle of children turning their backs to the teaching of their parents.

What could be their response when their own children later ended up out in the world with the divorces and the many other things out there that are not Christian? What could be their answer when their children retorted to their pleas to stay in the church thy had now chosen? "You didn't stay where your parents raised you, so why should we," was an answer that would often stab the hearts of those who started the license of going to other churches.

They got the pendulum swinging in the other direction, but it didn't stop where they wanted it to stop.

But this is still not all there is to the story. Those young folks taking a part in "having a merry good time" were sowing a seed that had to be reaped later. God Himself said in effect in the Ten Commandments that a curse and a punishment will follow the sins of a people into the third and fourth generation. (Exodus 20:5).

These barn-dancing people also grew up and are now also of grandparent age. They "settled down" at marriage and are not dancing with each other anymore. They are not getting drunk every Sunday evening.

A few of them are still smokers, but the cigarettes they now use are covered with a brown paper because at their age they would be ashamed to be seen smoking the white ones, which are somehow considered to be more worldly.

Unlike most of their "goody" counterparts, probably most of them stayed with the Amish Church. This has created a mindset prevalent among us that is hard to explain. Because most of the so-called "goodies" went to other churches what many of our people now believe runs in the same direction as what one Amish father actually expressed. — "I would rather see my teenaged boy with a beer can in his hand than with a Bible." Because many of those Bible-interested people have left our churches many of our people are now so sure that the boy with the beer can will "settle down" later on' while the one with the Bible "becomes too stubborn to be told differently."

The youth of fifty years ago; including myself and my wife, had then only a choice of three or four youth groups to chum with. With the several dozen different Lancaster County youth groups of today the children and grandchildren of those who are our age and older have the choice of joining a liberal group where nearly anything goes, to the very plain who are willingly keeping just about every one of the plain tenets of our churches.

Although there is no longer anything exactly like "the Group" to join, our young people have the chance of choosing any of the many different groups in any of the levels between the "very plain" and the "very high".

None of these youth groups are perfect. Composed of imperfect human beings they couldn't be perfect.

If we look deep enough we can find both good and bad in all of them. Satan has a different bait for everyone.

Some of these youth groups and their actions are repeats of the barn-dancing, band-playing and drinking of two or three generations back. However, among these it seems there is very little mockery and snobbing among them, and they are usually very respectable and sociable, which is more than can be said of some other very exclusive groups.

Some are making it easy for the church to keep our plain and unadorned way of dress, and it is heart warming that there are young people who very much believe in plainness and simplicity and in modest clothing. They seem to be free from wanting to impress others with what they wear, however, many people are shocked to learn that it is the plain groups who seem to have the most nicotine addiction. One non-Amish at a sale was heard to say that he was admiring a certain person he saw there for the plainness and simplicity of his clothes until he saw him light up a smoke. He said his plain clothes then suddenly meant nothing at all to him.

One plain-dressing group of boys was once asked by a non-Amish man if they could tell him why they were smoking. Their joking answer was that they wanted to do things differently from the people going to the worldly Mennonite Church up the road who do not smoke. Many older people insist that smoking is "an alt gebrach" (an old practice) that should not be stopped and they are smoking to let people know they are one of the humble ones!

Some of our youth groups are a fine example that fun with each other can be had without smoking and drinking, but when they overdo their joking we could get the impression about them that their only silly pastime is "dumb and dirty talk" upon which they all "laugh like crazy". I think we can read somewhere that a fool laughs overloud but a wise man laughs "just a little."

Us older people have often been asked by the parents of school-aged children if not something could be started in our churches before their children turn sixteen and get to be exposed to all the unrighteousness.

Couldn't something be done to shield them from, and make less, the strong temptations of their adolescent years; that short time of their life when they are developing from childhood to maturity?

Couldn't this behavior, which the young seem to be so unaware can cause such a remorse and regret in later life, be stopped among us?

Yes, something has been started, but because we are going through this world as a season of proving ourselves, it may not be quite as easy as what we had been hoping for, and it may not be quite exactly what we had been praying for.

We can read about what has been started to help our young people going through temptations in the first book in the Bible. One writer in a comment on the chaste life of the teenager Joseph, has remarked that "we must resist temptation with a strong and decided 'No' and then carefully take ourselves out of its range like Joseph did."

If we have already yielded to a temptation earlier, our reaction should be, "No, not again!"

A number of years ago I once told a father of several teenaged boys that my mother used to say that if anything is going on that we know is wrong we are to get away from there as quick as we can, like Joseph did, and we are to keep company with the "zurich haldichie" (Those who are keeping back).

This father said he thinks it is necessary that he should tell his boys to go one step further than that. They should beforehand firmly resolve to resist temptations, fully expecting that it may sometimes require standing alone. There may come times when no others will be there to help you support your convictions.

Since his sons are grown it looks like it may have been proved that his method has had a high degree of success.

Whenever even just one person will bravely take his or her stand only God knows how many others will be strengthened. Says one translation of the Bible — "Do not be misled; Bad company corrupts good character" (I Corinthians 15:33).

It is amazing how fast evil can grow and spread, but thanks be to God, good can do the same thing if it is practiced and promoted and taken care of.

All of God's creatures are created with the equipment that they need to protect themselves. For one example, rabbits can not claw and tear up their enemies with tooth and claw, but they have very keen ears and eyes and can run faster than most of their enemies.

That is why rabbits have not become extinct. God also gave all of us responsible humans what we need so that we do not need to live a sinful life that will kill the life of the spirit within us. God wants His people to live lives of moral power and He has given us what we need to do so, but we so often do not use it. That is the priceless gift of sound understanding (der gute ferstand).

When I hear people talking about the conditions among some of our communities as being "out of control", or in others as "they have things under control", I have to wonder if that is the way we should word it.

I don't think we should really want our young under our control, because none of us is wise enough to handle this controlling. Much better would it be for us all to be under the control of God's Holy Spirit. Then it could not fail.

However, our teenagers need boundaries. Even young people who outwardly appear rebellious, they at the bottom of their hearts, desperately want direction and guidance, and feel let down if they do not get it in a loving way.

There is one instance of a girl whose friends had planned to go to a place she knew she should not be going along. She wrote later that even while she was begging her mother for permission to go along "because everyone else is going" there was something inside of her that was crying out, "Please don't let me go." She felt let down when her mother told her that because all of her friends were going, she could also go. That mother missed out on the thankfulness of her children in later years who could have said, "I am thankful to God for having had strict parents."

One minister got a letter from a young girl who said she wishes a group of ministers would visit the places she goes to and would see what her group does every weekend.

"We would be hearing fiery sermons against sin for a long time afterwards", she wrote.

One boy whose best friend was suddenly killed in an accident said they had very quiet get togethers for the next several weeks. He thought what happened would bring them all to a repentance, "but it wasn't long till the most of us were worse than before," he said. Does this tell us that a pattern once started is not easy to break away from?

What you parents have started among your children is a new pattern. However, even though most other parents will admit that something like you have started is desperately needed, you will meet up with some slander and opposition. You may as well expect it.

But don't become discouraged. It can be done. Be thankful that you have other families for support.

Here we have another Biblical example. Noah and his wife did not have the support of these families to help them resist the drift of the godless world of those days.

What you are taking on does not have a promise anywhere that you will always have an easy going.

One instance is in the story of our first parents. Hebrew language scholars tell us that the words in the original Hebrew to Eve that "do sollst mit Schmerzen Kinder gebaren" would also include the raising of them, and the words to Adam about "Kummer" in the Hebrew manuscript are the same as "mit Schmerzen" to Eve. In other words, the raising of children will be a work and a care.

Our children may be at times the source of our biggest problems, but to more than balance it out, God in His mercy can make them also at times to be the reason of one of our greatest joys; both all in one.

Often when we learn of the things the youth of today are doing, how many of us can say we are not, at least in part, responsible for the sins in our midst? Is not much of it an actual continuation and extension of what many of us did years ago? At that time we had no thought that our actions would haunt us years later.

Here we can claim the promise coming right after

the curse which extends to the third and fourth generations of a sinful people. God has promised to show mercy "unto thousands of them that love me and keep My commandments." It is a comfort to know that there is a way that our children can be spared from the curse coming to them because of our misdeeds. Through God's grace and mercy the punishment for the sins of the previous generations can be lifted. There may be nothing more important for us to do than to pray for God's mercy upon us and the innocent people coming after us, even though we certainly do not deserve it.

I know that many leaving our churches tell us that they are doing so to spare their children from the influence of the unrighteousness of our own young people. This is the reason most often given for joining the churches of other faiths. This is taking for granted that not any of our young people are being a good influence, or that there are no other concerned parents among us; both of which are simply not true.

Then again, if these parents are people who in their young days helped to make our conditions worse they should be staying to help us build up what they were then helping to destroy.

The question for us parents is not if we are completely free from a past of doing wrong and taking a part in sinful actions. It is, "If you were, did you learn from it?" Are you open enough to your children and frank and honest enough to tell them why you do not wish them to make the mistakes that you learned from?

After reading your guidelines I was glad that the remark was included on "the appearance of the members, their mode of dress, their way of traveling, and their activities shall conform to the commonly accepted standards of the church."

This is something that some parents may judge to be not very important, because many of them may have had not-too-pleasant experiences in the past because of the "ordnung", or church guidelines. Many of our own people have come to the conclusion that our churches form their opinions of a person's spiritual character too much on how a person is dressed.

In too many cases the reason for accepting the candidates for baptism or for partaking of

Communion may have been on what they were wearing rather that on the inner transformation of heart.

We were all brought up somewhat differently. Among some parents the conviction on "staying away from hochmut" (pride) is pretty strong. This is probably why "the Group" of a generation ago, and also today's group of youth who are signing a pledge to stay away from nicotine, alcohol and drugs has had problems in recruiting new members. It is attempting a betterment without becoming a part of the church. Those who place a premium on a very plain garb are fearing mockery or a snobbing because of their conviction on plainness, so they are not interested in such a group. There are parents who fear the loss of plainness in their children if they were to associate too much with the children of those who are sure that "too much plainness is really not necessary."

However, ignoring the Scriptural tenet of our churches on plainness, simplicity and modesty will fail to get for us the support of the churches we are members of.

We do need that support. We cannot refuse to consider the fact that the way we are dressed does show on our outside what we believe in the line of modesty and non-extravagance on the inside. It may be possible for a proud heart to wear plain clothes, but it's really not possible for a humble heart to be wearing showy modes of dress which goes beyond that which our parents, our church and our God expect of us.

It is unfortunate that our church guidelines are so often considered a burden, which they are if they are taken to "be nothing but rigid man-made laws which dictate everything we are not allowed to do and wear." It is true that we have no need for stringent rules that spell out everything on "we cannot do this; we have to do that, and on and on", but really we can consider it a freedom to live among and be a part of a society, which can free us from desiring the ever-changing styles of the world.

We know the early Apostolic Church and the first Anabaptists were not followers of style. Style for the sake of impressing others or for calling attention to the God-given figure of the human form is indeed shallow. Our bodies are the part of us to which it

was said, "Dust thou art, and to dust thou shalt return."

Here it may be safe to say that how people are dressed starts out when they are very young children. They do not care then what is put upon them. How a teenager is dressed usually starts in the heart of a mother when that child was still a pre-schooler. The mothers buying the material and those at their sewing machines are making what our churches will look like in the future.

Putting clothing on their children made with material and style designed to impress other people is wrong not only because of church rules against it, but more importantly it distracts from the inner character of heart which is more important than showing off physical beauty and form. We may not all have good looks, but it is possible for anyone to have a sterling character of high value. May our young mothers keep the pride in their hearts from becoming stumbling blocks to humility in their children!

One of our duties as parents is to help to develop a conviction in our young people to dress neat and clean, and also to get across to them that they need not dress in a way to impress other people. Couldn't we teach them that simplicity has a beauty all of its own? Shallow indeed are friendships built solely on what people wear.

One instance comes to my mind of one set of parents who were concerned about the drinking and such among the Amish youth. The father told me he thinks drinking is in all the Amish youth groups except possibly in the very plainest ones, "But who wants to see their children dressed as plain as they are?" His wife never wanted her children "looking common", a term sometimes used for simplicity and non-extravagance.

These parents later left the church with their family, most of them still very small. These children are now grown, and it is ironic that not one of them is in the church of their parents.

This modest and plain garb is not to be taken too lightly. One writer, not even of the plain faith, remarks on how "the people of the world are dressed", and goes on to call modesty "a lost virtue of our time."

In actual adultery there are always two people in the sin. In the sin of a man or boy is adultery of the heart (Matthew 5:27 and 28) the other partner in the sin is often a girl or woman dressing outside the bounds of modesty.

We have every reason to believe that if all the boys and girls, and the men and women, of our churches were to remember that their relationships with each other were as brothers and sisters in Christ there would never be any inappropriate or sinful behavior among them.

In fact, in some of our Amish settlements the young are required to be baptized members of the church before they are permitted to date. Why is it that many boys, and even some girls, are putting off asking for baptism until they are well past the age of innocence?

Many of the boys and girls of the first Anabaptist churches could never be persuaded to stay out of the churches, even though they knew full well a martyr's death would follow being baptized. Their Christianity was deep and it was sincere.

Your printed young peoples' guidelines are becoming known about and are being discussed. One objection mentioned several times when I was present when what you are working on was being talked about was about having the supper gatherings and the singings at the same place. To some it would be something too different from what we were always used to.

Several people said that such would be too great a change from our having church in the forenoon, a light dinner for all, and then a supper only for a group of close married friends who had chosen to stay. The singing is then held in the evening for the young who arrive from having supper somewhere else.

However, Annie and I have been present at several Old Order Amish settlements where church, the supper for the young, and the singing were held at the same place. We thought it was a nice way of doing that could also be adopted here in Lancaster County if enough parents were willing to do so.

This is the practice at Bloomfield, Iowa, and at Aylmer, Ontario. At these places, no one would think of talking aloud to each other during the singing, even if there is a silence between the songs being sung. During this hour and a half or two hours of singing the quietness is like that of during church services, which is what a singing really is; a worship of God.

At Aylmer, after the time of singing is ended a light snack is passed around while all are still sitting and visiting together. Before anyone leaves to go home, one of the ministers or parents present gives a short talk and all kneel in prayer.

I can't think how any of the youth would feel like getting up and start carousing around before going home after ending their get-togethers in such a hallowed way.

Then also, wouldn't the young coming in for supper and visiting with the adults who had chosen to stay after church help to close a generation gap that is so unnecessary to be in existence? Would this not be a better way than what we were used to be having all these years?

In fact, I was once corrected in a testimony "zuignes" after the sermon for talking about "the young starting their running around years" "rum springa". To them it sounded too much like letting a bunch of rabbits go on the loose." Their young are not like a bunch of running around rabbits. They would say they were starting to go with the young folks.

There were several other paragraphs in your guidelines that stood out and said volumes in only a few words. One was in comparing the energy of a group of teenagers to the "critical mass" of an atomic reactor. The study of human nature is an extremely and fascinating application of the mind, and these paragraphs were a short course of that study in itself.

I have now gone back and read over what I have written. I am aghast at the number of pages it took me to "make a short comment" on your young people's guidelines.

I am wondering if I should not take out a number of the pages before sending them off. However, I guess I am like the inept newspaper reporter when he was asked by the editor why he had to write such a lengthy story when what happened could be described in a much shorter way.

"I didn't have the time to write a shorter story," he answered.

So, if you have stayed with me till now, please excuse my long and disconnected ramblings and my frequent interruptions in my train of thoughts, and my running off of target.

It would be interesting for us to sometime visit with some of your other concerned parent friends who are going out of their way to start their children out on a different route. It is clear that what you and your families are doing varies somewhat from the beaten path that nearly all of us were perhaps a little too used to.

I think I could learn from you all on how I could have corrected some of the many mistakes I have made over the years with my family.

Right away I could sense that here were parents who were open and would be interesting to visit with and learn from. I felt they were a heartwarming "one of us" as you might say.

Surely it is possible for a God-inspired reform to be started by a small group of sincere people within the larger church. Throughout the history of the Christian Church there were many needed improvements made by "a close society within the church" and by people who "considered their church an extended family and their families as little churches".

We are responsible to teach and pass on our faith to our children. They need answers to their many questions and need help to sort out their thinking about the times they are living in. To us a year is short, but to them time is long. The future to them seems to be too far away for it ever to become the here and now.

Let's be patient and not expect an instant reform. A perfect flower is a miracle of God, but it takes time for that flower to grow and unfold and become a miracle of fragrance and beauty. If we were to try to pry open that bud we would only put it all to ruin.

Keep up what you are doing. God can do miracles through people only if they give Him the glory for the results.

May God help us make that our aim, and of those coming after us, have a faith that has power, and is alive and growing.

Sincerely,

Ben Blank

"I will pour out my Spirit upon all flesh, and your sons and daughters will sing and speak under divine inspiration" — one translation of Joel 2:28 and Acts 2:17

Grief

This letter was written to friends Aaron and Mary Ann Beiler after a visit, both showing their feelings of grief. The book Ben mentions, was written by Aaron and is called "Light in the Shadow of Death." It is available at his address, 840 Peters Road New Holland, PA 17557

December 20, 2008

This letter kept getting longer until I finally sent it off several weeks later. – SORRY!

Dear Brother and Sister in the family of Jesus Christ,

Greeting of Christian Love from my home to yours. Thanks again from the bottom of my heart for your visit here last Monday and for introducing me to the book you got printed. I think God timed everything so perfectly because I was having one of my difficult days alone and needed something else to think. I must believe it was God who motivated you to come for a visit and leave one of your books here just then.

Thanks again for writing it. I know it could not have come easy to share your deep feelings of a family grief experience with others. I know there will be more people in the future who will be helped by how you handled your healing feelings of grief after Mervin was taken away from you, than you will ever find out in this life.

Soon after Annie's funeral a good friend of the family asked me to go with him to a big city bookstore and while there see if I could find something on dealing with grief. Sure enough, there was a whole shelf, probably six feet long, with dozens of books on that subject. The two I picked out and brought

home were helpful, but none of them touched my heart deep down like your book did; and tears can be healing.

I will share with you that several of my hankies got pretty well dampened while I was reading how you expressed your grief instead of just letting it build up inside.

I think God permits trials of different kinds to enter, and become part of our lives here on earth to become part of His master plan for our short earthly journey. We will be better Christians because of the trials we went through. It is God's way of making us fit for His kingdom, and to teach us how to be a blessing and a help to other hurting people.

After we ourselves have experienced how the hurts feel that with God's permission pass through our lives, only then can we learn life's lessons and later pass what we have learned on to others. So often God sends blessings into our lives through other caring people who have learned what hurts and trials feel like. God sees to it that the pain we go through does not get to be wasted. It is for our own ultimate good.

The difficult days that we would never have chosen to be a part of our lives were never meant to become like cracks that open up beyond fixing. They can become like blessings of rainy, fruitful

172

days so that the blessings of a long season of balmy and sunny days do not go on until our faith begins to dry up. Let us remember when we ask God that His will be done, we are really asking Him to send us both the pain and the joy that He, in His infinite wisdom, knows is for our own eternal good, and to teach us how to be truly an inspiration and a help to others without even being aware of it.

Early in this year we had a hospice nurse coming in to help with the medication Annie needed so that she could be at home with the family instead of at a hospital. Since the funeral another nurse, trained in grief counseling, comes occasionally to see how the family is doing. She suggested early on I keep a journal (such as you did), because to express our grief in words will help to relieve and heal it. However, with my other writing I didn't get started, although I now think I should have taken her advice more seriously. By now, many of my first feelings of grief can no longer be put to paper as accurately as they could have been right away.

In one way, the grief in your family when Mervin met his death so suddenly, and at such a young age so full of promise, was so different when Annie, the love of my life, parted from us after my many days at her bedside with her hands of love reaching out to mine. I had such a helpless feeling being unable to do more for her.

But in another sense, the grief is much the same. I still have many days when I wonder if I will ever come to fully realize that I will never, ever see her here on earth again. I don't want to believe it, but I know time will never again return to our happy days together here on earth. But because the Bible says so, I believe in a Resurrection from the sleep of death where God will make it possible for us to live together with Him in such an eternal bliss and contentment where we will not even begin to long for what we thought were happy times here on earth. Heaven will be beyond anything our limited minds here on earth can ever begin to imagine. The inspiring song (Heaven Will Surely Be Worth It All), often comes to my mind.

I had nine weddings this fall on nine different days; one at the other end of the house here. All of them were difficult, even though I tried to brace up for the sake of the young married couple starting out in life together.

Coming home to my empty end of the house after such a day was also not easy. I can't begin to tell you how deeply I miss those times of heart to heart talks with Annie. She was so easy to talk with about anything. I am not worthy that God led her into my life. She made happy memories that I will never forget.

Annie often told me she doesn't fall asleep until she hears I am sleeping. Until then we used to visit with each other, because it was interesting to me when she talked about who she visited with that day and what she learned. We would often talk about the insights the new couple were reminded of to make their marriage closer to each other; and closer to God.

Those times are now in the past. They are now over. I know the Bible says we are to thank God in everything, but it took me quite a while to learn to be thankful for the grief that came from God taking Annie away from me. I am now learning to be thankful to God that He permitted me to have her by my side for the fifty-three plus years we had together. The surviving partner of many couples who were together for only a short time could tell me I was truly blessed that God permitted us so many enjoyable years together. That song chorus often comes to my mind, "the best of friends must always part, and so must you and I."

So many of our friends, especially among the English, will ask how the family and I are doing since we lost Annie. I asked them if I may change the wording a little bit. We did not lose her; we have only parted for a while.

A little while before Annie passed on, the hospice nurse told me she thinks Annie is losing out and may not be with us much longer. However, she asked us to keep her updated by phone calls on how we think she is doing. Anyway, this one time I told her Annie seems to be stronger the last several days and we may have the opportunity to have her with us for a while yet.

She told me only God knows when our end here on earth is going to take place. "You may have each other for only two more hours, or two more days, or even two more years. We don't know. But as long as you have each other enjoy the precious time God gives you to be together. Make happy memories with each other together while you still are given the opportunity."

I told her, "Sandy, that would be a good reminder for all married couples; it wouldn't matter if they were together five days or fifty years."

Because her death did not come suddenly or altogether unexpectedly, Annie and I had this golden opportunity to make our farewells to each other before she left. I had the chance to express my thanks to her for the good work she so unselfishly did for the family and me over the years. I now regret I didn't show my appreciation to her more often. I could have brightened many more of her days by being more thoughtful.

During our years together she often apologized for things she thought she should have done better. Her apologizing was not put on; I knew it was sincere. I also sometimes apologized to her over the years, but I am now keenly aware I did not tell her often enough that I am sorry when I knew well enough I had hurt her feelings. Over our years together she cheered my heart many times more often then I cheered her.

Because her way was not to keep nagging me, she had this quiet, and firm but loving way of letting the children and me know what needed to be done, and then had patience with us until we did it. Because she showed her sincere appreciation for even the small things we did for her it made it easy for us and made us want to do even more for her the next time. My regret now is that I so often didn't honor her wishes sooner.

And it took me too long in our early marriage years to fully learn that a woman's feelings are much more sensitive and easily hurt than the coarse, and so often crude and unthoughtful feelings most of us men show. The big capacity that God built in a woman's heart for tenderness to others (often called a mother's love) is truly a reflecting of the love God has for His human family.

But when the time was here that she drew her last breath it was still so unreal to me. Her work on earth was now over, and her heart of mother love was now stilled. God honored her wish to be taken to a better life than this.

During the last years or so of her life Annie often had the experience of waiting in a doctor's waiting room. Of course, she was the kind who would start up a little visit with those next to her. A number of times she would remark to me later she feels her life here is like living in Heaven's waiting room. She wants to make the best of her time here until the door opens and her name is called to come in. She never showed a fear of death because she believed in a God of love.

And I am thankful to God for that better place on the other side where pain and tears and miserable feelings will be no more. The parting from our loved ones will be forever unknown.

When I think how the parting can get harder the longer a married couple is together I can better understand the story in the Bible of the first miracle that Jesus did which took place when a Jewish couple came together at a wedding where Jesus and His disciples were invited.

As the village of Cana is believed to have been not far from Nazareth where Jesus lived in His growing up years, I think it is possible that the wedding may have been when one of Jesus' younger half-sisters married her husband. Then also, Mary, the mother of Jesus was so worried when the wine they had prepared got to be all gone before the wedding was over.

I like to think Mary was a typical Mom. She was worried that everything would go well at her daughter's wedding.

I am aware that some people who would never touch any kind of intoxicating drink have not always been too comfortable thinking of this story in the Bible where wine was served at a wedding. I then think of a number of years back when Annie and I were invited to a wedding in a non-Amish family we knew well where intoxicating drinks were freely served, along with loud music and dancing for any and all who wished to take part. The mother of the bride did apologize to us and hoped we would not be offended when she saw things did begin to get a little out of hand. (The couple, by the way, have since been parted, not by death, but by divorce.)

But we need to have no problems with this Jewish wedding we read about in the second chapter of John, where Jesus did a miracle by serving the best wine last at this wedding. There are something like a total of ten root words for different types and grades of wine in the original Hebrew language of the Old Testament, and about four different words in the Greek of the original New Testament. These fourteen different words are all translated into our English as "wine", and in the German as "wein".

In other words, any drinks such as the aged fermented intoxicating wine, loaded with alcohol, on down to as mild as the juice of freshly pressed grape berries, are all called wine in our Bibles. The word also includes a refreshing drink made in those days by mixing a weak wine with water and spices, which was not more intoxicating than grape flavored soft drinks in our days. What we call sodas were not know in Bible times.

So none of us needs to have a problem with the wine being served at this Jewish wedding where Jesus was a guest. The Bible talks often enough against strong drink and the great evil of becoming drunk that we can rest assured that Jesus would not use one of His miracles to have an intoxicating wine served at a wedding that the guests could use to willingly damage their God-given blessings of a sound mind and clear unconfused thinking.

I think God saw to it that this story was included in the New Testament to teach us a great truth about God-blessed marriages to Christian believers in future years; which still pertains to us in our times. It is there to help us to understand that God's pattern and purpose of marriage is much better then the ways of the world.

The love (called wine in this story) between a couple being together in a marriage for a long time, under God's blessings can become more sacred and more spiritual to each other as the years go by. Yes, the first love, that beyond explaining attraction of physical looks and charming ways, is usually a part of God's leading two people together, but for true

love to last the glue holding the marriage together must move to a higher level. It must become the deep and dedicated love based on working to please and honor and appreciate each other for what they are; honest, with no deceit.

If a marriage does not move to a more enduring level than the Hollywood type of physical fascination for each other, the result will be a rocky marriage, or in worldly circles the marriage will end in a divorce with each going their own way. Both will so often make a wreckage of the duty of parents to provide a Godly home for the family. — Since Annie is gone, I can better understand the marriage miracle that only Jesus can do. I won't start another sheet, but will include a copy of several verses of the many hundreds she had highlighted in her Bible. It is my wish for you.

Ben Blank

Pſalm 115:13-15

13. er ſegnet, die den Herrn fürchten, Kleine und Große.

14. Der Herr ſegne euch je mehr und mehr, euch und eure Kinder!

15. Ihr ſeid die Geſegneten des Herrn, der Himmel und Erde gemacht hat.

Psalm 115:13-15

13. He will bless them that fear the Lord, both small and great.

14. And the Lord shall increase you more and more, you and your children.

15. Ye are blessed of the Lord which made heaven and earth.

Easter— When Is It?

51

This letter was written to Daniel J. and Katie Stoltzfus on April 29, 2009
A copy of the original letter in Ben Blank's own handwriting can be found on the following pages.

Dear Friends,

I want to start this letter out by thanking you for your visit here on Easter Monday along with your sister Rebecca. I think you also experienced some years ago how much visits mean after a death in the family.

The history of why we celebrate Easter, the Resurrection of Christ on different days every year instead of like celebrating the birth of Jesus on December 25th on the same day year every year is very interesting to me.

One of the first quarrels of the early Christian Church was over when to celebrate the Easter date. Some wanted it to be on April 9th which we believe was the day in our calendar system when Jesus arose from his tomb. Of course this, like Christmas Day, could happen to fall any day of the week. Others were just as strong in believing that Easter should always be on a Sunday every year because we do know from the Gospel of Matthew chapter 28, verse one, that the Resurrection happened on the first day of the week on a Sunday morning.

The church nearly split over a heated argument because on the same day that some were keeping

Good Friday, the day of the Crucifixion of Jesus Christ as a Holy day. The neighboring churches were already celebrating Easter the day of the Resurrection.

So in the year 325 A.D. a meeting of three hundred and eighteen learned Bishops met in the city of Nicea. One of the things they set out to determine is when the Christian Church would celebrate Easter and to make a church law that the churches all over would not do different from what they would propose to be the right way.

They went back to the Old Testament to find out when the Jewish Passover was held, because they knew Jesus was crucified on the very same day that the Jews sacrificed the Passover lambs at the Jewish Temple. The Jews determined the Passover date by the phases of the moon. Their month would always begin on the day on the calendar when the new moon appeared. Both the English word "month" and the German word "monat" are words that come from the word moon.

Their first day of the year was also not January the first as on our calendar system, but was on the first new moon after spring began, which was when day and night are equal all over the world. Their Passover was held on the 14th day of the first month of the Jewish year. (See Exodus, chapter 12 verses 2 and 6) Now fourteen days after the new moon is full moon, so we know the Passover was always held on a full moon.

That is why we know that on a full moon night Jesus was arrested in the Garden of Gethsemane. So there you have it; Easter was ruled to be held on first Sunday after the first full moon after the first day of spring.

So to this day we have the meeting of the Catholic Bishops telling us when to celebrate Easter. And I think that is okay with us all to leave it that way.

Sincerely,
Ben Blank

April 29, 2009

Dear Friends

I want to start out by thanking you for your visit here on Easter Monday along with your sister Rebecca. I think you experienced yourself some years ago how much visits mean after a death in the family.

But as you can see I am way on behind in answering my mail that needs a reply. You wouldn't have needed to, but thanks for sending an addressed and stamped envelope along.

The history of why we celebrate Easter, the Resurrection of Jesus Christ, on different days every year instead of like celebrating the birth of Jesus on December 25th on the same day every year is very interesting to me.

One of the first quarrels in the early Christian Church was over when to celebrate the Easter date. Some wanted it to be on April 9th which we believe was the day in our calendar system when Jesus arose from His tomb. Of course, this, like Christmas Day, could happen to fall on any day of the week. Others were just as strong in believing that Easter should always be on a Sunday every year because we do know from the Gospels in Matthew, chapter 28, verse one, that the Resurrection happened on the first day of the week; on a Sunday morning.

The Church nearly split over this heated argument because on the same day that some were keeping Good Friday, the day of the crucifiction of Jesus Christ as a holy day, the neighboring churches were already celebrating Easter, the day of His Resurrection.

So in the year 325 A.D. a meeting of 318 learned bishops met in the city of Nicea. One of the things they set out to determine is when the Christian Church would celebrate Easter and to make a church law that the Churches all over would not do different from what they would propose would be the right way.

They went back to the Old Testament to find out when the Jewish Passover was held because they knew Jesus was crucified on the very same day that the Jews sacrificed the Passover lambs at the Jewish Temple. The Jews determined the Passover date by the phases of the moon. Their month would always begin on the day on the calendar when the new moon appeared. (Both the English word "month" and the German "monat" are words that come from "moon".)

Their first day of the year was also not Jan. the first as in our calendar system, but was on the first new moon day after spring began, which is when day and night are equal all over the world. Their Passover was held on the 14th. day of the first month of the Jewish year (see Exodus, chapter 12 and verses 2 and 6). Now 14 days after the new moon is the full moon, so we know Passover was always held on a full moon. That is why we know that on a nearly full moon night Jesus was arrested in the Garden of Gethsemane.

So there we have it. Easter was ruled to be held on the first Sunday after the first full moon after the day spring begins

So to this day we have their meeting of Catholic bishops telling us when to celebrate Easter.

And I think it is OK with us all to let it be that way.

I won't start another sheet — Sincerely, Ben Blank.

179

Mother's Poem

A poem copied by Mother after her mother's death. It expressed our feelings since her death on February twentieth of 2008.

Our Mother

Oh, many lips are saying this
Mid falling tears today,
And many hearts are aching sore
Our Mother has passed away

We watched her fading hour by hour
As they slowly went by,
But cast far from us every fear
That she should ever die.

She seemed so sure, so good, so true
To our admiring eyes,
We never dreamed this glorious fruit
Was ripening for the skies

And when at last the death stroke came
So swift, so sure, so true,
The hearts that held her here so fast
Were almost broken, too.

And for the one still left to us
Our Father sad and alone,
Who hears, perhaps, by night and day
The old familiar tone.

We gather closer round him now
To guard from every ill
And near, the darksome river side
He waits a higher will.

And when the storms of sorrow come
To each bereaved heart,
Let faith glance upward to the home
Where we shall never part.

Where one waits with loving eyes
To see her children come,
As one by one we cross the flood
And reach our Heavenly home.

Our Mother

Oh, many lips are saying this
    mid falling tears today,
And many hearts are aching sore
    Our Mother has passed away.

We watched her fading hour by hour
    As they slowly went by,
But cast far from us every fear
    That she should ever die.

She seemed so pure, so good, so true
    To our admiring eyes,
We never dreamed this glorious fruit
    was ripening for the skies.

And when at last the death stroke came
    so swift, so sure, so true,
The hearts that held her here so fast
    were almost broken, too.

And for the one still left to us
    Our Father sad & lone,
Who hears, perhaps, by night & day
    The old familiar tone.

We gather closer round him now
    To guard from every ill
And near the dark, some rivers side
    He waits a higher will.

And when the storms of sorrow come
    To each bereaved heart,
Let faith glace upward to the home
    where we shall never part.

Where one waits with loving eyes
    To see her children come,
As one by one we cross the flood
    and reach our Heavenly home.

181